When the Other is Me

Emma LaRocque

When the Other is Me

Native Resistance Discourse
1850–1990

University of Manitoba Press

University of Manitoba Press
Winnipeg, Manitoba
Canada R3T 2M5

www.umanitoba.ca/uofmpress

Printed in Canada on chlorine-free, 100% post-consumer recycled paper.

Cover design: Doowah Design
Interior design: Karen Armstrong Graphic Design
Cover image: Margaret Boyle

Library and Archives Canada Cataloguing in Publication
LaRocque, Emma, 1949–
    When the other is me : Native resistance discourse, 1850–1990 / Emma LaRocque.

Includes bibliographical references and index.
ISBN 978-0-88755-703-3

    1. Native peoples—Canada—Historiography. 2. Canada—Historiography.
3. Canadian literature—Native authors—History and criticism. 4. Protest literature, Canadian—History and criticism. 5. Native peoples in literature. 6. Racism in literature. 7. Canadian literature—History and criticism. I. Title.

E78.C2L3733 2010   971.004'97   C2007-904067-5

The University of Manitoba Press gratefully acknowledges the financial support for its publication program provided by the Government of Canada through the Book Publishing Industry Development Program (BPIDP) and the Canada Council for the Arts, and the support of the Province of Manitoba through the Book Publishing Tax Credit, the Book Publisher Marketing Assistance Program, and the Manitoba Arts Council.

ENVIRONMENTAL BENEFITS STATEMENT

University of Manitoba Press saved the following resources by printing the pages of this book on chlorine free paper made with 100% post-consumer waste.

TREES	WATER	SOLID WASTE	GREENHOUSE GASES
10	4,680	284	972
FULLY GROWN	GALLONS	POUNDS	POUNDS

Calculations based on research by Environmental Defense and the Paper Task Force.
Manufactured at Friesens Corporation

FSC
Mixed Sources
Cert no. SW-COC-001271
© 1996 FSC

Contents

I Remember

Is there life after death? I asked as one by one those I loved so much were leaving the earth. Now I know there is—it sits in the deeps of our souls and rememberings. Over time, which is always like just yesterday, I hear them, I sense them, I miss them—

The great storyteller who taught me love of words and resistance discourse in Cree, my Ama Maggie (née Desjarlais) Larocque.

The grand and gentle man who taught me beingness, my Bapa Napoleon Larocque.

The sister I never walked with, who died when she was four, Josephine.

The sister I wept with when the northern lights called her, Delphine.

And to Harold and Erma Lauber, the quiet givers, whose caring home was mine away from home, who will always have a place in my heart.

And to that other great storyteller who I never saw enough of, my favourite aunt, Auntie Catherine (née Desjarlais) Bergman.

And to my always sister-in-law Carol Benson Larocque Rilling; she left us way too soon.

And to my good friend John Burelle, whose "side of life" wit awakened our laughter and sharpened our senses.

And to those little but extraordinary beings who heal and break our hearts, Grey Owl and Jasper.

Acknowledgements

Ni-teh-hi (my heart) resides with my beloved Ama and Bapa, who by allowing and supporting my intellectual and spiritual freedom, taught me that each generation has a duty to reinvent itself. I am grateful for my siblings: my dear sister Delphine whose lifelong struggle with poverty and tuberculosis ended in 2004; I am deeply grateful for my two brothers, Morris and Rene. To Rene for keeping our family's culture and blueberry meadows cultivated and beautiful. To Morris for his good-natured, open-hearted spirit. Among the great gifts my siblings have given me, the greatest are my many beautiful nieces and nephews, and now great-nieces and -nephews. My family's choices to live courageously and inventively, despite all odds, continue to nurture and inspire my work.

In addition to my family of birth, I have adopted other families along the many roads I have travelled. For their support and sustained friendship, my appreciation and affection must also go to Ike and Millie Glick, Juliana and Hans Kratz, Lydia and Menno Wiebe, and the late Harold and Erma Lauber. And special thanks to my childhood friends who speak to me in Cree: Mercedez Cardinal-Rizzoli and Tantoo Cardinal.

I continue to appreciate those many friends and colleagues who have followed my career and/or facilitated my works, among them Joyce Green, Jeanne Perreault, Sylvia Vance, Parker Duchemin, Jill Oakes and Rick Riewe, Hartmut Lutz, Paul de Pasquale, and the late Christine Miller and Carl Urion. And, of course, the entire staff from the department of Native Studies at the University of Manitoba.

Many people in their place of employ wish for a happy workplace. My wish came true when Dr. Peter Kulchyski joined us as our department head in the year 2000; since then I have been working with a dream team. I could not ask for more supportive, caring, erudite and always interesting, often entertaining co-workers than the ones who have become much more than colleagues. To each a special note of gratitude: Peter Kulchyski, for all that you perceive and do for Aboriginal culture and justice; Renate Eigenbrod, for your love of Aboriginal literatures, for your energetic gift of collecting diverse peoples together, and for the pizzas on your porch; Wanda Wuttunnee, for your laughter, for indigenizing meetings with your lovely "urban Cree" songs and drummings; Fred Shore, for always being willing to help. Or to send a joke. And Chris Trott, one of those rare characters who knows how to work at the centre and yet be at home off-centre. Thanks, Chris, for making yourself at home with my pod, for sharing your love of books, especially Pooh, and for all the extra miles of friendship. And for all the Xeroxing and extras, I thank our departmental assistants Kimberly Wilde and Shirley McFaren. And thanks too to Lucy Shore for her generous assistance with my computer glitches, and to our graduate student Vanda Fleury for her able and enthusiastic research assistance.

I started this book a long time ago, perhaps the moment I opened a "Billy the Kid" comic book at the age of five or six. Or when I first saw a cowboy and Indian movie, or had my first history lesson in school. Without my knowing, such signal events were the beginnings of my Otherness, of alienation in my own homeland. Both as an academic and a poet I have written much about marginalization and resistance. Naturally, *When the Other is Me* carries some ideas and argumentation or phrases that have appeared in previous publications, including my dissertation in 1999. A special mention must go to my dissertation committee members for whom I have the highest regard. Their critical contributions were invaluable. Their support was unstinting. I consider them my friends and thank Jean Friesen, Keith Louise Fulton, and Dennis Cooley.

Many unexpected and uncommon challenges have interrupted the writing of this book. For their patience and long-suffering I thank the University of Manitoba Press staff; to Pat Sanders, for the first edit; to Glenn Bergen for his considerate attention to detail, and for the easy conversations to bring text to the best possible place. I thank David Carr for the story about carpet makers of old who left one stitch undone as a reminder that no human creation is really ever complete—and so I have left many, many stitches undone to leave room for imperfection.

*   *   *

And for the orange tiger lilies by my "station," for all the wonderful aromas of coffee, and gourmet snacks, for all the sage and sweetgrass smudges and ceremonies to mark each important step in this stationary and protracted process, for all the gifts of beauty and excellence of words, for all the deadline deliveries, and for the idea to use her scarf for the cover design, my always *ni-ci-wagon*, as Bapa said it, Ruthie Lepp. And to Piper—for sweeping all the paperwork off my desk with her long, fuzzy, fluffy tail, or trying to figure out the computer mysteries with me in midnight hours.

Credits and Permissions

Jeannette Armstrong, "Death Mummer" and "History Lesson," from *Breath Tracks* (Penticton, BC: Theytus Books, 1991). Reprinted by permission of the author.

Chief Dan George, "I have known you…" and "No longer…," from *My Heart Soars* (Saanichton, BC: Hancock House). Reprinted by permission of Hancock House Publishers.

Alfred Groulx, "Savage Man," from *Steal My Rage, New Native Voices*, ed. Joel T. Maki (Vancouver: Douglas and McIntyre, 1995). ©1995 by Na-Me-Res (Native Men's Residence). Reprinted by permission of Douglas and McIntyre.

Louise Bernice Halfe, "I'm So Sorry," from *Bear Bones and Feathers* (Regina: Coteau, 1994). Reprinted by permission of Coteau Books.

Rita Joe, "A thousand ages we see…" and "Aye! no monuments," from *Poems of Rita Joe* (Halifax: Abanaki Press, 1978). Reprinted by permission of Breton Books.

George Kenny, "Rubbie at Central Park" and "Broken, I Knew a Man," from *Indians Don't Cry* (Toronto: Chimo Publishing, 1977). Reprinted by permission of the author.

Duncan Mercredi, "Occupied Territories," from *Wolf and Shadows* (Winnipeg: Pemmican Publications, 1995). Reprinted by permission of Pemmican Publications.

Duke Redbird, *"Old Woman" and "I Am the Redman," from Loveshine and Red Wine* (Cutler, ON: Woodland Studios Publishing, 1981). Reprinted by permission of the author.

Constance Stevenson, "Prejudice (Or, In-laws)," from *Writing the Circle*, ed. Jeanne Perrault and Sylvia Vance (Edmonton: NeWest Press, 1990). Reprinted by permission of NeWest Press.

Sarain Stump, "I was mixing stars and sand," from *There Is My People Sleeping* (Sidney, BC: Gray's Publishing, 1970). Used with permission under a non-exclusive licence issued by the Copyright Board of Canada in cooperation with The Canadian Copyright Licensing Agency.

"…and on the 18th of June we cast anchor at Tadoussac…It was here that I saw Savages for the first time."

—Father Paul Le Jeune,
Jesuit Relations, 1632

"[The] sinuous form of the first savage was raised above the gunwale, his grim face looking devilish…and his fierce eyes gleaming and rolling like fireballs in their sockets."

—John Richardson,
Wacousta, 1832

"The wild Indian was, in many respects, more savage than the animals around him."

—Alexander Begg,
History of the North West,
Vol. I, 1894

"His Indian blood gave him cunning, animal instincts, and a certain amount of ruthlessness…But always…his relentlessness was tempered by the white blood in him."

—Luke Allan,
Blue Pete: Rebel, 1940

"When *Brébeuf and His Brethren* first came out, a friend of mine said that the thing to do now was to write the same story from the Iroquois point of view."

—James Reaney,
Masks of Poetry, 1962

"Even in solitary silence I felt the word 'savage' deep in my soul."

—Howard Adams,
Prison of Grass, 1975

"I am not / What they portray me / I am civilized."

—Rita Joe, *Poems of Rita Joe*, 1978

"It is only a hundred years and now we stand before you in this great institution with our art work on the walls. Now we are civilized, aren't we?"

—Joane Cardinal-Schubert,
Racism in Canada, 1991

"I think I had this missionary zeal to tell about our humanity because Indian-ness was so dehumanized and Metis-ness didn't even exist."

—Emma LaRocque,
Contemporary Challenges, 1991

When the Other is Me

Introduction

Representation and Resistance

Racism...permeates the cultural life of the dominant society both
by its exclusive narrative of dominant experience and mythology,
and by its stereotypical rendering of the "Other" as peripheral and
unidimensional.

—Joyce Green[1]

Gerald McMaster and Lee-Ann Martin introduced the lovely resistance
book *Indigena* by stating, "To be an Aboriginal person, to identify with an
indigenous heritage in these late colonial times, requires a life of reflection,
critique, persistence and struggle."[2] The struggle is about colonization and,
for Native intellectuals, about the necessity of revisiting colonial records,
records that have largely negated and distorted Aboriginal history and humanity. This book is, in part, my revisitation of selected historical and literary
texts that have especially served to dehumanize Aboriginal peoples; however,
in larger part, this book is about the inevitable Aboriginal contrapuntal reply
to Canada's colonial constructs. What will emerge is a resistance born from
the contested ground upon which we, the Canadian colonizer-colonialist and
Native colonized, have built our troubled discourse.

It is taken here that Native-White relationships in Canada are rooted
in the colonizer/colonized complex, much as profiled in Albert Memmi's
The Colonizer and the Colonized. In this now classic work, Memmi, writing
from the context of Tunisia, focuses on the distance (both real and symbolic)
the colonizer employs to rationalize and to maintain his power over the
colonized. Memmi explains, "The distance which colonization places between him and the colonized must be accounted for and, to justify himself, he
increases this distance still further by placing the two figures irretrievably in

opposition; his glorious position and the despicable one of the colonized."[3]

This distance has been fashioned in terms of civilization confronting savagery (or as we might say, "savagism"), a super-myth that has provided the basis for the colonizer's psychology and institutions. This means that, as Canadian Native and non-Native peoples, we find ourselves, our respective cultures, lives, and experiences, constructed and divided as diametrically opposite to each other. We may then find ourselves, our respective stations, and places in our country reflected in Albert Memmi's portrait of the "colonizer and the colonized." The face of the colonizer is made visible through what Edward Said in *Orientalism* calls the "Western techniques of representation,"[4] in this case, the textual records colonizers have left and continue to perpetuate in the Canadian academy. It is also reflected in the continuing exploitation of "the Indian" in the media and marketplace. As I will show, the "Indian" as an invention serving colonial purposes is perhaps one of the most distorted and dehumanized figures in White North American history, literature, and popular culture.

Here, I focus on the face of the colonized. I address an important yet relatively unrecognized area of research: the devastating impact of White-written judgement on Native peoples *as sustained by Native writers and scholars*. Not surprisingly, Native intellectuals have taken particular exception to being portrayed as savages. Writers have countered this portrayal with a number of techniques, including humanizing the "Indian" by exhibiting Native faces and feelings, re-establishing the viability of Native cultures, and even reversing charges of savagery. This developing counter-discourse may best be understood as a resistance response to gross misrepresentation. This misrepresentation is no benign cross-cultural misunderstanding, though there was and is certainly that, but rather it was and is a war of words, words that have animalized and demonized Aboriginal peoples. Selected (but by no means marginal) Euro-Canadian historical and literary texts demonstrate how they are constructed to serve the material, cultural, and ideological ends of the colonial enterprise.

The colonizer's language employed against indigenous peoples is odious. To place Native resistance in context, Chapters 2 and 3 are given over to the study of textual dehumanization and its social consequences. These chapters are disturbing, and readers may be tempted to claim the material is exceptional, to protest it is selective, that it does not represent all the writing about "Indians." Specifically, one may protest that there have always been dissident, even anti-colonial, voices amidst the rubble of colonial forces. But when the records are re-examined with corrective lens, what comes into focus is an overwhelming presence of Eurocentric and hate material in our archives, histories, literatures, school textbooks, and contemporary popular cultural productions. This is indisputable, and, just as indisputably, this material remains protected and continues as currency for the colonizer's archives, art, and entertainment. But what is most important (and what is the central focus of the middle chapters) is that this institutionalization of warlike vocabulary has had severe repercussions for Native peoples. Even if only one-tenth of what is excessive existed, its impact on Native peoples would remain the issue. This cannot be overemphasized. Native rejection of the savage cannot be dismissed as mere bias on their or my part, or as overly reactive or emotional. Olive Dickason, in her comprehensive study *The Myth of the Savage and the Beginnings of French Colonialism in the Americas*, concludes,

> It would be difficult to overestimate the effect of Europe's classification of New World men as hommes sauvages, whether 'bons' or 'cruels.' The French, for all their policy of *douceur* toward Amerindians, never officially accepted that they were anything other than 'sans roy, sans loy, sans foy.' Like the Wild Men of the Woods, Amerindians represented anti-structure, man before the acquisition of culture had differentiated him from the animals. It mattered little whether these savage New World men were perceived as living in a Golden Age or as wallowing in unrelieved bestiality. The fact was that in the European folk imagination, denizens of the New World, like the Wild Men, were living metaphors for antisocial forces that could be brought under control only by...transformation into the spiritual and cultural conformity that Europeans acknowledged as the condition of being civilized.[5]

As to dissident, anti-colonial material, the Western world does have a noticeable prophetic tradition. Within Judeo-Christian and European theological and philosophical developments, there have always been dissidents and visionaries. And throughout the many phases and expressions of colonization, there have been those who abhorred European—and, later, White American—cruelty against indigenous peoples. Some also—Spanish theologian Francisco de Vitoria comes to mind—defended Native humanity and Native rights in the early 1500s.[6] There remain European scholars who continue to write and champion Native humanity and rights. In Canada today there are non-Native organizations and countless individuals who support and advance Native rights and well-being. We should never discount any individuals with a moral conscience who care about truth and justice, and I certainly do not. But my objective is to privilege Native perspectives, not get sidetracked by what Dickason refers to as "that strain of tolerance toward

Amerindians" in European thought, which "never dominated, yet was never entirely absent."[7]

It would be misleading to foreground what may be called Native-positive White constructions, for dealing with the fallout from Native-negative material is one of the defining characteristics, if not the core, of Native resistance response. But there is another point—it is debatable to what extent anti-colonial material was ever truly anti-colonial. Even those who spoke against European cruelties or European thefts did not call for an abandonment of colonial projects.

It is true too that a handful of Europeans, particularly within the primitivist tradition, have always expressed admiration for Native life. To this day there are communities of Europeans, for example in Germany, who believe they are emulating Native culture by imitating what are, in fact, Hollywood versions of the "Indian." Whether the primitivist tradition is positive is a question I raise in Chapter 6. At a purely emotional level, it is understandable that people of all sides of the colonial divide would crave for something "positive." Native intellectuals are anxious "to move on," as one colleague put it. I would think resistance is part of moving on, but what can be seen as "positive"? And can we ever move past colonization, especially when it remains as an active toxin in the lives of Aboriginal peoples? Is it not better to try to understand its workings than to deny its existence or to judge its analysis as being necessarily "negative"? For even if, at institutional and constitutional levels, decolonization was achieved, we know that the psychology of colonization lingers centuries after colonialism as an institution has expired. Perhaps more relevant to all Canadians, can we move on when we have barely begun to understand the colonial process, especially as lived and now being recorded by First Nation and Metis peoples? Is it possible that in our peculiarly Canadian haste to find the positive (often confused with "avoiding the negative" or expressed as "two sides to a story"), we short-circuit our understanding of our history and our assumptions? Might this be what Paulo Freire in *Pedagogy of the Oppressed* means by "false consciousness"?

A Word on Terminology

Terminology about identities is a minefield, given the history of stereotypes and legislative divisions, *real* cultural and historical differences. For example, the term "Indian" is, as Robert Berkhofer has shown in *The White Man's Indian*, the White man's invention.[8] The invention began with Columbus, full of his preconceptions, and later turned into a subculture of stereotypes for White North American entertainment and cultural productions. In Canada the designation also represents colonial power through the *Indian Act*. I therefore make an important distinction between "Indian" and "Native peoples." The difference between these terms is what Daniel Francis in the *Imaginary Indian* calls "the distance between...fantasy and reality."[9] There is little resemblance between the colonizer's Indian and the real human beings who are indigenous to this land. Although the terms "Aboriginal" and "Native" also reflect their colonial origins, I do use these terms, often interchangeably, but I sill prefer the phrase "Native peoples." My preference comes from my political origins in the 1970s when Status and non-Status Indians and the Metis of the Prairies embraced the name "Native peoples" with the shared understanding of themselves as a cohesive indigenous body in a common struggle against colonization. The word "peoples" identifies the phrase as a resistance self-designation in response to massive depersonalization to which *Ai-see-nowuk* ("the people" in Cree) have been subjected. I do specify self-designated First Nations terms whenever they are relevant. Although several Native Canadian scholars use the term "Amerindian," and though it is useful when referring to the indigenous experience throughout the Americas, this term obscures cultures and experience specific to Native Canadians. I use the term "Native American" when referring to Native peoples from the United States. Because of Hollywood connotations and the history of White frontier and military racist uses of the word "red-skin," I cannot use the term "Red" seriously. And the postcolonial designation "indigene" is no less problematic than the words "Indian," "Aborigine," or "Aboriginals" in that it is no less depersonalizing.

I also make a distinction between metis (or halfbreed) and Metis Nation peoples, the former meaning those individuals who are first-generation part Indian and part White; the latter referring to those peoples whose ancestors were originally White and Indian but who went on to develop as a distinct peoples with a distinct culture by marrying within their own group over generations and becoming a new race or ethnicity. Such peoples went on to develop regionally specific cultures, particularly in the Red River and far northwest areas. In western Canada, from about 1800 and up to the 1970s, the majority of these peoples grew up with Cree and/or Michif languages, combining land-based and wage-labour lifestyles.[10] Metis history and identity are variegated because, among other factors, most Metis of western Canada also have non-Status Indian linkages and lineages.

Frantz Fanon in *The Wretched of the Earth* has used the term "native" in opposition to the word "settler."[11] Postcolonial studies generally refer to "indigenous" in contrast to "invader-settlers." I take the view that Native peoples were the original settlers, in the sense of being a deeply rooted and settled indigenous presence on this land we now call Canada; therefore, I refer to all other state-created Canadians as immigrant "re-settlers." Europeans cannot own the notion of "settler" and "settlement." These words (and their kissing cousin "civilization") represent a perniciously colonialist phraseology that Europeans have always assumed and from which they have justified the conquest and dispossession of peoples native to their lands. There are obviously many ways of settling.

I am, for the most part, referring to those re-settlers with European colonizer origins. I use the terms "Euro-Canadian" and "White" to locate them within what J.M. Blaut, in *The Colonizer's Model of the World*, refers to as "Eurocentric diffusionism," with its racial politics that set the foundation of colonization.[12] The term "White" is, of course, problematic because it is in many ways as reductive, stereotypical, and obstructive as the word "Indian." But like the word "Indian," "White" was birthed at the site of colonization—which is located squarely on White social and racial doctrines. Most of the racially biased images, social arrangements, policies, and legislation that have had an irrevocable impact on Native peoples come specifically from European views and frameworks. It is, therefore, virtually impossible to deny either the term "White" or the existence of racism in any study concerning power relations between White and non-White peoples. To be sure, this may not be a comfortable discussion, but as a study of power relations in society, it certainly is not personal, as such. Of course, racism is personal when it is personally experienced, and Native peoples do experience racism virtually on a daily basis. But to expose and study racism is not to be taken as a personal attack against White or any other people. Racism is a social and ideological problem, not a problem that is unique to a certain "race."

The term "White" does appear throughout this discussion because the vast majority of Native writers use this term. They are conveying an experience that has come to them as "White." Alice Lee, in *Writing the Circle*, captures this "lesson" in one breath: "the year i turned six i began school i wanted to learn to read the first day i learned that the teachers are white the children are white in my new book Dick Jane and Sally are white i learned new words at recess squaw mother dirty halfbreed fucking indian i hope i know how to read soon i already know my colours."[13] No one can read Lenore Keeshig-Tobias's devastating postmodern treatment of "White" in an entry called "Trickster Beyond 1992: Our Relationship" without having to rethink what the term must mean to Native peoples.[14] The title is deceptively academic, but her multimedia conversation with the phantom Trickster is decidedly unbookish. But she implicates academia's traditional glorification of White frontierism and culture: "after three hundred years of prayer and missionaries, things were no better, and getting worse. The white folk kept getting cleaner and cleaner. Heck, they had the best food, cars and real culture—great literature, classical music, theatre—and God was always on their side."[15] Her opening quotation by Iktomi (trickster) provides a mirror for her dialogue: "He is like me, a Trickster, a liar... a new kind of man is coming, a White Man."[16] As a rule, Native writers use this word contrapuntally, sometimes ideologically, but not in a racist way. To charge these writers with "reverse racism," as some may be quick to do, is to miss entirely the point of their "White" experience.

Since there cannot be racial politics without some racists in the politics, I do use the word "racist" whenever applicable or unavoidable. However, I do not "employ it in a simplistic fashion as a diatribe," as Terry Goldie generalizes concerning its usage.[17] In *Fear and Temptation: The Image of the Indigene in Canadian, Australian, and New Zealand Literatures*, though he concedes that "the questions of racism, like those of imperial history, lie behind each line" of his analysis, Goldie takes sweeping exception to the usage of "racist" with the tired argument that no one is "beyond racism."[18] Perhaps no one is beyond racism, but not everyone is empowered by social or legislative means to exercise it. Moreover, strictly speaking, racism is a socially licensed belief in the genetic superiority of one's "race." Surely, not everyone from every culture carries such an ideology. I believe we as human beings are, as a rule, conditioned to be ethnocentric (not necessarily racist), Native peoples no less so, but racism, as it has come to be employed by colonizers and experienced by the colonized, is specifically European in origin. I am not suggesting that Native peoples may never be racist. Nor am I suggesting that only Whites are racist towards us.[19] I use the words "racism" or "racist" in the context of European colonization in that "racism as a specific social doctrine is an invention of the European peoples in the modern period of the expansion around the world."[20] Racism is both the foundation and justification of colonization. As Memmi writes, it "appears" not "as an incidental detail but as a consubstantial part of colonialism."[21] As such, it must be treated in relation to Native-White history in Canada.

Native Canadian Experience

I draw on White portrayals of Native North Americans from the United States to the extent that these portrayals have informed and influenced or parallelled Canadian productions. Perhaps because I lived in the United States for a number of years where few knew anything about Canada in general and even less about Aboriginal peoples, I feel quite strongly that Canadian Aboriginal writers and writing deserve focussed attention. We can be easily eclipsed by White and Native *American* profiles. I do not in any way intend to be parochial, but while we may share significant cultural and political realities, the Canadian

Native experience is not a replica of the Native American encounter. I think it is important for our country that our co-citizens, the non-Native Canadians, learn a lot more about colonial history as well as the rich creative literatures and criticisms they have been gifted with by Aboriginal writers and intellectuals. For these and other reasons I am devoted to bringing to the foreground our Native and Canadian context. Naturally, we have much to learn from our Native American colleagues, as well as from, to use a favoured Native expression, "all our relations" around the world.

But is there a "Native experience," particularly one that is unique to Canada? Given that some one hundred different indigenous cultures, representing ten unrelated linguistic families, or about fifty different languages, greeted Europeans (not all one once, of course) at the first sites of contact, and given all the changes undergone by Native peoples since (and before) this time, it may seem foolhardy to speak of a Native experience in the singular.[22] An incalculable amount of material exists detailing anthropological data as well as the historical development of relations between Euro-Canadians and Natives. These works point to a "kaleidoscope" of diversities among indigenous peoples, but also to some fundamental commonalities, especially in land-spirituality and use of resources.[23] Of course, under certain methodologically defined contexts, the differences must not only be taken into account, they must be highlighted. But the same can be said of their commonalities, which have become more important with time.

I have taken, perhaps perilously, a panoramic view, largely because both the Euro-Canadian textual dehumanization and Native response to it have been broadly, if not sweepingly, expressed. Colonial time has collapsed some fundamental differences among indigenous peoples in areas such as resources, economies, technologies, education, parental and kinship roles, governance, language, religion, and land base. The *Indian Act* has determined identity and locality, defining margins and centres even within the Native community. At the same time, Native peoples' persevering resistance to colonization has also bonded them and provided them with similarities, similarities intricate in their cultural and political workings. In other words, we can speak of the "Native experience" from a number of platforms, and certainly Native peoples can speak from their colonial experience. Native peoples' colonial experience is not uni-dimensional or inflexible. But it is there, as Native writers across many demarcations expressively reveal.

I, of course, share deeply with my Native colleagues everywhere the sense of horror about the extent to which we have been dehumanized. Clearly, no one, no human being, no individual, no group can find tolerable any form of dehumanization. Human beings want to be known as human beings. As sixteenth-century Shakespeare's Shylock, a despised and persecuted merchant, put it:

> I am a Jew. Hath not a Jew eyes? Hath not a Jew hands, organs, dimensions, senses, affections, passions? Fed with the same food, hurt with the same weapons, subject to the same diseases, healed by the same means, warmed and cooled by the same winter and summer as a Christian? If you prick us, do we not bleed? If you tickle us, do we not laugh? If you poison us, do we not die? And if you wrong us, shall we not revenge? (*The Merchant Of Venice*, 3.1.58–67)

In 1849, in a protest letter remarkably similar in tone to Shylock's, Ojibway leader Shinguaconse made his claim for his humanity and that of Native people: "We are men like you, we have the limbs of men, we have the hearts of men, and we feel and know that all this country is ours; even the weakest and most cowardly animals of the forest when hunted to extremity, though they feel destruction sure, will turn upon the hunter."[24]

Shinguaconse's colonially influenced patriarchalized humanity is problematic, but the call is clear: We Native peoples are human and cannot be treated as less than human. The task then is to humanize the "Indian" by, on one hand, de-normalizing the "savage" view, and, on the other, putting forward Native peoples' humanity through their writing. This, at the very least, entails the reframing of what Joyce Green, scholar and professor in Political Studies at the University of Regina, refers to as "the sanitised and partial 'school-book histories.'"[25]

Contrapuntal Space

Edward Said in *Culture and Imperialism* argues for a contrapuntal reading of colonizer texts. Such texts, he suggests, are incompletely understood unless read complexly with the counterpoint of the colonized's experience. Here I use the concept somewhat from the other way around; that is, I read Aboriginal resistance to Canadian textual techniques of mastery as contrapuntal. This does not mean a merely reactionary sort of response; it means that mainstream Canadians will not comprehend our decolonizing discourse unless they can identify the colonial ground from and against which we talk back. But there is nothing simplistic about any of this. Aboriginal theorists place the subjugated Natives at the centre of our investigations as we strive to understand the colonial forces, such as the use of language in the historical record and cultural productions, forces that have become, in the words of Bill Ashcroft, Gareth Griffiths, and Helen Tiffin, "systemic mediums through which a hierarchical structure of power is perpetuated, and the medium through which

conceptions of 'truth', 'order' and 'reality' become established."[26] In the tradition of my ancestors who come from "many roads,"[27] and in the tradition of
liberation resistance literature, which has provided the basis "for an examination of literary critical methodologies and the definitions whereby a literary
corpus is established."[28] I too challenge Western intellectual conventions with
their hegemonic, canonical assumptions of culture and knowledge, and I
most certainly reject any form of domination. I make no attempts to provide
solutions as such, although I do point to new directions, especially, in the final
chapters, around literary criticism; my objective is to highlight Native texts
because I wish to convey as much as possible the flavour and details of the
Native experience and insight, epistemologies and arguments. Native writers
are an extraordinary group of people whose critical, creative, and life writings
have, until recently, been ignored or relegated to ethnographic and personal
"narratives,"[29] which, if read differently, actually contain much anti-colonial
theory, or, at least, much theoretical possibility.

In fact, reading Aboriginal voice and discourse differently demands that
I cite generous portions from the Native documents and writing without
excessive intrusion. This is not to say that Aboriginal material cannot be
criticized or that it is either too transparent or too different, but it requires
a new critical approach and way of reading. Anne Zimmerman, specialist in New Zealand literature, argues for a critical approach that allows for
"extensive quotations…to stand for themselves, perhaps as voices that are
not in tune with the speaking subject's and allow for dissonances of a kind
similar to those which occur in conversation or discussion."[30] In the case of
an Aboriginal scholar treating Aboriginal texts, the issue may not be as much
about dissonance as about *mediation* and *reiteration*. In a way, I am re-citing
the documents because they have not been readily available to readers, nor
have they received the hearing they deserve.

To be sure, there are degrees of dissonance between any text and any
reading, even if there exist cultural and experiential similarities. As it will
become clear, I am no mere "facilitator" for these writings. I am committed to
my freedom of self-expression as an individual and an intellectual. However,
if I am restrained in my critique of Native texts, it is because my goal is not
primarily to perform criticism on Native writing; instead, it is to foreground
Native responses to centuries of misrepresentation. It is also to respect what
appears to be in the making among Aboriginal intellectuals: an Aboriginal-
based criticism within the community, one which seeks to be non-violent
and unintrusive. This is no doubt in reaction to the aggressive and sometimes
ruthless tradition of Western criticism. An Aboriginal approach to literary

criticism is now emerging, and I take up in Chapter 7 some of the issues that confront us as we seek to theorize our lives, our writing, and our discourse.

Writing, Arun Mukherjee reminds us, "is not just a matter of putting one's thoughts on paper. Writing is also about social power. How I write depends a lot on who I write for."[31] This is a point that may have escaped Penny Petrone in 1983 when she, in my opinion, misjudged Native social protest writing as "some of it written by militant patriots and couched in strident, sloganistic language."[32] For my part, though I take my place as a resistance writer and scholar, I am no militant patriot and I will not couch my language.

I avoid as much as possible obscure language, which has become such an uncontrollable part of postcolonial and literary criticism. The mystification of the English language provides no necessary proof that one comprehends the experience of colonization; likewise, it provides no support for the task of re-evaluating colonial writing. On the other hand, neither do I believe in oversimplification. I am an academic, after all, but I do want my scholarship to be useful to my audience, which must include those who form the backdrop to my research and writing, my family and my community, the Native peoples of Canada. I am thinking especially of future generations of Native students who will need intellectual traditions meaningful to their histories and perspectives. My long life in the university would certainly have been made more intellectually satisfying had I found a contemporary Native intellectual community in which to develop my thinking, teaching, and research.

Finally, I believe that inasmuch as we must seek to recognize the faces of both the colonizer and the colonized, we must at the same time acknowledge that we are human beings and, as such, are more than the sum total of our colonial parts.

There is much here that can dishearten even the most optimistic reader or researcher. I did not even include anywhere near all the combustible and hate material against Native peoples that is extant in our sacralised institutions as well as in popular culture. It is stunning.

At the same time I found hope that my generation and subsequent generations—of students, scholars, and artists, Native and non-Native—are producing a vociferous counter-discourse. This material from so many different fields and disciplines is not only disputatious but reconstructive, inventive, cogent and often elegant. The depth and scope of the scholarship is inspiring. An then there are all the new novels, short stories, poetry, plays, essays and dissertations coming out by a new 'coterie' of Native writers and intellectuals. But beauty and inspiration by itself cannot make the change required. So a lot of work remains to be done.

I believe the majority of non-Native peoples in our country want to be fair and caring, not just replicating a history full of mistakes and some malefaction. Native peoples, a dynamic and engaging peoples, also take exception to being restricted to colonial models or experience. Nevertheless, our encounter is informed by colonization. Colonial texts are offensive. In fact, many of these texts constitute hate literature. Few scholars, comparatively speaking, have challenged, much less excised, these records in any direct way. That this is so serves to alienate Aboriginal intellectuals from the Canadian intellectual community. It also dampens the desire to engage in reading offensive material. How many potential Aboriginal scholars have these records turned away? Shakespeare's Shylock cried out for a recognition of his humanity in the sixteenth century; here we are in the twenty-first century still having to demand respect for our humanity. I have struggled with the ramifications of my exposition because I would like to be generous. I was raised to be polite and tolerant. But how does one read hate literature—or the selective inattention to it—generously?

Today, there is a rapidly growing, consciously alert, decolonizing scholarship, much of it inspired through Native Studies, feminist, postcolonial, and indigenous criticism. We all stand on the shoulders of such works—these writers in turn stand on the sloping shoulders of the colonized. But even this, however significant, has only begun to address in any sustained way the concerns here expressed by Native writers. While much is in the process of changing in White scholarly, critical, and constitutional treatment of Native peoples, much more work remains to be done. Aboriginal scholarship and creative writing are in a unique position of advancing this work; however, all scholars and other intellectuals are challenged to attend to decolonization in keeping with our respective legacies. Native resistance to dehumanization challenges the academy to re-examine its privileged position. The assumption is, of course, that decolonization is a dynamic process requiring introspection and critical change. Our collective aspiration must be the ending of our (Native) marginalization in society and in scholarship. Finally, it is my hope that this re-examination of both White and Native Canadian writing may generate new frameworks of interpretation, certainly dramatically new perceptions concerning the power of text as it speaks to the White-Native encounter in Canada. It should also remind us of the extensive contribution Native writers have made and are continuing to make to Canadian culture, especially to intellectual development in history, literature, anthropology, and criticism. For me as an Aboriginal writer and scholar, all this is home now.

*　　*　　*

Because of the sheer volume of Native writing and of historiographic and critical material available on Native history and literature, I limit the time period of study from about 1850 to 1990. Even so this is a huge span of time but it is made more or less manageable by the fact there were very few published Native writers until the 1970s. I go back to the mid-1800s largely because I want to include George Copway (1818–1869) and Pauline Johnson (1862–1914), the two most expressive and well-known Native writers of their times. Since there was an absence of Native presence in Canadian culture from the 1870s to the 1970s, most of the writers selected for this study fall roughly within 1970 to 1990. This twenty-year span of time saw the beginnings of what has become a vibrant, inventive, and growing community of contemporary Aboriginal (First Nations and Metis) essayists, novelists, poets, playwrights, and humorists, many of them also educators and scholars from a variety of disciplines. I stop at about 1990 because this seems to represent a turning point in Aboriginal writing not only in terms of creative productivity by writers but also in themes, direction, and critical treatment. This exciting development has resulted in many changes for writers, academics, and critics alike. And I believe also for Canada at large, as may be indicated by John Ralston Saul's opening declaration in his recent book *A Fair Country,* that "We are a metis civilization." I can't argue with that.

On the other hand, there is much to argue against a book such as *Disrobing the Aboriginal Industry* by Widdowson and Howard.[33] These two books were both published in 2008, quite beyond the period under study, but they do remind me that Canada seems split in its attitudes towards Aboriginal peoples. In important ways much has changed from early exploration literature era. But clearly, not nearly enough has changed—some relic colonial attitudes are still in circulation as can be found in *Disrobing* which when put next to Dick Pound's Olympian judgments that Canada was once a land of savages, to say nothing of the *The Globe and Mail*'s shameless support for Pound,[34] jars me into a discomfiting reassurance that my call to "extinguish" Canada's Civ/Sav master narrative is more than relevant for scholarly dissection.

Like uncontrolled wildfire this particular master narrative has raged on long enough, and as abundantly evidenced in the following chapters, has burned into the hearts and minds of Aboriginal peoples. The Civ/Sav doctrine permeates Canadian culture and is obviously very powerful. Yet I am noticing that scholarly references to it, while increasingly critical, are still fairly indirect. Post-colonial theorists in particular seem especially shy to deal with dichotomies and binaries, as if such ideas or their aftereffects no longer exist. It is not enough to simply make a nodding acknowledgment of the Civ/Sav's radioactive lifespan; this would be the place and time to redirect the colonial gaze, and give it a microscopic examination. It is incumbent on us all to understand its twisty workings in our cultural productions. There is no "metis civilization" for Canada otherwise.

Chapter One

Insider Notes: Reframing the Narratives

The prairie is full of bones.
The bones stand and sing
and I feel the weight of them
as they guide my fingers on this page

—Louise Halfe, *Blue Marrow*

In the summer of 1974, I worked for the Native Curriculum Resource Project, part of the Province of Alberta's Department of Education. My job was to research alternatives to Alberta's provincial curriculum with respect to its treatment of Native peoples. I was struck immediately by the endless layers of stereotypes in both elementary and secondary textbooks, particularly in history and social studies. I easily connected what I was discovering—and in an important sense, re-discovering—with what I had known as a Metis student in public schools. I was connecting my knowledge with my experience, or, as I have written earlier, my footnotes with my voice.[1] This research enabled me to write *Defeathering the Indian*, which addresses the problem of stereotypes in schools and in society.[2] *Defeathering the Indian* is, on one level, a curriculum handbook for teachers. On another, perhaps more important level, it is a resistance book without the political language to mark it as such. What I was protesting—that is, resisting—was the portrayal of Native peoples as befeathered savages. I pointed out the prevalence of the stereotypes in school textbooks, classroom politics, and in society, particularly as promoted by the media and marketplace. I explained how dehumanizing it is to be seen and treated as savages, as less than human creatures bereft of valuable culture, coherent language, and multidimensional personalities. I turned to facts of biography and cultural information, and used humour, among other things, to highlight our (Native) humanity and challenge the Canadian historical record and its gamut of culturally produced stereotypes. I turned the tables to point out, however meekly, who the "real savages" (meaning the American cavalry) were. In the end, I optimistically (naively, some would say) appealed to our common humanity, to common sense and common decency. I tried to be subtle rather than explosive, but I think such a concern was more a mark of my colonization than of my liberation. And, certainly, I was unaware of sexist language. I was young and in the early stages of decolonization. In many ways I was not particularly aware of Western-defined politics. I was just beginning to shore up my Plains Cree-Metis–based youthful knowledge with another kind of knowledge, the outside world of many voices and the protocols of Western scholarship.

I was also entering a particular kind of discourse. I was quite unaware, at the time, that I was well within an established and ever developing Native resistance tradition, in facts, process, tone, and approach. Indeed, the unity of experience, presentation, and argumentation across the centuries of this tradition is dramatic. Whether in the form of social and historical commentaries, autobiographies, short stories, legends, poetry, or plays, whether it is in the 1790s or 1990s, whether it is lands, reserves, homesteads, homes, parents, children, or women personally invaded, or whether it is languages, ceremonies, epistemologies, or faiths suppressed, there is a striking unity of occurrence. Native writers record historical and personal incursions, social upheavals, a range of emotions, and unique individual and cultural backgrounds, and struggle for hope and determination. The earlier style of recording these many realities is often a mixture of rhetoric, extraordinary insight, moral outrage, and dignified poignancy. Literary devices are both inventive and prosaic. The argumentation combines historical and current Aboriginal traditions, including resistance and postcolonial strategies. The writing is more complex than first meets the eye.

Is Native Writing Resistance Literature?

Native activists and intellectuals have long been *resisting* Canada's political and intellectual treatment of Native peoples. However, situating Native writing as resistance literature requires some discussion because, for a number of historical and cultural reasons, Native writing does present its own unique problems, approaches, and features. In *Resistance Literature*, Barbara Harlow traces the development of the theory of resistance literature to organized resistance militant movements for national liberation and independence "on the part of the colonized peoples in those areas of the world over which Western Europe and North America have sought socio-economic control and cultural dominion." These movements have produced "a significant corpus of literary writing, both narrative and poetic, as well as a broad spectrum of theoretical analysis of the political, ideological, and cultural parameters of this struggle."[3] The writers, ideologues, and theoreticians of these movements "have articulated a role for literature and poets within the struggle alongside the gun, the pamphlet and the diplomatic delegation."[4]

Given these parameters, Native writing does not strictly follow "resistance literature within the early Third World"[5] terms. In the first instance, Native peoples of Canada did not have written languages;[6] therefore, they did not leave their own written records of their resistance activities against the early European intruders. Indeed, it is not until the late 1700s and early 1800s that a few individual Natives were able to write in English, having learned the skills of Western literacy from missionaries. Reflecting the complexity of the Native people's relationship with the missionaries and the Canadian school system, be it public or residential, Native writing as a form of any significant collective expression was not possible until about the 1970s, if not the 1980s.[7] This is not to imply that English literacy is a necessary foundation to resistance, for clearly Native people resisted the European oppressions long before they took up the English alphabet. Indeed, resisting colonial languages has been an integral part of the resistance.

Native writers have a complicated relationship with the English language, a relationship that reflects more than 500 years of cultural, linguistic, and political appropriations, exchanges, and confrontations. As Albert Memmi points out, literacy is a linguistic, political, and psychological challenge for colonized peoples of oral traditions who move on to the technique of writing—that is, adopting, and surely tweaking—the colonizer's language.[8]

Many Native writers have certainly commented on the difficulties of adopting the colonizer's language(s). This awareness is perhaps why many Native writers and speakers have felt compelled to acknowledge our oral traditions. Apparently self-conscious of the fact Native North Americans presumably did not have written languages, Native writers have extolled their spoken languages as well as their methods of recollection. But, more than self-consciousness or concession, we are assigning equal value to oral traditions which, of course, include an array of communication signs and systems that may form a "sort of text." One of the earliest Native writers, George Copway (1818–1869), begins his cultural defence in 1847 by what at first appears to be concession: "I have not the happiness of being able to refer to written records in narrating the history of my forefathers." But he also immediately stakes out the value of oral tradition by calling on his memory: "but I can reveal to the world what has long been laid up in my memory."[9] Similarly, a century later, Chief Dan George wrote, "My people's memory / Reaches into the / Beginning of all things."[10] The final report of the Royal Commission on Aboriginal Peoples, issued in 1996, also highlights an anonymous statement by one of the Native presenters: "I have no written speech. Everything that I have said I had been carrying in my heart, because I have seen it. I have experienced it."[11]

In 1969 northwest coast folklorist, artist, and actor George Clutesi (1905–1988) introduced his collection of Tse-Shat traditions, traditions he translated into English, by declaring that he avoids documentation: "This narrative is not meant to be documentary. In fact, it is meant to evade documents. It is meant for the reader to feel and to say I was there and indeed I saw."[12]

It is often taken for granted that literacy is an enormous improvement in human evolution. Those of us who come from oral traditions have quite different perspectives on literacy (and evolution). In fact, literacy becomes the enemy when printed words are used for "extinguishment" purposes, as nineteenth-century Ojibway activist Catherine Soneegoh Sutton (1823–1865) put it so poignantly.[13] Not only is English (or French) the vehicle for the extinguishment of Aboriginal rights, it is also the expressive means of dehumanization. Mohawk lawyer, educator, activist, and writer Patricia Monture-Angus explains that "it is probably fortunate for Aboriginal people today that so many of our histories are oral histories. Information that was kept in people's heads was not available to Europeans, could not be changed and molded into pictures of 'savagery' and 'paganism.'"[14] For these reasons, and as George Clutesi knew so well, in certain contexts documentation must be assiduously avoided. My parents, who were of Clutesi's generation, but, unlike Clutesi, never attended school, knew this too. This is why my father refused to let me go to school until he had no choice. This is why my grandmother and my mother told us stories deep into the winter nights. Clearly, it is not by accident that I grew up so close to my language, a language that remains closest to my soul, and just as clearly I have my parents to thank for their insightful resistance, a resistance I did not fully appreciate until I began to understand that language is the epistemological basis of culture.

As Ojibway writer and ethnographer Basil Johnston argues, it is through our languages we carry our world views, which are, in turn, expressed in our epistemologies.[15] This means, then, that our approaches to the notion and application of knowledge may be quite different from those that inform Western conventions. Anthropologist Robin Ridington has posited that oral-based, hunting Aboriginal societies approach knowledge rather than materials as technology and "they code information about their world differently from those of us whose discourse is conditioned by written documents."[16] These "differences," as Ridington appreciates, are much more involved than the oversimplified comparative charts that have become current in discussions on Aboriginal cultural differences or "traditions."[17] Among non-Native scholars, Ridington has among the most perceptive understandings of how northern hunting societies conceive of and apply knowledge, and that this knowledge is intimately linked to language, land, and skills. Land-based Aboriginal cultures are nuanced and intricate, and this should raise questions about how we translate them into our urban lives, literatures, and criticisms.[18] In any event, the indigenous *eh-tay-ta-moowin* (in Cree it approximates "hypothesizing") and *eh-too-ta-moo-win* ("praxis") have implications for those of us engaged in scholarly activities. Cree writer and educator Janice Acoose finds "writing in the colonizer's language simultaneously painful and liberating."[19] Painful because English provides her "the only recourse… to convey the reality of the Indigenous peoples." Painful because our words have been infantilized, stolen, silenced, or erased. Yet, "writing in the colonizer's language" is also facilitative (I am not sure I can agree that it is liberating), for as Acoose puts it, "doing research and writing encourages re-creation, renaming and empowerment of both Indigenous peoples and non-indigenous peoples."[20]

There is no question but that literacy and the art and politics of documentation present us with cultural problems when, for example, literacy steals the nuances of oral expressions, and with political problems when words are used to vilify or to dispossess. But literacy in and of itself is a great human achievement; obviously, literacy is a two-edged sword dependent on whether humans use it for oppressive or emancipatory purposes. In certain contexts I can certainly appreciate George Clutesi's strategy of avoiding documentation, but those of us today engaged in scholarship and writing cannot and must not avoid documentation. For now we are here. And document we must, for much of the "war" is in the words. And document we do.

Further, we are in the twenty-first century, and English (or French) is as much our birthright as our Aboriginal languages. English is in many respects our new "native" language, not only because English may become the only language known to future Native generations (I shudder at the thought) but also because it has become the common language through which we now communicate. English is now serving to unite us, and, in many ironic respects, serving to decolonize us. In this sense, perhaps we can say literacy is liberating. Our usage of English is, of course, not necessarily that of the colonizer. Since we have a painful and political relationship with this language, we attend to the task of "reinventing the enemy's language" as Native American poet Joy Harjo has so aptly put it.[21] To reinvent the enemy's language is a re-creative process, and for Cree poets, a Cree-ative process, and, as such, English is now as much our vehicle of creative expression as it is our vehicle of resistance.

Assessing Native resistance writing is also complicated by the fact Natives are still expressing the presentness of their colonization. It is apparent that Native peoples are not uniformly conscious of or resistant to their colonized condition, one expression of which is the internalization of the colonizer's standards and stereotypes. One consequence of this internalization is the Natives' sense of shame concerning their Indianness, a theme many Native writers treat. This sense of shame is another indication of having taken on the images, standards, or expectations of the colonizer, which Metis historian and social critic Howard Adams referred to as the "White Ideal" in *Prison of Grass*.[22] Powerful media through which White North Americans' conceptions of beauty, status, acceptability, privilege, or reality become established have had damaging effects on both White and Native self-images. Whereas for Whites the White Ideal has, as a rule, provided them with an exaggerated self-assurance, Native peoples, much like other oppressed or "minority" groups,[23] have struggled with self-acceptance in the face of formidable racial and cultural rejection. And such racism continues to harass contemporary generations even if it appears to some that there is an Aboriginal "industry" of privilege! There are no socio-economic privileges for Aboriginal peoples, but more, they are still being hounded and haunted by White North America's image machine, which has persistently portrayed them in extremes as either the grotesque ignoble or noble savage. Internalization is just one of our struggles against misrepresentation, which in our literatures are reflected in both overt and subtle ways. The study of Native writing must take into consideration this not so inconsiderable problem evident in our works and across generations, a point to which I return in Chapter 6.

In any case, resistance literature is no longer limited to specific historical liberation movements in Africa, Central and South America, or the Far and Middle East; it has broadened to include what is now generally referred to as postcolonial literatures. Ashcroft, Griffiths, and Tiffin use the term "postcolonial" to "cover all the culture affected by the imperial process from the moment of colonization to the present day" in which there is concern "with the world as it exists during and after the period of European imperial domination and the effects of this on contemporary literatures." And they suggest that "it is most appropriate as the term for the new cross-cultural criticism which has emerged in recent years and for the discourse through which this is constituted."[24]

Native peoples certainly fall within (and outside) the inclusive terms as set out here, although Native Canadians hardly enjoy "postcoloniality" since their colonial experience is imbricated with the past and present. Neither is the Native experience of colonialism universally understood nor has Native writing as resistance been consistently recognized at home or abroad. Nevertheless, we have been protesting being othered or dominated by re-settler colonies. We have certainly been articulating the experience and, to rephrase Ashcroft, Griffiths, and Tiffin, *talking back* "to the imperial centre."[25]

Articulating the experience and "talking back" constitutes, according to Peter Hitchcock, a "dialogics of the oppressed," and while dialogics does not end the oppression, it does "constitute a significant logic of resistance and an array of contestatory practices."[26] Native peoples of Canada have been engaging in contestatory practices right from the initial contact with Europeans to the present. But more to the point, Native writers and critics are not going to depend on external definitions as to whether they have written resistance literature. It is to Native writing and theorizing that critics must turn to be able to assess the cause and nature of the resisting Native in Canada.

To be sure, resistance may not always be immediately apparent to the unstudied; for examples we can turn to a range of works by authors that include Chief Dan George, Ruby Slipperjack, Tomson Highway, Tom King, Richard Wagamese, Richard Van Camp, or Eden Robinson, among others. With respect to producing literature along with armed resistance, no one Native nation or peoples has produced literature from an "organized resistance movement" within a "specific historical context," as defined by Harlow.[27] This is undoubtedly due to the vast cultural, linguistic, and geographical differences among the indigenous peoples of Canada. Perhaps Louis Riel, who today would be understood as a liberation resistance fighter, came closest to producing literature within an organized resistance movement, but he had no colleagues in this pursuit. Certainly, many Native works cannot be considered works of resistance in the tradition of liberationist Third World thinkers and writers or the explosive American Black writers of the 1960s, such as Eldridge Cleaver or Malcolm X, but, as I have argued, a simple assertion of one's (Native) humanity is a form of resistance, given the magnitude of dehumanization over a span of 500 years. In this overarching history of colonization, Native peoples have developed a collective sense of relationship to the land and to each other, and to the common cause of decolonization. In this sense, every politically aware Native teacher, scholar, writer, artist, filmmaker, poet, or activist is ultimately a producer of resistance material. In fact, precisely because Native writers have not written "alongside the gun,"[28] their writing is all the more the form of articulate resistance in Canada.

Native Writers Resisting Colonial Practices

Not only is this writing articulate, it is in fact quite extensive, as Penny Petrone documents in *Native Literature in Canada: From Oral Tradition to the Present.*[29] Petrone produced the first comprehensive study of Native literatures and showed how much and how long Natives have been writing. Although she acknowledges the social protest element to this literature, her reading is more an ethnography than a study in intellectual agency. But Native writing is much more the story of strategic contestation than it is of ethnographic testaments, and when cultural information is provided it is usually a device of contestation.

Now, of course, an increasing assortment of scholars are paying increasing attention to Aboriginal perspectives. But I am not sure to what extent these scholars appreciate the oppressive nature of colonial canons and their pernicious workings in our respective intellectual lives. The problem has centrally to do with the "civ/sav" ideology,[30] which dichotomizes Native-White relations in terms of civilization inevitably winning over savagery, as most Western writers have assumed throughout the centuries. This ideology circles the wagon, so to speak, on any Native action and reaction as something infantile or less than human. Historical and literary treatment of so-called "Indian Wars" is a case in point: Aboriginal Nations fighting to save their persons, communities, cultures, and lands was propagandized as simply irrational violence of bloodthirsty savages.

But once the Native-White encounter is understood as colonially framed, and once Native peoples are accorded humanity, we can find their many contestations in a variety of genres going back to the earliest encounters. So read, the subtext to the very records that sought to denigrate Native humanity is a power struggle between newcomer and indigenous discourses. For example, as recorded in the *Jesuit Relations*, Father Brébeuf remarks on Huron challenge to the Jesuit tenets of creation and "our other mysteries." Apparently miffed that the "headstrong" Huron approached this discussion with cultural relativism, Brebeuf points out to them "by means of a little globe… that there is only one world," to which the Huron "remain without reply."[31] This is a fairly classic instance of early Europeans resorting to technical trickery to strengthen their claim to superiority, especially when they were confronted with Native cultural and intellectual scepticism or resistance. Parker Duchemin in "'A Parcel of Whelps', Alexander Mackenzie among the Indians," explains that, as a way of establishing White authority over Native peoples, "a charade of white omniscience and omnipotence...was played and replayed" by European explorers.[32] It had to be replayed because Native peoples were not so easily impressed. The point is Native peoples were not glazed-eyed savages sitting on their haunches by the seashore waiting for European gods and baubles. In the understated words of Olive Dickason in *Canada's First Nations*, "most authorities agree that it is highly unlikely that 'civilization' was brought over whole to a welcoming population waiting to be enlightened."[33] A decolonized critical review of archival records shows Native peoples resisted ideological impositions, economic exploitation, cultural insults, and personal abuse.[34]

Similarly, a critical review of contemporary Native writing shows that Natives have been resisting colonizing practices as long as they have been writing. The depth and scope of Natives engaging in contestatory literature is such that we can refer to it as a tradition in the sense of canon. We can trace this tradition from—as Petrone puts it—the "first literary coterie of Indians in Canada" of the mid-1800s.[35] Of course, the most dramatic growth of Native writing has taken place since 1969 when Harold Cardinal signalled the arrival of contemporary resistance writing with his *Unjust Society*. If any era birthed Native resistance literature proper, it is the 1970s, for, on the heels of Cardinal came, first, a steady stream of socio-political commentaries, then poetry, and autobiographies. Also published in this era were a miscellany of collections that presented a cross-section of biographies, essays of social and literary criticism, interviews, government reports or proposals, newspaper articles and editorials, short stories, plays, and poetry.

This was followed in the 1980s, finally, by novels. Beatrice Culleton's *In Search of April Raintree* (1983), Jeannette Armstrong's *Slash* (1985), Ruby Slipperjack's *Honour the Sun* (1987), and Lee Maracle's *I am Woman* (1988)— which is not a novel—became popular reading and made it into mainstream classrooms studying Canadian Native peoples. These works have gained considerable attention, especially as resistance works. Since then, streams of novels have been published, most of them after 1990; among the most well known include Thomas King (*Medicine River; Green Grass, Running Water*), Ruby Slipperjack (*Silent Words*), Lee Maracle (*Sundogs; Raven*), and Richard Wagamese (*Keeper 'n Me; A Quality of Light*), Richard Van Camp (*The Lesser Blessed*), Tomson Highway (*Kiss of the Fur Queen*), Jeannette Armstrong (*Whispering in Shadows*), and Eden Robinson (*Monkey Beach*).

Poetry has continued to pour in from a host of writers, much of which is to be found in current anthologies on Native literature as well as in literary journals and periodicals. A number of poets have also published books of poetry (e.g., Rita Joe, Duke Redbird, Louise Halfe, Marilyn Dumont, Beth Cuthand, Annharte Baker, Duncan Mercredi, Gregory Scofield). Short stories and plays are also to be found in both old and new anthologies. Entertaining short-story writers include Richard Van Camp, the humorist and prolific writer/playwright Drew Hayden Taylor, and veteran writer and ethnologist Basil Johnston. And, of course, plays by Tomson Highway (*The Rez Sisters, Dry Lips Oughta Move to Kapuskasing*) have received international recognition. Other notable playwrights include Margo Kane, Floyd Favel, Daniel David Moses, Ian Ross, Armand Ruffo, and Monique Mojica.

There are resistance themes common to all these works, irrespective of genre, gender, era, or even chronology. They engage fairly overt postcolonial and decolonization themes that include the re-establishing of Native cultures and the challenging of historical and cultural records. The texts also expose destructive government policies and social injustices. Many novelists, short-story writers, poets, and biographers recount cultural fragmentation in the form of community and personal crises. Others analyze colonial records, and some focus on the struggle for revitalization and self-determination. Finally, I take note that Native literary criticism is forming into a new formidable intellectual genre since the arrival of *Looking at the Words of Our People: First Nations Analysis of Literature* (1993), edited by Jeannette Armstrong.[36] A first of its kind, this Native Canadian-published collection of critical essays situates Native North American writing in American and Canadian intellectual life. Although many of the essays focus on American material, essays by Janice Acoose, Kateri Damm, and Gerry William treat Canadian writers such as Maria Campbell, Howard Adams, Beatrice Culleton, and Thomas King. Since then a number of other publications of critical essays authored largely by Native writers and academics have appeared, and they include: *(Ad)dressing Our Words* (2001), ed. by Armand Garnet Ruffo; *Creating Community: A Roundtable on Canadian Aboriginal Literature* (2002), ed. by Renate Eigenbrod and Jo-Ann Episkenew; *Aboriginal Oral Traditions* (2008), ed. by Renée Hulan and Renate Eigenbord.[37] In addition to Native-authored literary criticism published in journals, anthologies and some books, Native peoples have been producing other kinds of critical works as well; for example, there are numerous theses and a considerable number of dissertations produced by Native graduate students. There are also legends, children's stories, ethnographies, arts and crafts manuals, and so forth. I have previously considered these as "soft sell literature," but they are, in fact, forms of resistance as they too represent contemporary efforts to re-establish the validity of Aboriginal aesthetics and formats.

Voice as Resistance Scholarship

Many of us who are writers are also scholars. As a writer and a long-standing professor in Native Studies, I have per force been dealing with issues that confront resistance writers who work inside the academic community and mandates.[38] For me, there has always been an insider/outsider tension, although much of my three decades in the university I have experienced as an outsider. To this day, in fact, the only time I feel more or less like an insider is when I am mentoring grad students or meeting with my colleagues. Arun Mukherjee's *Oppositional Aesthetics*, describes experiences strikingly similar to my own, particularly the struggle to assume intellectual agency in the face of Western scholarship's continuing practice of universalizing Western experience and knowledge. Take the notion and politics of theory, especially in the study of literature. In the context of discussing rankings and promotions in universities, Mukherjee points to the pressure to "write in sanctioned ways," and to get "published in the right places," which, she explains, is not simply a matter of "disagreements with other scholars in a dialogical mode."[39]

To write and research in sanctioned ways often involve the invocation of theory. Barbara Christian questions what she calls "the race for theory" in an article of the same title. Christian notes that "there has been a takeover in the literary world by Western philosophers" such that "they have re-invented the meaning of theory."[40] She believes that this has served to silence and to intimidate "peoples of color" whether they are creative writers or academics. She argues that this represents a new version of Western hegemony: "I see the language it creates as one which mystifies rather than clarifies our condition, making it possible for a few people who know that particular language to control the critical scene." She adds that this took place "interestingly enough, just when the literature of peoples of colour…began to move to 'the centre.'"[41] And like Mukherjee, Christian argues this is political. "It is difficult to ignore this takeover," she explains, "since theory has become a commodity which helps determine whether we are hired or promoted in academic institutions—worse whether we are heard at all."[42] Christian further argues that "people of color have always theorized—but in forms quite different from the western form of abstract logic."[43]

Cree Metis people engaged in abstract logic, but not necessarily or totally in the same way or about the same things as Western peoples. That this is so must make a difference in our theories and research. I have been investigating how and where these places of difference emerge for someone like me who carries an indigenous ethos and epistemological basis and also works within Western scholarship, yet calls for decolonization (for everyone and on many levels). Needless to say, I have been confronted with extraordinary pedagogical and canonical challenges, contradictions, anomalies, and, at times, insults. In my earlier years at the university, practising positionality of resistance in scholarship was sacrilege, and not fashionable as it now appears to have become.

How well I remember a particular letter of reference in my application for doctoral studies in history. A professor I trusted and held in some regard (who was also a colleague, as I had been publishing and teaching long before I was able to take up doctoral studies) characterized my work as suffering from "too much introspection and the facts of her own biography." He patronized me as a "remarkably talented" but "undisciplined scholar," and ended with a gratuitous slap by asking the department to "assist [me] in taking this step towards realizing [my] full potential as a scholar." This was in 1990, when it was not uncommon for mainstream academics to undermine the work of Native scholars with charges of parochialism, "advocacy history,"[44] or even reverse racism. This was done with the confidence of objectivity, a confidence only colonialist scholars have enjoyed.

To say the least, such accusations are glaringly ironic, given the racism evident in White texts on Native peoples and cultures, a racism unabashedly inflammatory, patronizing, and subjective. And yes, there is advocacy history—it is stitched into the very core of the re-settler canon. Plainly, there is overwhelming evidence that the Western argument for "objectivity" is a self-serving tool of those accustomed to managing history.

The discourse of "bias"—or its apparent opposite, "objectivity"—is of particular interest to Aboriginal scholars. The essence of the dominant Western narrative is its claim to "objectivity." As Russell Ferguson writes, objectivity is simply assumed by utilizing techniques of supposed absence: "In our society discourse tries never to speak its own name. Its authority is based on absence. The absence is not just that of the various groups classified as 'other,' although members of these groups are routinely denied power. It is also the lack of any overt acknowledgement of the specificity of the dominant culture, which is simply assumed to be the all-encompassing norm. This is the basis of its power."[45]

This technique of absence, or what may be called the subterranean Western voice, as practised especially by earlier anthropologists and historians but still echoed by many mainstream intellectuals, is a tool in the politics of power. While Native voice in scholarship has been swiftly stigmatized, White North American voice over Native history and cultures has been normalized. Techniques of absence are nowhere more present than in the classically colonial, archival, and academic descriptions and data about Natives' tools, physical features, beliefs (which are often degraded to "rituals"), or even geography. There is, as Parker Duchemin explains, an "appearance of impartiality" to these descriptions, and it is this appearance that has been mistaken for objectivity.[46] Such appearances are in fact imperial and are not at all objective or impartial (see Chapter 2). To the point here, such airs of detachment are in direct contrast to my Plains Cree-Metis socialization, which encourages integration between the "self" and the "word."

Cree clearly differentiates *achimoowin* ("fact") from *atowkehwin* ("fiction"). It allows the speaker to speak in his or her own voice without assuming that voice is mired in what Kathleen Rockhill calls "chaos of subjectivity."[47] One's own voice is never totally of one's self, in isolation from community. At the same time, one's self is not a communal replica of the collective. The Cree knew themselves as *Nehiyawehwak*, the Exact Speaking People.[48] As a *Nehiyohsquoh* (exact-speaking woman), I choose to use my exact-speaking voice whether I am writing history or whether I am writing poetry. Or teaching in a university classroom. Of course, voice is not primarily about oneself or even of "one's people" (a favourite colonial expression)—it is more a recognition of the relationship between power and knowledge, which then reveals positionality. From this theoretical base I have pursued my academic career.

I am in good company, for many scholars and writers from non-Western traditions (and feminists from a variety of traditions) are refusing to remain alienated from their "selves."[49] Likewise, by refusing to remain distant from my words and works, I am not only attempting to remain true to my heritage, I am also seeking cultural agency. Peter Hitchcock's exploration of dialogics in which "both subject and object are decentered" is helpful here: "Rather than assume subaltern subjectivity as forever the concern of what has been derisively called 'victim studies' a dialogic approach emphasizes the cultural agency of the oppressed and also shows what political implications this might have for literary analysis in general and cultural studies in particular...the underlying concern is to develop a critique of the epistemological bases of the academy that marginalize or ghettoize those cultures that would call its authority into question."[50]

But I do not approach scholarship only from a cultural location, especially one that is often reductively and categorically classified as "different," which I take to be the colonizer's strategy. Rather, as one who comes from a dispossessed people, I engage with my research. A key part of this necessarily and unavoidably means disturbing the re-settler canon.

Palestinian writer and critic Ghassan Kanafani challenged Western scholarship by arguing that research of the subjugated was finally legitimized only by the researcher's engagement in the language and resistance of the subjugated. Kanafani asserted that "no research of this kind can be complete unless the researcher is located within the resistance movement itself inside the occupied land, taking his testimony from the place in which it is born... the lips of the people." Kanafani, as Harlow explains, "not only disclaims any pretence to 'academic objectivity' or 'scientific dispassion,' he rejects too the very relevance in a study of resistance literature of such critical stances or poses."[51]

Kanafani's stand is not entirely unprecedented, even in Western practices. The questions and debates concerning the study of history that came out of Michelet's passionate and engaging *History of the French Revolution* (1833–1867) comes to mind. In his introduction to Michelet's translated work, Gordon Wright argues that "Michelet could never be the impartial judge, weighing evidence and letting it guide his decision. He was an historian *engagé*, the impassioned evangelizer of a new gospel."[52] Michelet would have taken to Kanafani. Or perhaps Said.

Edward W. Said wrote extensively on the relationship of power to knowledge. In *Orientalism*, he points out that while the West's requirement for knowledge to be non-political, that is, "scholarly, academic, impartial, above partisan or small-minded doctrinal belief," it is an "ambition in theory." In practice it is "much more problematic" because no one "has ever devised a method for detaching the scholar from the circumstances of life, from the fact of his involvement (conscious or unconscious) with a class, a set of beliefs, a social position, or from the mere activity of being a member of society."[53] He challenges too the "general liberal consensus that 'true' knowledge is fundamentally non-political (and conversely that overtly political knowledge is not 'true' knowledge)." In fact, he cautions, "No one is helped in understanding this today when the adjective 'political' is used as a label to discredit any work for daring to violate the protocol of pretended surprapolitical objectivity."[54]

Said's observations are certainly applicable to the Canadian academic community and its treatment of Aboriginal history, text, and scholarship. The political nature of the colonizer's language(s), his/her ownership of "history" (or who qualifies as "historian"), "objectivity," and other hegemonic practices have inspired what should most appropriately be understood as Native resistance scholarship and discourse. Much like other non-Western scholars before us, we are grappling with the relationship between knowledge and power, between misrepresentation and resistance.

Resistance is in me and in the literature I document and analyze. However, at multiple levels, I am constantly negotiating practices and canons of the colonizer and yet remaining one of the voices of the colonized. Obviously, I value and enjoy university scholarship and at the same time I respect my Plains Cree-Metis knowledge and ways of approaching knowledge. For example, I try to maintain orality both in my style of teaching and, in certain contexts, also in my academic writing.[55] I find it useful to make a distinction between scholarship as a disciplined way of approaching knowledge that requires training in certain academic skills and language, and scholarship (purportedly) that advances a particular ideology. The question is whether we can separate skill or craft from ideology.

In order for me to exercise liberation, I must create an intellectual practice that claims my own humanity and style, one that builds scholarship based on this humanity. I consider my use of "voice" good scholarship, not a contradiction, as some might argue. My use of voice is a textual resistance technique in that it concerns discourse and presentation, not simply or necessarily personal or familial matters. Voice is much more than about introspection or even about "sounding differences," to borrow the phrase from Janice Williamson.[56] It is, in large part, corrective scholarship. Native scholars and writers are demonstrating that voice can be, must be, used within academic studies, not only as an expression of cultural agency, but as a form of resisting misrepresentation in Canadian scholarship and popular culture.

The implication for me as a practising academic is that when I use my voice (say, through references to first-person commentaries, or to community, family, experiences, perceptions, anecdotes, or facts of biography for instructional purposes), I am assuming a contrapuntal space concerning Western conventions; I am not in any way abandoning the canon of scholarly circumspection. In fact, as a scholar, I am exposing bias—in this case—Western bias. I am, as Barbara Harlow writes, "imposing a review" of what is understood as "literature, literary studies and the historical record."[57]

Does it need saying that my exposition of bias is not restricted to White partisanship? Native intellectuals are not immune to their own forms of bias, but they are no more predisposed to it than are Western intellectuals. What's more, as part of claiming my own distinctiveness and exercising my ideals of scholarship, I will not serve merely as a conduit of other voices, Native or otherwise. I am observing that as various Native communities are flexing their political or cultural muscles, Native scholars may find themselves in difficult positions. We are no different from any other human community in that we hold dearly some beliefs and assumptions, which if challenged, even with all the best data and argumentation, may evoke responses that could affect our research. Studies of violence, traditions, women, spirituality, or even images of "Indians" are fraught with potential politics. The Native community is as vulnerable as the White community in its internalization and perpetuation of stereotypes, an issue I return to in my discussion of romanticism in Chapter 6.

Even though stereotypes exist, we are a diverse peoples criss-crossing geographies, languages, culture areas, faiths, legally divided identities, politics, and so forth. We do not have a uniform Native identity even if we have a common experience under colonization. Of course, in important ways, we have many things in common, which come from our colonial experience as well as shared indigeneity. But we are also truly different from each other, not only as individuals or cultures, but also in our personal socio-economic circumstances and perspectives. It is as important to name our differences as it is to articulate the common experience of invasions in our lives. We have all experienced colonial intrusion, but we have not all experienced it at the same time or in the same way or to the same degree. I, for one, cannot entertain racist, sexist, or ideological injunctions that I must be a carbon copy of other colonized persons and colleagues. For that matter, nor do I unquestioningly accept postcolonial buzz labels such as "essentialist," "subaltern," "hybridity" or "mimicry," which can be similarily universalizing. At some point, agency has to mean something actual, like having the right and the freedom to name one's identity without someone theorizing it and us to yet newer forms of erasure and generalization.

It is imperative that we treat with respect other people's works upon which we build our dialogics and, for many of us, our academic degrees; it is also important to maintain our right to disagree. Writers owe much to each other, and I acknowledge my debt to all these writers (and scholars) I use, but I must also retain my right to debate and to question. My goal is not to settle for politically correct or kitschy notions. My objective is to offer valuable criticism. Edward Said in *The World, The Text, and the Critic* writes that "criticism must think of itself as life-enhancing and constitutively opposed to every form of tyranny, domination and abuse; its social goals are noncoercive knowledge produced in the interests of human freedom."[58] The important thing is that we all have the right to speak, the right to be represented fairly, as well as the obligation to represent fairly, and the right to express ourselves true to our lives, experiences, and research. As Abenaki resistance filmmaker, poet, and singer Alanis Obomsawin explains,

> The basic purpose is for our people to have a voice. To be heard is the important thing, no matter what it is that we are talking about... and that we have a lot to offer society. But we also have to look at the bad stuff, and what has happened to us, and why.... We cannot do this without going through the past...because we are carrying a pain that is 400 years old. We don't carry just our everyday pain. We're carrying the pain of our fathers, our mothers, our grandfathers, our grandmothers...it's part of this land.[59]

I too carry "the 400 year pain," a "pain" that is part of this land; I too carry the pain of my mother, my father, my sister, my brothers, my nieces and nephews, my grandfathers and mothers, my aunts and uncles. And I carry my own pain. Here I offer vignettes of life experiences relevant to the profound sense of alienation I have experienced in the world of education, an experience that has propelled me to pursue scholarship—particularly, the story of dehumanization—so passionately. I must emphasize that, to me, it is not enough to simply tell the story, it is equally important that we name, locate, and situate the "story."

Neegan (First) Narrative

"Get 'em, Daniel Boone, get 'em." My eyes were wide open, my hands clutching the sides of my desk. I waited breathlessly as America's mythic frontiersman Daniel Boone, with a cast-iron frying pan in hand, stood readying to spring upon a hideously painted Indian stealthily crawling into his boathouse. Then "BOINNG"—and our grade four (mostly Metis) classroom burst into gleeful applause—the gallant frontiersman had "got 'em."

Of course, it was not my first and certainly not my last exposure to such imagery. My relatives and I were well acquainted with the scene of the tomahawk-swinging savage who took shrieking delight in rushing upon wagon trains and defenceless White women and children.

Niso (Second) Narrative

When my brothers and I were in elementary school, we were required to draw Columbus's ship. I drew a large, detailed picture of a multi-storeyed clipper, its tall white sails fluttering against a cerulean blue sky, the sky touching the deep blue sea. It must have been then that I had to memorize the famous ditty: "in 1492 / Columbus sailed the ocean / deep and blue."

I was a northern Canadian Cree Metis child with a political and cultural heritage in contradiction to the Columbus narrative. At the time I, of course, had no knowledge of the ramifications behind Columbus's ship, but I was left with the distinct impression that he was some godlike White hero who had done the universe an inestimable, not to mention irreversible, favour by "discovering" the "New World."

Neesto (Third) Narrative

In Goshen College, Indiana, the showing of the 1969 BBC film series *Civilisation*, written and narrated by Kenneth Clark, was a campus-wide mandatory event. Clark begins by arguing that Greco-Roman cultural accomplishments defined civilization against the powerful but impermanent achievements of African masks or wandering Viking ships. What has stayed with me about this series is how Clark compared a surviving "pitifully crude" stone baptistery to a wigwam by saying: "But at least this miserable construction is built to last. It isn't just a wigwam."

I could not speak.

Nehwi (Fourth) Narrative

In the summer of 1976, prior to enrolling in Canadian history at the University of Manitoba, I had an occasion to visit the Martyr's Shrine in Midland, Ontario. From the outside the Martyr's Shrine looked like any eastern Roman Catholic cathedral—stone-built, large, and reminiscent of edifices shown in Kenneth Clark's *Civilisation* television series. On the inside, it looked like a large version of the Catholic churches my parents and teachers had made my siblings and me attend—dark, echoing, and full of flickering candles. I really had no idea what the Martyr's Shrine represented until my eyes adjusted to the darkness—there, at the very front of the pews, were looming life-sized wax museum figures. I slowly realized what they were: kneeling priests angelically looking up, hands folded, praying for mercy as open-mouthed, hideously painted, evil-eyed savages tower over them, about to bury hatchets in their skulls!

Postcards and pamphlets were handed out—still photography to lock in the master view, perhaps to keep it safe from exposure. Inside myself, I resolved to know the truth behind such soul-numbing presentations. I walked out of that structure with fire in my head. Consciousness was seeping in. Liberation resistance scholarship was in the making.

Rediscovering the Narrative

Of course, Columbus or the Jesuits were but the beginning of an endless string of White heroes who filled the pages of my comics and my school textbooks. The Explorers, the Conquistadores, the Missionaries, the Fur Traders, the Pilgrims and Puritans, the Daniel Boones, the American Cavalry and the Cowboys, the Fathers of Canadian Confederation—they were all presented as "great" and their greatness was and still is directly related to the degree to which they othered, killed, dehumanized, or de-Indianized Indians.

Hollywood put in motion the glorification of the White man. While Whites could experience a vicarious greatness watching Cowboys beat the Indians (no matter how ferocious and "cunning"), Native audiences crouched in their seats, grateful for the theatre's darkness. Similarly, in so many of Canada's signal places, Native peoples have had to cringe within themselves, having to cope with the re-settler's heroic point of view. I have noted that at every important juncture and place in my life, or in that of my family or community, our worlds have been either deleted, belittled, or decontextualized by an assortment of White North America's propaganda machines.

As can be surmised from my narratives, my student life was filled with considerable distress.[60] Before I was in any position to critically examine the history and sociology of racism, I experienced a sense of shame and alienation from teachers, textbooks, comics, and movies that portrayed Indians as savages. Later, as I pursued "higher" education, I soon discovered that many university professors and most textbooks presented Native peoples in as distorted and insulting ways as the elementary texts had done. The racist theme of Western civilization/Indian savagery was ever-present. Some professors were less subtle than others.

I have been a professor for three decades, and I continue to battle this epic myth. Indeed, I continue to be astonished by some White academics' obsessions in the defence of "civilization." For instance, Tom Flanagan flagrantly waves his star-spangled civ/sav banner in his book *First Nations, Second Thoughts*.[61] In a chapter called "Whatever Happened to Civilization," he bemoans the contemporary enlightened direction of assuming cultural equality for Aboriginal peoples. Further, not only does he actually believe the civ/sav construct is objective, he argues his thesis is not racist. Of course, throughout he draws on the American expansionist doctrine of Manifest Destiny.

As Joyce Green points out, "Flanagan's book is arguably not in fact about second thoughts, but about first thoughts: the justifications that have always legitimated colonialism on Turtle Island."[62] The notion of "civilization" and its antithesis "savagery" are invariably defined and measured by Euro-White North American standards. It should be needless to point out that such an unscientific belief is racist because it sets up Whites as superior and non-Whites as inferior. Yet such racialized evolutionism has not entirely disappeared from the Western intellectual tradition. In disciplines of anthropology, history, political science, psychology, sociology, religion, and even in earlier Marxist thought, theories on human development were and still are largely premised on patriarchal, Eurocentric and evolutionary ideas about so-called primitive peoples.

I have not been impressed. I have experienced Canada's archives, libraries, cathedrals, martyrs' shrines, museums, movies, forts, and university hallways—all places that reflect Eurocentrism—as places of exile.

Reframing the Narrative

My liberation has come from rediscovering the Columbus narrative for what it is: a self-serving White cultural myth, which has been effectively transmitted from generation to generation and institutionalized by White North America's powerful educational and cultural systems. The other aspect of my liberation has come from the "knowing" that Native peoples were not as they were imagined.

I have always known that there was absolutely no connection between the othering of "the Indian" and the consummate humanity of my parents, brothers and sister, my *nokom* (grandmother), my aunts and uncles, my nieces and nephews. It is this unsung humanity, as much as the vilification of Native peoples, that has compelled me to this place of engaged research and discourse. It is important that we understand colonial subterfuge behind the fantastic hero-ification of the White man. It is imperative that our understanding is taken from the words of those who have suffered from this proselytizing, the Native peoples of Canada. In *There Is My People Sleeping*, Sarain Stump speaks movingly to the significance of understanding:

> I was mixing stars and sand
> In front of him
> But he couldn't understand
> I was keeping the lightning of
> The thunder in my purse
> Just in front of him
> But he couldn't understand
> And I had been killed a thousand times
> Right at his feet
> But he hadn't understood.[63]

Before "he" can "understand," we must situate Native response in the context of colonization; in particular, room must necessarily be given to the exposition of what Parker Duchemin calls "textual strategies of domination" in Euro-Canadian writing.[64]

Chapter Two

Dehumanization in Text

dehumanize: "to divest of human qualities or personality"

dehumanization: "the act or process or an instance of dehumanizing"

Colonization has required rationalization, which, in turn, has produced an overwhelming body of dehumanizing literature about Native peoples. Colonial writing, Joyce Green argues, has been "legitimised not only through racist construction but through creation of language celebrating colonial identities while constructing the colonised as the antithesis of human decency and development."[1] Colonizers require a system of thought and representation to mask their oppressive behaviour. In other words, they require an ideology to legitimate and to entrench the unequal power relations set up by the whole process of colonization. Memmi in *The Colonizer and the Colonized* characterizes the colonizer as a "usurper" who "needs to absolve himself" about his "victory." He therefore "endeavors to falsify history... anything to succeed in transforming his usurpation into legitimacy." This can be done, Memmi continues, by "demonstrating the usurper's eminent merits, so eminent that they deserve such compensation. Another is to harp on the usurped's demerits, so deep that they cannot help leading to misfortune."[2]

White North American writers have supported their "eminent merits" by constructing "evidence" of Natives' demerits. In Canadian scholarly and popular writing a number of such constructions centrally dehumanize the subjugated "native." This dehumanization has been effectively advanced through what I have come to call the "civ/sav" dichotomy, which provides a framework for interpreting White and Native encounters. The framework is really an ideological container for the systematic construction of self-confirming "evidence" that Natives were savages who "inevitably" had to yield to the superior powers of civilization as carried forward by Euro-Canadian civilizers. Since the civ/sav paradigm undergirds, encases, and permeates colonizer texts, it obviously requires much greater inspection than it has received thus far in Canadian writing. In this chapter I pay particular attention to lexical strategies of belittlement that especially serve to degrade and infantilize Native peoples.[3] These are textual techniques often veiled by a set of scientific-sounding classificatory words and images that can be found in much of imperialist writing; here I examine selected Canadian archival sources and, to a lesser extent, Canadian historical and literary writing. I more or less focus on western Canada in the nineteenth century.

I am also interested in the powerful instrument of demonization (next of kin to animalization). This too can be found in much of nineteenth-century White literature that juxtaposes in Manichean dualism Whites as agents of divine elevation in moral combat against subhuman, demonic, shrieking savages. Perhaps demonization is the ultimate expression of dehumanization, the ultimate textual "technique of mastery," to borrow Parker Duchemin's phrase.[4] I point to several works from John Richardson and Ralph Connor because they represent some of the grossest examples of the colonial practices of demonology to produce othering, another thread to the colonizer's web. Richardson and Connor were also, each in their respective eras, widely read, and continue to influence the Canadian literary community as well as discourse between Aboriginal and non-Aboriginal peoples. Their dualism and invectives, though, were not atypical, for as Fanon observed, "the settler paints the native as a sort of quintessence of evil."[5]

I concentrate on exposing what is, in effect, textual warfare, and while I obviously must draw on the "enemy's language," namely, the relevant archival, historical, and literary works such as exploration, fur trade, and missionary journals, *the emphasis is on the textual constructions*, not on the authors, eras, or genres, per se. I especially inspect the key traits or apparatus of the civ/sav dichotomy, then I make some critical observations concerning its function and its social and intellectual influences in our respective culture(s) and understanding. Of course, care is taken to place specific data in their proper contexts as appropriate or relevant, but again it is not my goal to rewrite Canadian history or even to offer literary criticism as such; the objective is to expose textual constructions instrumental to racism. Also, since providing "context" to racist material can have the effect of legitimizing it, I approach with extreme care anything with inflammatory material.

What is being advanced here is nothing less than the deconstruction of the very foundation of imperialist writing concerning White and Native relations. The metaphor of rebuilding a roof may be helpful. Rebuilding a roof entails first deconstructing it, which is to say, taking it apart shingle by shingle. Then, it means reconstructing it. But I find the very frame that holds the shingles is so rotten that it too needs to be gutted, and a whole new structure needs to be built before any new shingles can be nailed in. Simply repairing the roof would be poor carpentry. Good scholarship, in other words, must call for the disassembly of the very frame that houses the roof.

The Frame: The Civ/Sav Dichotomy

Behind the dichotomy of civilization versus savagery is the long-held belief that humankind evolved from the primitive to the most advanced, from the savage to the civilized. With respect to the Americas, there are great similarities between a widely circulated ethnological classification done in 1576 by Spanish Jesuit Jose de Acosta and an anthropological theory published in 1877 by American lawyer-ethnologist Lewis Henry Morgan.[6] Both placed Amerindians at the lowest level and Euro-Whites at the highest in their respective constructs. The main difference between them was that, for Acosta, the Spanish were the highest of the high and, for Morgan, White Americans had achieved that level.

The civ/sav formula is succinctly stated by Morgan: "savagery preceded barbarism in all the tribes of mankind, as barbarism is known to have preceded civilization. The history of the human race is one in source, one in experience, one in progress."[7] Eventually, as Roy Harvey Pearce, in his revised study of *Savagism and Civilization*, submits, White Americans latched onto such creeds to elevate their expansionist conquering practices into theories of progress: "American civilization would thus be conceived as three dimensional, progressing from past to present, from east to west, from lower to higher."[8] It was actually four-dimensional in that civilization was synonymous with White and savagism with the Indian, the non-White. To be non-White was to be "lower," or savage, which, as Pearce states "was at best an hypothesis which called for proof."[9] But "proof" meant using Euro-White criteria to measure non-European peoples and cultures, making the civ/sav model obviously doctrinaire and self-serving.

Ethnohistorian Francis Jennings discredits this "proof" in his 1976 publication, *The Invasion of American: Indians, Colonialism, and the Cant of Conquest*. This is an outstanding work, which revisits seventeenth-century Puritans and their version of the Holy Crusades against the "wilderness" and its "savage heathen." It is a masterly analysis of Europe's colonizing "master myth" of civilization encountering savagism, which was first applied by various warring bands in Europe, then brought to the Americas for colonial purposes. Jennings traces variations of the civ/sav construct to "very ancient times" of the Greeks and Romans to Europe's pre-feudal history and shows that at every point there was political conflict the "enemy" was always cast as the antithesis to human fitness, or "civilization." At each and any convenient turn, attempts were made to prove "the factual difference between civilization and savagery," but often "the difference was political and no more," as in the case between "Englishmen" and "Irishmen."[10] Jennings points out that while there was no "substantial difference" between the English and the Irish except "tribal government on the one hand and a feudal state on the other," the rulers of England "set themselves up as carriers of civilization to a savage people."[11]

Jennings spells out how "powers bent on conquest made "floundering attempts at explanation" to substantiate cultural differences between themselves (the civilized) and their opponents (deemed uncivilized). "Most frequently," he writes, "the difference has been one of religion. At other times it might have been nomadic instead of sedentary habitation or one mode of subsistence versus another: communities without agriculture—or those possessing horticulture but lacking animal husbandry—were barbarous or savage."[12] These arbitrary distinctions reflect "moral sanction" rather than "any given combination of social traits susceptible to objective definition." Jennings bluntly concludes: "It is a weapon of attack rather than a standard of measurement."[13]

However floundering or arbitrary, nineteenth-century social scientists did make efforts to define and measure civilization—or its converse, savagism. The extremes of this led to a movement known as Scientific Racism, the most obvious pretension to science being the measuring of cranial structures of different "races."[14] While craniology was relatively short-lived, the attempts to measure "uncivilized" or "primitive" "cultures" has remained, if not any longer in actual physical terms, certainly in overall anthropological and other intellectual speculations, including genetic studies and theories about Native people, especially regarding alcohol.

During the heyday of scientific racism, Lewis Henry Morgan looked to the Iroquois in an effort to establish "empirical criteria with which to distinguish one stage [of human evolution] from the other,"[15] that is, from savagery to barbarism to civilization. What would be the ultimate cultural marker that would place the Iroquois on one of those three evolutionary rungs? Jennings explains that at times Morgan waivered between metal technology and literacy as the final indicators of civilization.[16] Finally, Morgan showed his hand and turned to White hegemony as the ultimate proof of White superiority. He applied the social Darwinist, survival-of-the-fittest theoretical rave of his time to seal his argument that "the American aborigines are possessed of inferior mental endowment," whereas "the Aryan family represents the central stream of human progress, because it produced the highest type of mankind, and because it proved its intrinsic superiority by gradually assuming the control of the earth."[17]

What exactly formed the basis of White superiority, or "civilization," was indeed a wide-ranging debate, but the very essences of each stage were to be defined solely by White, Christian, and European cultural standards. As Jennings so definitively shows in *The Invasion of America*, constructs of civilization and its supposed antithesis are inherently biased, for "*civilization* necessarily implies not only technical but moral superiority over the stages assumed to be lower on the evolutionary scale. Civilization is rarely conceived of in terms of empirical data, and although its phenomena might vary as widely as those of ancient Sparta and Victorian England, its essence is always its status on the top of the evolutionary ladder."[18]

While the term itself can have many meanings, Jennings takes pains to point out that "civilization" in its "mythical sense" is "omnipresent in American history and literature" and is treated as "an absolute quality that cannot be grammatically pluralized." Here, "a myth of social structure" was developed "in which civilization and savagery stood as reciprocals, each defined as the other was not, and both independent of any necessary correlation with empirical reality."[19]

Canadian historical writing and literature have been very much influenced not only by British advancements of imperialist "civilization," but also by White Americans. Then, of course, Canadian writers have not been free from their own biases and vested interests. Generally, in Canadian writing as in American publications, the civ/sav dichotomy is spelled out in terms of cultural "traits" that reflect binary opposites, each civilized trait corresponding, inversely, with a savage one. In Canadian terms, civilization is consistently associated with settlement, private property, cultivation of land and intellect, industry, monotheism, literacy, coded law and order, Judeo-Christian morality, and metal-based technology. Civilization stands for what is illuminated, progressive, and decent, while savagery is its shadowy underside. Such a "civilization" is repeatedly outlined against "Indian savagery," in which savagism is seen as a psychosocial fixed condition, the antithesis of the highest human condition. Indians, then, by contrast, are delineated as wild, nomadic, warlike, uncultivating and uncultivated, aimless, superstitious, disorganized, illiterate, immoral, and technologically backwards.

A number of nineteenth-century writers on the Canadian West, many of them missionaries, provide astonishing examples of the civ/sav master narrative. The missionaries represented here were not obscure bigots on the fringes of society. They were well-known, well-read, well-travelled men who saw themselves as "agents of a superior civilization."[20] They played the role of "experts" on matters "native," and were often consulted by colonial officials if they themselves did not become the officials. Of course, they had differences of opinion about a host of things, but as fellow actors on the colonial stage they were in concert in their mission to superimpose their super culture over indigenous "savagery." With this same sense of mission and confidence, the Anglican clergy in Red River society in the period from 1818 to 1870 "struggled to recreate...a little Britain in the wilderness," preaching the virtues of civil law, settlement, cultivation, industry, puritanical morality, and Christianity against "barbarism."[21] In 1820, Anglican missionary John West arrived in Red River. He served mainly as chaplain to the Hudson's Bay Company. West reflected prevailing attitudes in his 1834 *Journal*:

> Savages talk of the animals that they have killed...but they form no arrangement, nor enter into calculation for futurity. They have no settled places of abode, or property, or acquired wants and appetites, like those which rouse men to activity in civilized life, and stimulate them to persevering industry....Their simple wants are few, and when satisfied they waste their time in listless indolence... and the scarcity of animals that now prevails...is a favourable circumstance towards leading them to the cultivation of the soil; which would expand their minds, and prove of vast advantage.[22]

Writing in the late 1860s, John McDougall, son of a missionary to western Native peoples, and himself a missionary as well as husband to a Plains Cree woman, envisioned that "the wild nomadic heathen life" will "give way to permanent settlement, and the church and school will bring in the clearer light."[23] Similarly, Methodist missionary John McLean, a highly educated man, even an apologist for Indian traditions, proposed "guiding" Indians "out of nomadic life into the stationary residence attending a life of agriculture." "Our motto must be," he declared, "Religion, Education, Self-Support—the Bible and the Plough."[24]

The persistent civ/sav doctrine was also recited by secular authors. Alexander Ross, fur trader, sheriff of Assiniboia, and chronicler of the Red River Settlement, anticipated that once the buffalo were extinct, the "wandering and savage life of the halfbreed, as well as the savage himself, must give place to…the husbandman and the plough, the sound of the grindstone, and the church-going bell."[25]

It must be noted that besides harping on the Indians' nomadism, Ross variously slanders them as barbarous, savage, wild, vile, wretched, superstitious, and degenerate children of nature.[26] Neither Ross's Native wife and children, nor the "settled and industrious" Natives around his colony garden seem to have tempered his harsh judgement.[27]

Nothing seems to have tempered Alexander Begg's racist judgement of Aboriginal peoples. Journalist, novelist, and advocacy pioneer Begg reviles "Indians" as scalpers, thieves, liars, and plunderers, and abusers of the elderly, women, and the sick—all this in a four-page passage of bile in the first volume of his 1894 so-called *History of the Northwest*. Begg's hatred turns to classic colonial dehumanization: "The wild Indian was in many respects, more savage than the animals around him."[28] Presumably, as Volume II of his *History* implies, the Indian's savagery was related to his [the Indian's] "wine of life" of buffalo hunting, and most especially to the "unsettled conditions of the Indians."[29] In the manner of early American writers and historians, Begg refers to the Saskatchewan country as "wild and uninhabited," even though there were certainly many more than the expansionist estimate of 60,000 Aboriginal peoples between the Rocky Mountains and Lake Superior.[30] Begg and the other writers were laying ground for their expansionist vision of transforming the "wilderness," fancied as "empty land," for their own land acquisitions and economic gains. And it served them well to elevate nitty-gritty expansionism to social doctrine.

The idea of an abstract civilization inevitably winning over savagery neatly served the White North American usurper. Everything the White man did was legitimized by "civilization" and everything Indians did was "explained" by their supposed savagery. This was ideology at its brutal best, and clearly fits the profile of what Memmi calls the "Nero complex."[31] As Pearce has established, Americans developed a doctrine of savagery as a moral antithesis to progress. In the United States it became a morality script in which the cowboys finished what Columbus, the conquistadores, or the Puritans began. Cowboys—and before them the Puritans, the frontiersmen, and the cavalry—moving west and killing "Indians" could then be equated with moral and human progress.

Whether Whites crushed the Natives (as in United States) or dispossessed them largely through legal means (as in Canada), they have justified their "victory" by creating a myth that Indians were only a handful of vicious savages who "roamed" rather than inhabited the "virgin" land.[32] As Jennings describes so incisively in *The Invasion of America*:

> The basic conquest myth postulates that America was virgin land, or
> wilderness inhabited by nonpeople called savages; that these savages
> were creatures sometimes defined as demons, sometimes as beasts
> 'in the shape of men'; that their mode of existence and cast of mind
> were such as to make them incapable of civilization and therefore
> of full humanity; that civilization was required by divine sanction
> or the imperative of progress to conquer the wilderness and make it
> a garden; that the savage creatures of the wilderness, being unable
> to adapt to any environment other than the wild, stubbornly and
> viciously resisted God or fate, and thereby incurred their suicidal
> extermination; that civilization and its bearers were refined and en-
> nobled in their context with the dark powers of the wilderness; and
> that it was all inevitable.[33]

The myth that Indians "roamed rather than inhabited" the North American
country was pronounced at least as early as 1612 when Jesuit missionary
Pierre Biard wrote of northern Aboriginal peoples: "Thus four thousand
Indians at most roam through, rather than occupy, these vast stretches of in-
land territory."[34] Such a portrayal became a convenient ideology in the hands
of colonizers such as the Puritan Samuel Purchas, whose phrase "range rather
than inhabite" validated killing Atlantic Native Americans throughout the
seventeenth century[35] and was to be repeated by countless American White
men whose interests ran counter to those of indigenous peoples.

Similarly, John Quincy Adams's rhetorical question—"What is the right
of a huntsman to the forest of a 1000 miles, over which he accidentally ranged
in quest of prey?"[36]—is a classical note of self-exoneration in pursuit of
"virgin land." So is Canadian writer Alexander Begg's reference to Native-
populated Saskatchewan country as "wild and uninhabited," as is William
Butler's depiction, albeit nostalgic, of the western landscape as the "great lone
land." Subsequent White Canadian writers have referred to White expansionism as "peopling" the West, a most telling expression.[37] Such wording,
while patently political in nature, has been elevated to theoretical absolutes
in Canadian courts concerning concepts of property vis-à-vis Aboriginal
rights. A contemporary example of this is to be found in the 1991 case of
Delgamuukw v. the Queen. The Supreme court of British Columbia's Chief
Justice Allan McEachern ruled against the Gitksan and Wet'suwet'en peoples
on old European preconceptions that "natives" lived "nasty, brutish and short"
lives (he was quoting Thomas Hobbes), that is, too primitive to qualify for
land rights.[38]

Re-settling expansionists have argued—and continue to argue, as does Tom Flanagan in *First Nations? Second Thoughts*—that agricultural (and, as it became convenient, industrial) peoples represent a superior stage of development, such that by divine sanction or "natural law" have, as Pearce has explained, claimed the right to "dispossess hunters from their sovereignty over nature."[39] In other words, it was morally mandated to disinherit them. And the moral mandate was often rationalized by portraying native hunters as disorganized and brutal "bands" aimlessly wandering over land. Various Canadian parties with economic interests in the West certainly promoted the image that Indians were uncultured primitives who lived solely as disorganized foragers. Such views were often noted matter-of-factly. Alexander Ross, in support of Sir George Murray, quotes Murray to that effect: "The white people, by their habits of cultivation, are spreading everywhere over the country… they [the Indians] will be gradually swept away."[40]

Hunting, according to colonialist justifications, was endemic to savagism except as condoned in their own self-interest. Colonialists reserved for themselves the right to hunt whenever they needed to, whether to eat, make a profit, or annihilate the buffalo as a military strategy against the Plains peoples. In Europe, hunting had largely become a sport enjoyed by the upper classes. Overlooking the fact that a wide variety of indigenous cultures across the Americas cultivated the lands, among other things, and that many White people were hunters, the colonialists blithely judged Native hunting as savage with the added assumption that, as savages, "Indians" wandered and warred in the "wilderness." It was obviously convenient to dismiss even the most glaring discrepancies and contradictions. In the words of Doug Owram, "wilderness, by definition, implied a region where the natural dominated the works of man, whether those works be put in technological, legal, or spiritual terms.… [W]ilderness was irreconcilable with civilization."[41] But, as Bruce Morrison and Roderick Wilson point out in *The Canadian Experience*,

> In the European conception of things, America was a wilderness and Natives were part of that wilderness. That idea could be maintained despite all the evidence: the obvious concentration of indigenous populations, the obvious control and management of unfenced pasture areas in which native people harvested mammals for food, the practice of agriculture, the military power and skills of indigenous groups and the extensive trade networks. The country was no wilderness, and given the evidence, it is a wonder that Europeans could see it as one.[42]

Similarly, Olive Dickason in *The Myth of the Savage* contradicts the expansionist view of the Indian as anarchic and without governance. She writes that whatever "the differences may be between 'tribal' societies and 'civilizations', the presence or lack of order is not one of them. The people of the New World all led highly structured lives."[43]

Clearly, Old World notions served "New World" needs, and, like their American counterparts, Euro-Canadians set for themselves the task of "civilizing" (or subduing) the land whose Native-populated regions symbolized the anarchic and the sinister. As Nash writes, "Civilizing the new World meant enlightening darkness, ordering chaos and transforming evil into good. In the morality play of westward expansion, wilderness was the villain, and the pioneer, as hero, relished its destruction."[44] The "Indians" were viewed as part of the foliage; in Roderick Nash's words, "savages were almost always associated with wilderness." They were the "terrifying creatures… sweeping out of the forest to strike, and then melting back into it."[45] To Owram, the Canadian "missionary's attitude to the wilderness determined his view of the Indian," and this view was the Indian "as a degraded savage who endured all the miseries and privations inseparable from a state of barbarism."[46] The Euro-Americans—and later the Euro-Canadians—believed their destiny was to master the "wilderness," and this, of course, meant mastering the "Indian" as well.

And so it was for White Canadians moving west. Although they worked out, and are still working out, their westward trek somewhat differently from the Americans, they certainly ascribed moral properties to the wilderness, regarding it variously as a "heathen and moral desert," a "barren waste," and the "dreary land" that kept Indians in a "degraded state."[47] Yet, despite themselves, many missionaries could not help but marvel at "nature's grandeur and beauty" and ultimately had to make a theological concession that all the earth, even the "howling wilds," was God's handiwork. But as Owram observes in *Promise of Eden*, "the fact that it was a heathen wilderness" demanded the light of the Gospel and European civilization.[48] Of course, once the Euro-Canadians began to realize economic interest and settlement rights over this area, the wilderness no longer "howled" but beckoned. For the expansionists, "the charm of the wilderness lay mainly in its potential for development."[49]

Both the missionaries and the secularists were confident that the "Indians" and their land would succumb to the "resistless tide of progress."[50] Some, like McLean and Butler, could express sadness for the Indian, but greater happiness in the anticipation that White civilization would impose itself upon the Canadian landscape.[51] Egerton Ryerson Young, a missionary in northern

Manitoba in the 1870s, actually exulted over Canada's future prospects in the West:

> In fancy's ear I heard the lowing of cattle from the hillsides, the hum or industry from a 100 towns and villages, the merry shout of children returning from school, and in the distance the thundering tread of the iron horse as he sped swiftly across the plain. As I looked again the whole scene was transfigured. Everywhere quiet home-steads dotted the plains and nestled among the hills, the smoke of factories rose thickly on the air, a hundred village spires glittered in the rays of the setting sun, while golden fields… waved in the pass-ing breeze; and I said in my heart: "Lo, here is a dominion stretching from sea to sea."[52]

The issue of transforming the savage was, of course, central to most discussions on "Indians." Although the distinctions between "Civilage" (my invention) and "Savage" were profiled as a binary trait-per-trait phenomenon, the reverse logic of using the process of elimination was not extended when-ever Native peoples assumed "civilized" characteristics. The question—how many civilized traits would a savage need to qualify as civilized?—was not asked nor were the implications of asking it taken to their logical conclusions. Instead, a double standard was developed in response to contradictions that inevitably came out of the civ/sav polarity.

The Double Standard

James St. G. Walker, in a germinal essay "The Indians in Canadian Historical Writing," notes that archival sources and historians judged Native people using a double standard.[53] In the uses of the double standard, we see more clearly the extent to which Canadian writers have clung to their beliefs about themselves in contrast to Native peoples. An analysis of contradictory White treatment of "White vices" in relation to "Indian virtues" demonstrates how the double standard works.

For all the vilification of Indians expressed in archival sources, there is also a great amount of praise, and even admiration and respect (though often qualified, as I will explain). And for all the emphasis on White civilization, there is a lot of concession concerning White "vices." The cumulative list of both Indian "virtues" and White "vices" is considerable, but the manipulation or tendentious use of such traits is what is revealing about the original writers. This was not Native-positive or anti-colonial writing.

A quick list of positive Indian characteristics as gleaned from the very same works that vilify includes these terms: generosity, helpfulness, compassion, trustworthiness, openness, communality, fairness, wisdom, and spirituality, and even some allusion to non-violence. Also recognized, though at times begrudgingly, are technical skills demanding precision and keen judgement, such as navigation or marksmanship in hunting. Missionaries, beginning with the Jesuits, also had to contend with Native specialists possessing knowledge in medicine, human psychology, and religion.

It is significant to note that these Native "virtues" were not offered in the context of romanticism that defined the noble savage. As a rule, these nineteenth-century Canadian writers insisted that they did not believe in the noble savage. In fact, most were aware of it as an invention, and Young, McLean, Butler, and Ross explicitly claimed to present the "true Indian." That these men made a point of making this distinction attests to the fact that not every positive description of Aboriginal peoples was a fabrication to bolster the device of the noble savage, as some historians seem to suggest.[54]

On the matter of White "vices," there is also much evidence that a hefty number of White men were not paragons of "civilized" human behaviour. They engaged in murder, pillaging, scalping, torturing, sexual assault, deceit, dishonesty, drunkenness, laziness, and generally "lawless" behaviour. They exhibited cruelty, cowardice, greed, ignorance, bigotry, and irreverence. Many were fully or semi-illiterate, and most wandered from place to place. In fact, they were so much like the very traits they purported to see and hate in "Indians" that a psychological study of their projections would add to our historiographic inquiries. Given that these Canadian writers liberally (though inconsistently) recognized positive, if not "civilized," qualities in Native peoples and cultures, and, on the other hand, also acknowledged that the "civilized" showed signs of the "savage," the logical outcome here, one would think, would be that these writers would abandon the belief that Euro-Canadians were universally civilized and Indians savage. If traits were counted, it would be difficult to see the difference between the *civilages* and the *savages*. Was there nothing to be reconciled here? How could they hang on to their civ/sav notions?

As products of Western culture, these Canadian writers assumed their superiority. To them, there were no contradictions to be reconciled. They did not seem to notice that to maintain their framework, they had to do considerable scurrying from mental corner to mental corner. The construct within which they were encapsulated was a locked system of dogma. It was an ideology veiled as an objective and judicious moral understanding of human development. Although some of these writers, especially McLean and McDougall, did notice Indian "virtues" against White "vices," and they at times reflected conflicting attitudes and inconsistent judgements, and some, like Butler, perceived deep contradictions, they never waivered from their given framework. John McLean, for instance, perhaps one of the most liberal and enlightened missionaries of his time, even chided his contemporaries for being "guilty of judging these people in light of our own customs, and not estimating them from their own standard."[55] But as a missionary he believed in the idea of progress as set out by Lewis Henry Morgan, and that all peoples, given the Gospel and the plough and education, would ultimately progress to the "ideal race," "speaking a universal language and accepting a common faith."[56]

There is absolutely no question that McLean's ideal race would look and live like his race, the universal language would be English, and the common faith, Christianity. He, like Butler and McDugall, all men who found much to admire in Native peoples, entertained no doubts that the Whites had a superior intelligence and a "nobler system of morality and religion."[57] The same is true of most other Euro-White writers cutting across the centuries; for example, the writers in the *Jesuit Relations*. In fact, to maintain the framework against evidence to the contrary, they resorted to ingenious mental constructs of exceptionalizing (in both directions). While the offending Whites were liberally criticized (and even called "savages" or "brutes"—in behaviour, not in evolution—by Butler and Mclean), White savagery was never extended to all Euro-Canadians. However, (presumed) Indian savagery was applied to all Indians. Native persons modelling "civilized" and Christian behaviour or traits were seen as exceptions (and, under certain contexts, and not usually by the men mentioned here, even romanticized, especially if "vanishing," which could occasion nostalgic eulogies), and invader re-settlers exhibiting "savage" behaviour or traits were viewed as aberrants, usually as "ruffians."

This explains why even when Whites and Indians behaved the same—say, in warfare, religion, or trade—positive values were assigned to Euro-Canadians and negative ones to Natives. And when it was conceded that Native peoples had displayed "positive" behaviours, various textual techniques or themes were used in order to be able to maintain the civ/sav construct. When Whites displayed "negative" traits, they could become "wicked" or "ruffian," but such name-calling never implied that they were outside the civilized fold. Only rarely could a White man become "savage," and usually only in fiction, such as John Richardson's Wacousta. He is allowed to be a savage in order to beat the Indians at their own game. But his savagery is more situational than fundamental. However, like Indian savages, all White savages must also die.[58]

Such double standards were employed politically as well. Once typecast as "roaming" "huntsmen" Native peoples were not allowed the right to defend themselves. Nowhere is John McLean's cultural blindness more apparent than on the topic of warfare. In the same breath (or stroke of pen) that he itemizes White scalping and torturing—acts normally associated with savagery—he insists that "the superior intelligence of the white race should always be sufficient guarantee for the prohibition of cruel and savage rites."[59] In contrast, Native resistance to White encroachment was always framed in terms of innate "bloodthirsty"-ness. In turn, Indian violence was blamed for the destruction of Indians.[60] Yet, despite all the atrocities of war and human torture in the history of Europe, including horrific violence against indigenous peoples on a global scale, colonialists believed their form of warfare was, in Jennings's words, "a rational, honourable and often progressive activity while attributing to the latter [the Indians] the qualities of irrationality, ferocity and unredeemable retrogression. Savagery implies unchecked and perpetual violence."[61]

Native peoples were neither "bloodthirsty" nor "insanely irrational." Nor was the land "virgin," neither in the United States nor in Canada. Nor were Aboriginal peoples "wild" or anarchic. But no matter. The myth proved indispensable. Specific words and categories were (and are) chosen to indicate the ranking of Indians as less evolved, less developed, and less ordered in their social and political lives. Nouns, pronouns, or adjectives used in both scholarly and popular writing to describe Whites could not be used to describe Native peoples. Native men are "bucks" or "warriors," women are "squaws."[62] All political leaders, no matter how diverse their roles and functions, remain "chiefs" or "headmen," spiritual specialists are "conjurors," "shamans," even "sorcerers." There are "Indian villages," not hamlets or towns; Natives are "tribes" or "bands," not nations, and sometimes, not even "peoples."[63]

In this war of words, Whites explore, Indians wander; Whites have battles or victories, Indians massacre and murder; Whites scout, Indians lurk; Whites go westward, Indians go bloodthirsty; Whites defend themselves, Indians "reek revenge"; Whites appear as officials who simply assume authority, Indians are "haughty," "insolent," "saucy," or "impudent" (when they assume equality); Whites have faiths, and so they pray; Indians have superstitions, and so they conjure; Whites may be peasant, Indians are primitive; Whites may be "brutes," but Indians remain savage and barbaric in their "heathen" lands.

In effect, Indians could not win. Every aspect of their life and culture was censured. An example of the degree to which this could be carried is to be found in Alexander Mackenzie's writings, as outlined by Parker Duchemin. Duchemin challenges the "heroic point of view" of exploration literature and lays bare Mackenzie's attempted "techniques of mastery" over the Indians.[64]

Employing various means, including threat, force, bribery, the "appearance of benevolence," liquor, or "the talismanic value of his scientific instruments," which "helped to create an impression of awe" Mackenzie sought to establish his authority over the Indians.[65] Ultimately, he was most successful in his journals: "By writing about them, defining them and explaining them, he could assert to himself and to his readers that he, as a white man was ultimately in control, that his authority, or at the very least, his superiority, remained intact. Information about the Indians…was necessary for the development of the fur trade, and, in a broader sense, for the process of extending European hegemony into every part of the globe."[66]

Consistent with the dehumanization process endemic to the colonial purpose, Mackenzie showed no interest in the Indians as individual human beings with personalities. Instead Mackenzie turned to impersonal descriptions of their physical features and material culture. In these descriptions, Mackenzie adopted a technique of absence by "a deceptively impartial appearance, skilfully blending a selection of 'facts' and value judgements."[67] Duchemin's meticulous analysis of Mackenzie's descriptions of the Sekani men and women merits an extensive quotation here:

> "Low stature," "meagre appearance," "small" eyes and a "swarthy yellow" complexion are ugly and repulsive by the standards of Mackenzie's society. However, these images do not constitute a merely aesthetic judgement: they strongly impute qualities of cunning, deceit, and treachery to the unfortunate Sekani. Even worse are the moral qualities implied in his images of their "dingy black" hair, "hanging loose and in disorder".… By European standards, women ought to be small and fastidious, but among these people, Mackenzie implies in richly suggestive imagery, the normal distinctions of gender have been inverted, the women being "of a more lusty make than the other sex".… Their physical appearance (which he constructs) is a mirror of their moral condition (which he also constructs). While appearing to be neutral, Mackenzie's language and imagery is in fact highly evaluative and judgmental.[68]

From imperial heights, Mackenzie provides details of what he considers the "more 'identifiable savage' customs": the "cartilage of their nose is perforated.… The organs of generation they leave uncovered." Such "details," Duchemin notes, are "calculated to provoke the scorn of his readers, violating so clearly their notions of decorum, common sense and reason." Further, Mackenzie's select, "almost scientific," vocabulary gives him that air of "objectivity" and "intensifies the impact.… The message assumed or implied, is that these customs are grotesque, primitive and reprehensible. This is a judgement fully anticipated and mutually acknowledged by writer and reader; in an important sense, it exists already before it is stated, since it is, in reality, based on their shared cultural experience."[69]

Duchemin also analyzes Mackenzie's fascination with the Indians' material culture, whereby the "Indians' tools acquired a significance of their own while becoming oddly disconnected from the people who employ them."[70] Providing "mind-numbing" ethnographic details, Mackenzie "resembles one of the eighteenth century virtuosi whose cabinets were stuffed with costumes, utensils, ornaments, and other ethnographical curiosities from around the world, divorced from their social context."[71]

Duchemin's insights on Mackenzie bring to mind David Mandelbaum's treatment of Cree "tools" in his book *The Plains Cree*.[72] Mandelbaum, one of the earlier anthropologists in the 1930s to study the Plains Cree, divides Cree technology into disparate pieces, giving the impression of a people frozen in time with only a handful of "simple" (meaning primitive) tools. I well recall my introduction to what may best be called "soul-stealing toolography" in my first years as the only Native graduate student in history at the University of Manitoba. This book was first published in 1940, but I do not recall any discussion about its Eurocentric assumptions. My history and actually my living culture (as my parents were still using a number of the tools in question) were treated as prehistoric, inferior, and alien. That they most likely were received as such by my classmates only intensified my sense of being othered.

Similarly, according to Duchemin, Mackenzie's language and ethnological speculations have their cumulative effect of freezing the Sekani: "they are fixed, by their culture and their environment, and they exist in a kind of timeless ethnographic present, where everything he has noted about their appearance...defines them for all time."[73] Finally, the "effect of this is to lend powerful support to his textual strategies of domination...Mackenzie's terms of reference for his 'ethnography', therefore, as well as his language, tend to diminish and dehumanize the objects of his description."[74]

Even when Mackenzie concedes positive aspects to Native peoples, Duchemin points out that Mackenzie resorts to "an especially subversive" technique. He used a "rhetorical stratagem of allowing the Indians to have, among their vices, a few virtues, which he proceeds at once to qualify severely. Although the Beaver are 'excellent hunters', the physical demands of this activity reduce them to 'very meagre appearance'.... They 'appear' to be fond of their children, but they are 'as careless in their mode of swaddling them as they are of their own dress'. The effect of these qualifications is to give an appearance of balance to his portrait while at the same time preventing it from conferring on them a full measure of humanity."[75]

This is consistent with the technique of exceptionalizing, in which "positive" features of Natives are set up, only to smash them down. This does not negate the positive qualities or "Indian virtues" that missionaries (and other archival sources) recorded, but it does remind us that not all words are as they appear. When explorers, fur traders, missionaries, or historians conceded that Indians were intelligent through skill, trade, or theological discourse, they often immediately qualified the concessions by undermining Natives with words like "shrewd" (rather than intelligent), "simple" (rather than, say, efficacious within Native cultural context, e.g., referring to the design of canoes), or "cunning." For instance, fur trade historian E.E. Rich persistently uses colonial phrases such as "crafty," "shrewd enough," "sophisticated enough," or "hardened enough" when describing Indians taking advantage of competition.[76] Even the more objective John C. Ewers similarly qualifies his compliments about Natives for their business acuity with the phrase "sharp enough."[77] James Walker notes the contradictions: "Because they yearned after European goods, Indians are described as 'grasping' and 'greedy.' Not one of the histories I consulted talks of Cartier in the same way, yet he and his colleagues travelled thousands of miles to gain easy Eastern wealth."[78]

There was nothing that "Indians" could be or do that would meet with approval because the judgements, contradictory as they were, were cemented within colonial dogma, not objective accounting of behaviour or ethnography. Some such instances are more brazen than others. After receiving hospitable treatment from "Chief Pigewis" (a "settled" Christian Indian), John West mixed insult with "gratitude": "Our hungry party put the liberality of the Indians to the test, but it did not fail; as I believe it seldom does, in *their improvidence of tomorrow*."[79]

Alexander Ross was completely incapable of accepting Indians as anything more than inferior. In the following passage, he begins by pretending to praise the Cree, but in the end twists their "positive" qualities to undermine them:

> After a settled life of twenty years with the advantages of religious instruction…the Swampies were universally allowed to be docile… people…and obliging in their manner…. [T]heir sole study, as it appeared, was to make themselves useful to their employers….
>
> But time developed their true character. When they…got accustomed to our people…they…began at once to compare themselves with the whites, and to have a great itching for dress and finery. The blue coat, frilled shirt…were no sooner adopted than they became

saucy, tricky, dishonest; and in place of their former docility, they now showed themselves to be proud.[80]

And, in the imperious words of Ross, "If they have become less notorious for their drinking propensities…they are now *proportionately expert in cheating*."[81] Typical of colonialists, Ross is assuming familiarity and knowledge of "the Native," but feigning mystification when the Native does not behave according to his predictions.[82] Such "knowing" carries a sense of authority over the Native.

By using these various textual techniques at every turn, Whites always secured for themselves a sense of mastery, quite at the expense of Native peoples. Walker also found this to be true. He writes,

> Before the arrival of the European, Indian life is pictured as simple, honest and free, a childlike existence shattered by the intrusions of civilization. Unfortunately even such sympathetic references serve to reinforce the image of the Indian as a man of inferiority to whites. Using material culture as the only criterion, a judgement is made that a technological stage through which Europe had passed centuries before represented an earlier stage in human development. The stone age implements of the Indian are taken as a reflection of some lower level of evolution.…
>
> Their intricate stone implements, their invention of the canoe and snowshoe, their longhouses and tipis… their forest and hunting sense, all are given fair credit.… Often this is done in negative terms and in contrast to European technology, as in Wrong's statement that the pre-contact Indian had "no vehicles, no wheels, no pulley's nor derricks, and no machinery." *The bottle may be half-empty or half-full.*[83]

In this 1971 article, "The Indian in Canadian Historical Writing," James Walker provides one of the first scholarly attempts to criticize the treatment of Native peoples in archival and historical material.[84] Walker studies eighty-eight titles, ranging in publication date from 1829 to 1970.[85] He reports that these sources presented "the Indian as a human being… in confusing, contradictory and incomplete ways."[86] He also finds that Indians are given significance only in relation to White history, appearing "so fleetingly in our national story." Indian differences are generalized and Indian actions are placed out of context. Although some "noble savage" qualities are attributed to the Indian, his base savagery is assumed and emphasized.

In attempting to explain the reasons behind this "neglect and generally poor treatment" of the Indian, Walker points to the double standard for Whites and Natives in both the archival and historical sources, the need for heroes in Canadian historiography, and a belief in the "manifest destiny of European civilization." He especially pays attention to the "unwise use of sources" by historians who failed to take into account the beliefs, objectives, and ambitions of the original narratives. From such sources, historians repeat a "long string of epithets," the term "savage" predominating.[87]

Demonization/Animalization in Canadian Literature

The Indian as "savage" was especially carried to extremes in early Canadian literary productions. It is there that we find even more startling examples of the civ/sav ideology, which, when carried to its logical extent, results in the demonization of Indians. With respect to early English Canadian literature proper, numerous writers have demonized Native peoples, but perhaps no writer will ever equal John Richardson's sensational portrayal of Indians as grotesque cannibals that tear into human organs and slurp human blood. Richardson (1796–1852), born and raised in Upper Canada, advertised himself as "the first and only writer of historical fiction the country has yet produced."[88] He is best known for his personalized history of the War of 1812 (in which he was engaged as a teenager), as well as for his fiction, particularly for his novel *Wacousta*.

Sounding much like the early historical sources, with which he was familiar, murderous dark savages stalk Richardson's pages.[89] Margaret Turner suggests that savages stalk Richardson's mind because as "the savages drop shrieking from the trees… it is clear that something has gone wrong in Richardson's imaginative transition to the new world."[90] But more than imaginary fear is at work here. Turner points to the "failure of the discursive construction of place and culture" and "of the gap between the experience of the place and the language available to describe it" for Richardson's world of "paralyzing fear and potential madness."[91] The fear of "Indians," Turner explains, comes from the "European inability to discern an intelligible (and familiar) reality."[92] But more, she suggests that there was a basis of reality to Richardson's fear: He could not accommodate his (civilized) self of "Gothic" novels of "love" and honour" with what he experienced "in the new world savagery and violent cultural confrontation."[93]

Herein may lie the crux of the disagreement between Native and White Canadian intellectuals in our reading of White treatment of the "Indian." To suggest that Richardson, or his characters, could make no sense of the New-World (i.e., "Indian") violence, is to suggest that Europeans—or British

Canadians, as was Richardson—were innocents in the face of Native violence. In effect, it is to embrace the Old World Structure (Civilization)-meets-New-World Anti-Structure (Savagism) prototype. Nor can we simply explain away Richardson's sensationalist language as merely reflective of the gothic novel—gothic or not, what stays in the mind of readers is the "Indian" as savage beast.

It is certainly understandable that Whites (like anyone else, for example, Native peoples), would experience fear, even terror, in a threatening wartime situation, but neither gothic sensationalism nor fear nor dislocation explains sufficiently Richardson's unrestrained treatment of "Indians" in *Wacousta* or *Wau-Non-Gee* as "fiendish," "demonic," "shrieking," or "swimming savages." It is not as if warfare, brutality, and mayhem were alien among Whites, either in Europe or North America. If Europeans could not "discern intelligible reality" in the "New World," it is because they imagined unintelligent savages long before they ever set foot in the Americas, and long before they ever fought with any real Native men. White terror against presumed Indian depravity and irrational violence is a theme so prevalent in White North American culture that it constitutes a genre all its own. Given this, Richardson did not offer anything so different from most other White writers before and during his lifetime. Perhaps far too much has been given to his psychological state; he was actually borrowing an already established tradition, which today we might consider Hitchcockian horror. He may have been personally troubled, but was he really lost in a new world without a narrative? He was born in North America, not in Europe.

Reminiscent of captivity narratives, the Jesuits' Iroquois, and James Fenimore Cooper's Mohicans, *Wacousta* is typically peppered with nightmarish savages terrifying in their stealth, and heart-stopping in their sudden bursts of "mingled fury." Richardson's repeated descriptions of Indians as "fearless devils… brandishing their gleaming tomahawks… ejaculating… a guttural ugh," or "swimming savages" whose "grim" faces and "fierce eyes" are "gleaming and rolling like fireballs in their sockets" are really not that original.[94] But what Richardson lacks in originality, he more than makes up in intensity. As if there is not enough sensationalism in *Wacousta*, Richardson provides in his *Wau-Nan-Gee* what Leslie Monkman refers to as "the ultimate portrait of degenerate savagery" (presumably of the Pottowotamies).[95] Richardson writes:

> Squatted in a circle, and within a few feet of the wagon in which the tomahawked children lay covered with blood, and fast stiffening in the coldness of death, now sat about twenty Indians, with Pee-to-

tum at their head, passing from hand to hand the quivering heart of the slain man, whose eyes, straining as it were, from their sockets, seemed to watch the horrid repast in which they were indulging.... So many wolves or tigers could not have torn away more voraciously with their teeth, or smacked their lips with greater delight in the relish of human food, then did these loathsome creatures who now moistened the nauseous repast from a black bottle of rum.[96]

Richardson may have set the standard for portraying Indians so savagely, but he was by no means the only Canadian fictionalist to exploit the civ/sav tradition. Ralph Connor (1860–1937), a Presbyterian minister also known as the Reverend Charles William Gordon, built a successful literary career, in part based on such exploitation. Almost a century separates these two men, but their characterizations of Indians are thematically similar. Connor also indulges in sensationalism, though to a lesser extent than Richardson. Connor compares Indians not so much to demons as to animals; in fact, there is virtually no difference among animals, savages, and Indians in his treatment. Whites are terrified of Indians, or "halfbreeds," as the case may be, because Indians can turn into animal types, that is, savages, at any time. And "halfbreeds" can turn into Indians, ergo Savages, at any time too.

Connor often uses "halfbreed" characters to highlight White civilization against Indian savagery. In *The Foreigner*, one of Connor's characters is a Scot-Cree halfbreed named Mackenzie. In one scene, a teenage boy, Kalman "the foreigner," tries to tear a bottle of whiskey away from Mackenzie. Mackenzie goes through a palpable transformation: "The change in Mackenzie was immediate and appalling. His smiling face became transformed with fury, his black eyes gleamed with the cunning malignity of the savage, he shed his soft Scotch voice with his genial manner, the very movements of his body became those of his Cree progenitors. Uttering hoarse guttural cries, with the quick crouching run of the Indian on the trial of his foe, he chased Kalman... there was something so fiendishly terrifying in the glimpses that Kalman caught of his face now and then that the boy was seized with an overpowering dread."[97]

But at his English master's appearance and command, Mackenzie's "fiendish rage" fades "out of his face, the aboriginal blood lust dying in his eyes like the snuffing out of a candle. In a few brief moments he became once more a civilized man."[98] Kalman, though, is not the only foreigner. Mackenzie too is a foreigner when he turns "Indian," that is, a savage. It is an ironic treatment that a character, at least half native to the land (according to Connor), becomes an alien to humanity when "the Indian" in him comes out in the form of an animal! He stops being a savage, that is, a "foreigner," only when he returns as a Scot, that is, as a "civilized" man. Is Connor really not aware who the real foreigner is?

In another novel, *The Patrol of the Sun Dance Trail*, Ralph Connor continues very much in the same vein with his characterization of Jerry, a "halfbreed" scout caught between his White and Indian "blood."[99] This novel is set against the Riel "Rebellion" of 1885; the tension is between the Northwest Mounted Police and a Sioux "chief" Copperhead, whose intention is to rally a political movement of Piegans, Blackfoot, and Crees in support of Riel. In a scene where the White hero and his halfbreed scout are listening to Copperhead's "machinations," a transformation similar to Mackenzie's comes over the scout: "For that hour at least the half-breed was all Sioux. His father's blood was the water in his veins, the red was only his Indian mother's. With face drawn tense and lips bared into a snarl, with eyes gleaming, he gazed fascinated upon the face of the singer. In imagination, in instinct, in the deepest emotions of his soul Jerry was harking back again to the savage in him, and the savage in him thirsting for revenge upon the whiteman who had wrought this ruin upon him and his Indian race."[100]

Connor may as well have been describing a mad dog—the savage Jerry's physicality resembles rabid ferocity (lips are "bared into a snarl") with hints of the devil (eyes "gleam"), and Jerry regresses to unadulterated animal instinct. It is disturbing that so few scholars have really noticed the stark dehumanization that is engineered so casually. Is it that the hate and the racism in these types of novels are so risibly overstated, so off the charts that mainstream academics, perhaps more secure in the art of restraint or mystification, or simply inured to "shrieking," find in these works everything but the obvious? To Native readers and critics, what is here obvious is not laughable and it cannot be shrugged off.

Chapter Three

Currency and Social Effects of Dehumanization

Perhaps John Richardson and Ralph Connor were only trying to make money and become famous by using sensationalism. Perhaps, as Canadian colonialists presumably with inferiority complexes, they were trying to gain recognition. The point is, whatever their intentions, the impression left by their spectacular dehumanization of Native peoples is that of hate. The imagery their words and phrases evoke can sear the hearts of the most experienced Native readers. As Howard Adams puts it, "Even in solitary silence, I felt the word 'savage' deep in my soul."[1] Yet, in the guise of art and research such works, which, at the very least, should qualify as hate literature, are protected and perpetuated. I have long been concerned about the hate content in these type of productions; writers and educators unconsciously (and for some, not so unconsciously) transmit this racist and hate material. Even examining hate literature has potential for misreading. But, ultimately, it is better to expose hate writing to enlightened criticism than to keep using it to fortify colonial history. Arguably, it is better to study it than to burn it. However, *how* we study this material may be an offence. In Canada, hate literature is a federal offence, and were we to apply the law to sources routinely used for research and teaching, we would certainly notice diminished archives.

Given the extent of hate expressed against Native persons and cultures in Canadian writing, I find James Walker's assessment of Canadian historical writing conservative and inadequate. While "The Indian in Canadian Historical Writing" is an eye-opening and groundbreaking reassessment of Canadian historiography, it does not go deep enough into the underlying assumptions that both cause and justify the dehumanizing treatment of the Indian. It is disappointing that after all the racism and bias Walker studied and exposed, he concludes, "Generally speaking the times in which these early accounts were written made prejudice and ignorance inevitable."[2] Does any time ever make prejudice (to put it mildly) "inevitable"? Canadian historiography is not that benign. The broader purpose and effect of all these constructs of control was colonization.

It is neither "inevitable" nor by happenstance that much White intellectual and literary tradition is founded on name-calling. How else to explain Canadian historiography and literature that is replete with incendiary writing against Native cultures, peoples, and persons? "Savage" is not the only word that predominates in the epithets ascribed to Native peoples. As Walker himself establishes, standard archival and historical sources indulged in a lexical orgy, defaming Natives at every turn.[3]

To say the least, deprecating terms indicate political intentions, not to mention bias, slander, and just plain hatred. Terms or techniques construct, as well as express, hatred. Hatred, though impossible to quantify and difficult to pinpoint, must certainly be a factor in all this name-calling, especially in the demonization (and animalization) of Native characters. We may even speculate on behalf of these writers that they were afraid and that their insults were projections, perhaps were attempts at taming their fears of the unknown. Such speculations may or may not serve Aboriginal history because they can take the direction of absolving the colonizer of his racial (or sexual, as the case may be) hatred, instead of questioning the presumed objectivity and authority of such works. I worry about making dead people's racist and at times genocidal prejudices "inevitable" or "human" by over-exploring their psychological state and social or cultural conditioning, especially when this is done without any challenge to either the vocabulary, the images, or theories that advance racism, sexism, or hate. If we explain away the many and chameleon hatreds of the past, the implication is that such hatreds today are also explained away.

By "challenge" I do not mean simply to "contextualize." It is of course the province of scholars to contextualize. However, I find it most unsettling when scholars can readily and even conscientiously acknowledge—as does Germaine Warkentin in *Canadian Exploration Literature*—the "horrifying effect" of European "discovery and settlements of Canada" on Aboriginal populations, and, at the same time, rehabilitate exploration writing without so much as a whisper about its racist vocabulary.[4] Is it not possible to treat the complexities of historical figures and circumstances without skirting the dirty politics and problematics of power relations? If "the very way we read the texts themselves has been transformed"—as Warkentin asserts—then I am not comfortable with the ever-more insidious ways the "heroic point of view" is maintained by this "transformation."[5] It is not enough to contextualize people's heroics or prejudices, society's stereotypes, or governments' policies when these are so clearly racist or destructive to certain populations. Merely contextualizing offensive literature—or policy or outcome—can have the effect of defending, normalizing, neutralizing, or even legitimizing it. If this is not apparent to the researcher, it is certainly apparent to the target group.

It seems to me that White scholars forget that Native scholars will most likely read archival and other texts very differently from their own readings. A number of years ago I did a short critique of a journal written by George Nelson, a missionary to the Cree and Ojibway in the 1840s.[6] As a young scholar, and a member of a "target group," I took some exception to his terminology; for example, his description of the Cree shaking tent ceremony as "conjuring." I explained that the cumulative effect of his acceptance of the civ/sav framework results in the belittlement of Native life. I received some chiding from an established scholar who wrote (to another colleague): "In doing much needed corrective history and commentary, there is a great risk of reverse stereotyping… [George Nelson] had his biases and ethnocentrism; but he and other European traders varied considerably from one another as individuals and thinkers, just as did the Indian people whom they met."[7] She especially disputed my reading of "conjure," arguing over its meaning, and defending Nelson as one who "does not usually belittle Indians." I had in fact acknowledged that Nelson was not only noticeably liberal for his times but also that his faith was shaken, so to speak, by Cree beliefs; the thing is, no amount of contextualizing the word or the missionary could undo *how I read*, not only the individual words, but the colonial constructs from which Nelson and other exploration writers framed their understanding. Quibbling over the "positive" parts of the word or the good intentions of certain Europeans misses the point. Let me be clear: It is the overarching, accumulative effect of Eurocentrism that sticks. To say this is not to deny anyone's individuality or specificity, or even basic goodness. Nor do I promote reverse stereotyping of the European by which he is painted as the proverbial grabby White man, oppressing poor hapless little savages. None of us should be so caricatured. However, that we are all potentially more than the sum of our colonial parts does not erase colonial history, and this empirical reality does compel us to interrogate archival sources as well as scholarly readings of these sources.

I am, of course, raising the issue of ethical responsibilities for scholars who use racist or hate material in our research. We are members of society and we are not immune to societal or governmental pressures. Who, after all, has made possible the building of weapons of mass destruction? And it has been pointed out by sociologists who study the nature of prejudice that, often, programs (or pogroms) of ethnic destruction begin with verbal and written campaigns of hate. While this observation has often been applied to Nazism, it has rarely been applied to the textual/political dehumanizing treatment of indigenous peoples of the Americas. That few scholars have noticed the connection between hate literature and violence against indigenous peoples is testament to the powers of prejudice and propaganda. Are scholars to be exempt from having to address the historical and social consequences of textual dehumanization? Texts do have social consequences; the thought that social scientists can be so alienated from the social purpose of knowledge is not a comfortable one.

There are serious conflictual situations between White and Native Canadians, and institutionalized racism is not an insignificant contributing factor. According to Canadian sociologist James Frideres, in his book *Aboriginal Peoples in Canada*, unmistakable evidence "reveals that racism widely distorts the attitudes of white Canadians toward Aboriginal people."[8] In turn, he writes, such attitudes result in a domino effect of related attitudes: "Whether blatantly or covertly, most Canadians still believe that Aboriginals are inferior; as a result, these people believe that there is a sound, rational basis for discrimination against Aboriginals at both the individual and institutional level."[9] We see clearly the results in Natives' struggles for land rights and self-government, to say nothing about social inequality. Frideres highlights biased Canadian historical treatment of Native peoples as an institutionalized expression of racism: "To legitimize its power, the dominant groups must reconstruct social history whenever necessary... today, most Canadians continue to associate 'savage' and 'heinous' behaviour with Canadian Aboriginals."[10] That Canadians continue to associate "savage" with Natives goes back to hate literature in Canadian writing.

By "hate literature" I do not mean writing that merely expresses the emotion of hate; I mean it as a particularly pernicious racist point of view that is transmitted from generation to generation through systemic forces of colonization (language, history, schooling, media, marketplace). The Euro-Canadian point of view is a self-perpetuating, profoundly institutionalized machine of thought we often refer to as "Eurocentrism." J.M. Blaut's distinction in *The Colonizer's Model of the World* between Eurocentrism as "a sort of 'prejudice'" and Eurocentrism as a "set of empirical beliefs" is significant to our understanding of this machine. Blaut argues that Eurocentrism as an attitude could be "eliminated from modern enlightened thought in the same way we eliminate other relic attitudes," but he explains, "the really crucial part of Eurocentrism" is that it "includes a set of beliefs that are statements about empirical reality, statements educated and usually unprejudiced Europeans accept as true, as propositions supported by 'facts.'"[11]

I am not convinced that European bias as a relic attitude has been eliminated, but the point is that European prejudices have enabled Western peoples to believe their attitudes have some basis in empirical reality. This is where the media and the marketplace come in, most handily at that. In no small way, the graphic presentation of re-settler encounters with "natives," however imaginary, are simultaneously an expression of and constant reification of Eurocentrism. In other words, prejudices and what social scientists refer to as "the social construction of reality" (thought to be empirical reality) feed off each other, especially through the dissemination of images.

Through pulp fiction and other cultural productions, commercial exploitation of the "Indian image" continues unabated. Hollywood, for example, keeps on producing and reproducing movies that still largely depict "Indians" in the tradition of captivity narratives, James Fenimore Cooper's *Leatherstocking Tales*, and Buffalo Bill's Wild West Shows.[12] And although the movie-making industry is slowly showing signs of moving to more contemporary directions (*Smoke Signals* [1998], *Windtalkers* [2002], *DreamKeeper* [2003]), stereotypical treatments in both old and new movies remains a problem.

Michael Hilger, in *The American Indian in Film*, points out that "the repetition of these techniques through each historical period is what really impresses the fictional Indian on the minds of audiences."[13] Movies are plastic, and their stories are often fabrications, but because Hollywood has bombarded the global public with thousands of cowboys and Indians movies (and off-shoots of such movies), the image of the Indian as a primitive, blood-thirsty savage terrorizing good, innocent and, to boot, glamorized White men, women, and children has become more real in the minds of the public than any *real* Native peoples as human beings.[14]

Textbooks, too, continue to depict a world that revolves around, and out of, Europe and its descendants. As Blaut explains in *The Colonizer's Model*: "Textbooks are an important window to a culture; more than just books, they are semi-official statements of exactly what the opinion-forming elite of the culture want the educated youth of that culture to believe to be true about the past and present world."[15] Blaut continues that while "in the main" racism has been discarded in textbooks and "non-Europe is no longer considered to have been *absolutely* stagnant and traditional," prominent historical scholars

continue to maintain and focus "on Greater Europe as the perpetual foun-
tainhead of history."[16] Always presented as makers of history, Blaut writes,
Europeans are accorded "permanent superiority": "Europe eternally advances,
progresses, modernizes. The rest of the world advances more sluggishly, or
stagnates: it is 'traditional society.' Therefore, the world has a permanent geographical center and a permanent periphery: an Inside and an Outside. Inside
leads, Outside lags, Inside innovates, Outside imitates."[17] This "Eurocentric
diffusionism," he argues, "lies at the very root of historical and geographical
scholarship. Some parts of the belief have been questioned in recent years, but
its most fundamental tenets remain unchallenged, and so the belief as a whole
has not been uprooted or very much weakened by modern scholarship."[18]

In Canada, racism in textbooks is by no means a thing of the past.[19]
Insightful, well-documented studies of textbook bias was provided by Native
analysts, writers, and educators as early as the 1970s.[20] Native peoples consider
textbook bias in the school curriculum so unacceptable that even Native organizations have published material on the matter.[21] What is troubling is that, as
a rule, Native analysis has not been taken seriously by non-Native Canadian
readers, scholars, and educators. This is reflective of an ongoing colonial tactic
of denial: Erase by selection (by simply not noticing the relevant parts) not
only the records that attest to hate and racism, but also the Native documentation and analysis of it. Here again, we see the power of prejudice. Frideres
points out what Native scholars know so well, that readers "react quite differently" to books by Native authors such as Harold Cardinal and Waubageshig
"than they have" to books by authors such as W.L. Morton or Arthur Lower.
"The layperson typically rejects the conclusions" of the Native authors "as the
products of bias," but, explains Frideres, "the same layperson tends to accept
the explanations provided by... 'established academic' authors."[22]

Obviously, if it takes a White person (usually an educator) to say there
is a problem with racism in textbooks before other Whites, including many
scholars and educators, will find the statement credible, then Canadian society has not even begun to deal with its colonizer's face of racism. By denying
even Native documentation, a vehicle much sacralized in Western culture,
Canadian colonialists are showing both their colours and their inabilities to
deal with history and its legacies. They are I believe feeling represented by
Canada's national myths. Muffling, containing, or ignoring Native evaluation
is a huge part of maintaining the Eurocentric point of view.

The combined effect is powerful. The "heroic point of view," with its
tendentious use of words and classifications, has served to de-grade Natives
and their societies, and to infantilize and objectify them, thus, "verifying" the
very assumption that set them up as savages in the first place. But these sets

of ingenious rationalizations were not just playful mind games. They were required in the service of subjugating Native peoples. They served to justify invading Aboriginal lands, resources, and cultures. Demonizing has served to erase any sense of responsibility for the destruction of Aboriginal peoples, places, and cultures. The cumulative effect of all this is staggering. To come back to what should by now be a glaring point, Native peoples are perhaps the most debased and misrepresented peoples anywhere, if not in archival and scholarly sources, certainly in popular culture.[23]

The Colonizer's Culture

This puts into perspective whatever changes (or anti-colonial material) has been produced about "Indians." To begin with, the changes have been extremely slow and uneven. For example, while Canadian novels of the 1960s and 1970s ease up on the ever-present dark savages shadowing the landscape, a number of Canadian writers from the period resort to other disturbing stereotypes in their literary presentation of "the Indian." Mort Forer's *The Humback* (1969), David Williams's *The Burning Wood* (1975), and Betty Wilson's *Andre Tom MacGregor* (1976) immerse Native characters in cliché-ridden misery and dissipation. The objectification of Native women as sexually unrestrained, indiscriminate, or servile is particularly noxious but classically colonial. In Williams, the treatment is couched as mystical; in Forer, Metis women merely serve as biological but blurry-eyed vehicles for sex and species; in Wilson, "Indian" women are shamelessly presented as repulsive. The Native men in all these novels are stilted, Hollywood-ish, stock caricatures, often named Joe with a surname of an animal.

To say the least, such novels are depressing and predictable. And then there is W.P. Kinsella's treatment of Native characters in works such as *Dance Me Outside*. At best, he caricatures; at worst, he draws on popular societal stereotypes and prejudices, and, in this, his works confirm existing racist images. And sexist ones. In "Iliana Comes Home," the Native women have no sense of privacy or decorum as they climb into bed while others are watching. However, Kinsella does also caricature White society and characters in ways that expose White arrogance, hypocrisy, and stupidity. But does his cynical treatment of White culture outweigh Frank Fencepost's broken English? Or the over-sexualization of Native women?

Of course, there have been exceptions. Anne Cameron, Margaret Laurence, George Ryga, Rudy Wiebe, George Woodcock, Margaret Atwood, Margaret Craven (who is not Canadian, but whose *I Heard the Owl Call My Name* is set in Kwakiutl country), among others, have treated Native characters and themes much more respectfully and, some, elegantly. In *Dreamspeaker*, Cam

Hubert (Anne Cameron) foregrounds and elevates Native humanity, humour, and knowledge (although her ending is troubling, overdramatic, and perhaps somewhat stereotypical). While Laurence and Wiebe have produced some compelling portrayals of Native themes or characters, they are not all free of problems and stereotypes, either. Laurence, particularly in *The Diviners*, treats Native/Metis characters with considerable ambivalence; on one hand, she ennobles Morag's predictably elusive, temperamental, but long-suffering and passionate Metis lover, and yet she stoops to typically social-problem stereotypes of the much fragmented Tonnerre family. But, like Wiebe, she certainly takes Native presence in Canada seriously.

Intriguingly, Cameron, Laurence, and Wiebe all emphasize Native spirituality, especially as an antidote to the implied spiritual vacancy of modern White Canada. A continuation of this treatment is discernable in a number of self-consciously postcolonial Canadian writers who continue to simply rearrange old and familiar themes that draw on and perpetuate stock images of "Indians" or "Natives" (Natives includes the Metis). Often, Indian characters are created to act as spiritual or mystical guides to the landscape so that Canadian colonists can more deeply and completely appropriate the land.[24]

Richardson and Connor appropriate the land and the "Indian" violently rather than spiritually, but they were within the Canadian tradition of using the "Indian" or "halfbreed" from which to build their personal reputations as well as Canadian art and culture. This is a point cogently treated by Leslie Monkman in *A Native Heritage: Images of the Indian in English-Canadian Literature*. Canadian writers, explains Monkman, "have repeatedly found in the confrontation of native and non-native heritages a unique focus for the exploration of their own concerns and culture."[25] Whether they found in the Indian an enemy or an alternative model by which to develop their identity, writers "in each era of Canadian literary history... have turned to the Indian and his culture for standards by which to measure the values and goals of white Canadian society, for patterns of cultural destruction, transformation, and survival, and for new heroes and indigenous myths."[26] We can find a parallel in Said's analysis of the role of the constructed Orient "as a sort of surrogate and even underground self" for European identity.[27] As such, Orientalism was a cultural investment that brought to Europe "a created body of theory and practice," or, a "mode of discourse with supporting institutions, vocabulary, scholarship, imagery, doctrines, even colonial bureaucracies and colonial styles."[28] By no means as exotically treated as the "Oriental," the "Indian" or "native" nonetheless has served Canadian identity and culture quite extensively.[29]

If the "Indian" was for Canadians cultural clarification and development, it certainly has been quite something else for Native peoples. But before we turn to the Native writers' experience of the "Indian," we must attend to another layer of the colonizer's culture. I must again bring up the fact that it has taken White intellectuals half a millennium to begin to sense the extent to which Native peoples have been assaulted in colonizer texts and productions. Obviously reflecting profound association with the Western myth of civilization, the majority of Canadian scholars and fiction writers are still reluctant to acknowledge the racism and hate material that informs their views, attitudes, and works about Aboriginal peoples. Indeed, some not only remain entirely impervious to the thought that colonialism might be racist, they continue to fortify it! I have already mentioned the more recent examples. I repeat this because it is important to comprehend the stunning degree to which Native peoples have been subjected to degradation.

White scholars and writers have not easily understood or accepted Native intellectual or political response to systemic racism. Instead, many have traditionally rationalized, if even they recognized, the use of what is, in effect, Eurocentric hate literature as sources to advance their own research, theories, and fiction. Focussing on ethnography or using Indian motifs with stock themes of good and evil, light and darkness, and the "primitive" or the "savage" in "man" has served to detract from or dilute what should be intolerable in much of the writing on Native peoples. For instance, Gaile MacGregor's *The Wacousta Syndrome*, a book full of entertaining and important insights concerning the Canadian psyche, does not confront the racist hideousness of Richardson's *Wacousta*. MacGregor focuses on the White Canadian's "colonized" position vis-à-vis the Americans, rather than recognizing Native presence in the country, and, when this is offered, it is only in relation to the White Canadian's experience and response to the landscape.[30]

Margaret Turner, in *Imagining Culture: New World Narratives and the Writing of Canada*, does dutifully acknowledge Native peoples, but largely as a backdrop to her main study. She devotes her examination to four classic Canadian writers, among them John Richardson. She departs from MacGregor slightly in her emphasis on Richardson's virtual madness due to his sense of presumed displacement in the "new world." But like others before her, she does not deal with Richardson's "shrieking savages" as hate literature. This omission, plus the fact she makes no mention or use of contemporary Native criticism, is disappointing. Laura Groening, on the other hand, turns to Native writers and critics in her study of the voice appropriation controversy in *Listening to Old Woman Speak*. She departs from the usual inattention to Indian hating in early Canadian classics in her confrontation of anti-Indian literature. Applying Fanon's "Manichean Allegory" to a number of classic Canadian colonial texts, Groening concludes that "as we move through the century, the ideology of nation building appears to shift, but the colonial dialectic ... nevertheless remains constant. The allegory is as concrete as a table: one may need to reposition it, but apparently one need not throw it out."[31]

Again, and perhaps this is a rhetorical question, how could intelligent Canadians have missed so much racism in their research and writings? It is not as if it were obscure. To go into the many historically rooted reasons for all this tolerance of suspect literature is to go right back to the point of the struggle: that colonial constructs are for the purposes of conquest, not knowledge, and that they serve to blind and condition subsequent generations to see through "stereotypic eyes."[32]

The essence of the colonial relationship, as Canadian political essayist Peter Puxley explains, is that the colonized are "unilaterally defined by the other."[33] The colonizer then cannot accept "any move toward real autonomy on the part of the colonized." And any such move is either "ignored, defined as unacceptable, or reprimanded, depending on the degree of institutionalization of the relationship."[34] With some exceptions, the colonial forces attacking Native peoples in Canada have not been military, but rather, have been institutional, through economic, religious, educational, legislative, and media systems. Not surprisingly, the colonial relationship between White and Native peoples is profoundly institutionalized, and has grown more so with time. One of the indices of such systemic control is the extent to which Native peoples have been defined outside themselves, and, when they seek to change this definition, meet opposition in many forms.

Reception to Native readings and writings, particularly from the 1970s to the 1990s, has often been oppositional. This perhaps explains why Penny Petrone, in *Native Literature in Canada*, seems unaware that she is undermining Native social protest writers, particularly those from the 1970s, by repeatedly labelling and psychologizing them as "bitter."[35] She impresses upon this point further by praising those works that (to her) show no "anger" or "rage" or "sentimentality."[36] She goes so far as to accuse these writers (by indirect reference) of "self-pity" and even reduces Sarain Stump's aesthetically rich protest poetry to "laments."[37] While Petrone understands that Native writing "has always been quintessentially political, addressing their persecutions and betrayals and summoning their resources for resistance," she judges this writing in a patronizing way: "Already many are able to deal with the culture clash and their own identify not only with perception but with some detachment and control, moving beyond the worst excesses of emotion and diction that marred much earlier protest writing."[38]

There are a number of such patronizing comments throughout the book, which detract from an otherwise exceptional and valuable work. It is revealing that Petrone feels most comfortable with Native oral traditions, which she largely treats as a thing of the past. Her obvious respect for Native languages and oral traditions, is, at times, marred with stilted ethnological generalizations.[39] But she also criticizes Westerners for failing to appreciate the "highly developed and extensive body of native Canadian oral literature," and explains that this literature was "misunderstood because, although it did not conform to the conventions of Western literary criticism, scholars still treated it as Western literature."[40] It is puzzling why Petrone does not apply this observation to Native social protest writing, because she does provide insightful "reasons" why Western scholars have "neglected and ignored" Native literature generally. She introduces her work by listing the reasons: "European cultural arrogance, and attitudes of cultural imperialism and paternalism that initiated and fostered patronizing stereotypes of the Indian; European antipathy and prejudice towards the oral literatures of so-called primitive peoples; the European belief that the Indian was a vanishing race; the purist's attitude of Western literary critics towards literature that does not conform totally to their aesthetic criteria; and finally, the difficult problems of translating native literature."[41]

Petrone is not the only critic who has reprimanded Native writers. In the 1980s, Native writers were variously rebuked for "blustering and bludgeoning society," or were generalized as "minorities" who were "strangling in their own roots." Even what I call "soft sell" literature, such as Beatrice Culleton's *Spirit of the White Bison*, was received with little discernment.[42] The confrontation between the Writers' Union of Canada and Native writers on the issue of cultural appropriation was revealing for its oppositional politics. This important debate, which flared up in the late 1980s, quickly broke down into counter-accusations: some White writers cited Natives with censorship in response to the charge of racism.[43]

As writers, we struggle enough with White Canadian judgement and labelling about our presumed bitterness, anger, or militancy, legitimate as such responses to untenable situations may be. Our works are further gauged with a language of containment. Bruce Trigger's foreword to George Sioui's *For an American Autohistory* provides a typical example of containment: "While this is a polemical work, it never descends to recrimination and vituperative condemnation, even when that might seem justified... it is a polemic written at the level of philosophy."[44] So long as established academics can determine for us when or how our resistance might seem justified, White Canadians need not worry about a revolution. But what is resistance if it cannot be expressively resistant? Are we now to resist only in metaphors? Not all Native writers wish to couch their resistance through their Tricksters. Resistance is not about making resistance palatable to the colonizer! As long as Native writing is defined within or limited to preferred colonizer terms, it is neither free nor resisting.

I am not suggesting that all Native expressions of protest are lovely or that they are easy to receive. I can appreciate that protest is difficult to absorb; Native resistance does reflect poorly on the Canadian self-image. Nor would I ever suggest that Native writing can not be criticized or reviewed. But academics and critics must make it their mandate first to comprehend the noxious nature of colonization before dismissing utterances of decolonization merely as "sloganistic," "bitter," "biased," or "polemical." These are high-handed charges that reflect an ideology that only Whites are "objective" and only they are able to discern balance, emotional or intellectual. In most instances, such accusations, especially when redundant, are patronizing labelling techniques consistent with the phenomenon of White backlash to minority groups.[45] To call Native writers "bitter," "angry," or any number of related labels is to imply there is something emotionally or psychologically wrong with them. Labelling or psychologizing them discredits the basis of their resistance or their research. Such ad hominem tactics reflect the colonizers' wish to neutralize the "negative" or "accusatory" tones that *they* hear. It is their wish to sidestep the uncomfortable truths that the anger, in oppressed people mirrors. "Anger" as used by oppressed people is not a psychological problem to be diffused by therapy; it is not just a feeling, it is an expression of moral outrage against injustice. In this spirit Jesus expressed anger, as did the Old Testament prophets. Anger is a tool of liberatory potential. It is a political sign. In this context I wince when I see or read Native peoples advocating a socially disconnected spirituality as a way of pacifying or replacing Native anger. Of course, anger can be dangerous. Oppressed people in a politically unaware state tend to internalize this anger and turn it upon themselves. Then, too, it can be externalized and turned into a revolution (as Fanon so brilliantly explicated), and so is threatening to all, perhaps more so for the colonizer.

Social protest cannot be beautiful; neither is the ground from which it is born. Aesthetics cannot be the primary concern for Native resistance writers, even if much of their writing is in fact elegant and gracious. Resistance is about exorcising the "400 [500] year pain" that filmmaker Alanis Obomsawin spoke about. We are engaged in nothing less than an intellectual revolution. And if Native writers have been angry or polemical in their counter-discourse, it is only because so much Eurocentric material requires excision, a work White Canadian intellectuals have barely begun to perform.

Only in the last several decades have scholars in specialist fields and other pockets of the academy produced an impressive body of deconstructed material. The respected scholar Olive Dickason has led the way in bringing to the foreground a Native presence in Canadian history and culture. Other scholars, Native and non-Native, are highlighting our political relationships, and still others are concentrating on specific histories. However, with respect to mainstream writing, Native histories, issues, and literatures are still largely marginalized and ghettoized. Ken Coates and Robin Fisher, editors of *Out of the Background: Readings on Canadian Native History*, express optimism that there is "historiographical vitality of this field," but concede that "enormous historiographical gaps remain."[46] Given the record, we are largely at the beginning stages of correcting and balancing Canadian historiography.

Exciting and extensive changes are especially underway in the study of contemporary Native literatures, but, again, much remains to be re-examined, particularly in the area of cultural studies in English departments and in the use of obstructive jargon in postcolonial theory. I caution that we not relax, that, as indispensably significant as the new works are, we have much more deconstructing and reconstructing to do. Like Blaut, I find "the sheer quantity" of Eurocentric material daunting. Refutations, as Blaut says, no matter how persuasive, "cannot be placed, so to speak, on one arm of a balance and be expected to outweigh all of the accumulated writings of generations of European scholars, textbook writers, journalists, publicists, and the rest, heaped up on the other arm of the balance."[47]

Canada has taken some significant constitutional and legal steps to accommodate Aboriginal peoples' rights to lands and self-government, and Aboriginal peoples have shown tenacity, as reflected in their political and cultural reawakening.[48] But it is difficult to be overly optimistic, for even as the specialized White scholars, writers, reviewers, and audiences are beginning to appreciate the complexities of Native histories, cultures, and characters, we are all still under the effects of more than 500 years of textual and political domination. Even as we are tackling racist sources, such sources remain uncritically open to the public and to all students. Almost worse, new versions of racism pop up and come at us through politics, legal judgements, Olympian pronouncements, stupid editorials, and spurious uses of scholarship.

The impact of White judgement and dehumanization remains current. To the extent this literature is archived (or revived), the hate/fear techniques are recycled. As long as we continue to go to our archives, textbooks, and theatres, we are constantly confronted with it all. And, if we do not truly transform how we read and critique these sources, our scholarship can be as much about reproduction of racism as about rooting it out. How many people (both

Native and non-Native) are trained to read (in the fullest sense of the word) critically such material? Teachers, beginning in grade school, must learn and teach the young how to evaluate information, and school systems must provide anti-racist textbooks and online materials. Students and the Canadian public in general should not have to go to universities before learning the art and skills of critical thinking. It is troubling though that even those who have higher education are not necessarily aware of racism in texts. It appears not all academics are prepared to engage in decolonized criticism, either in historiography, literature, or in other fields of research.

I must live with the reality that this material will continue to exist. But unlike Terry Goldie in *Fear and Temptation*, I cannot have the luxury of avoiding the term "racist" in my study. Perhaps, and I feel ambiguous here, those of us who bear the brunt of this racist literature must view and treat the scurrilous material as monuments of our experience, of our dispossession, of our destruction. Indigenous peoples of the Americas have been destroyed in numbers beyond words, yet not only has this not received much notice by anyone (certainly no huge annual commemorations, no massive monuments), but worse, the war of words against us continues.

Chapter Four

Native Writers Resist: Addressing Invasion

The national mythologies of white settler societies are deeply spatialized stories.

—Sherene H. Razack[1]

Subjugation of Aboriginal peoples is, of course, the context both to the subjugator's justification literature and to the subjugated's resistance response. To appreciate Native resistance, we need to understand the "long walk" of Native people as they have experienced it and as they have told it, and now as they are recording and analyzing it.

"My people are a storytelling people"—so begins Mohawk lawyer, academic, and writer Patricia Monture-Angus in *Thunder in My Soul*. And Native people have been telling a story. The "story" they have been telling is not a legend, not *atowkewin*, but rather *achimoowin*, a factually based account. A retelling, really. In recording these accounts, these writers are, in effect, challenging the Canadian canons of history, culture, and representation. In this, the story is a political narrative. Like all revelations having to do with unequal human relationships, this story or series of stories is, of course, involved and difficult to hear. But it is unmistakable. And if it is difficult for Euro-Canadians to hear, imagine how difficult it is for Native writers to have to reiterate.

Peoples in "occupied territories," to use Duncan Mercredi's poetic phrase, tell us that, on a fundamental level, colonizers invaded, stole, and exploited natural and human resources, the consequences of which left the colonized dispossessed, demoralized, objectified, and marginalized. When the dust settled, indigenous peoples across the Americas were massively destroyed and exiled in their own lands. For the last half-millennium, White colonization of North America has been nothing short of catastrophic for Aboriginal peoples. The numerical loss alone is staggering. Contrary to the mythmakers' blithe estimates that there were only one million pre-Columbian Indians north of the Rio Grande, Jennings, for example, places these indigenous populations at 10 to 12 million.[2] More recently, in the context of discussing "the incalculably devastating effects of early epidemics" anthropologists Bruce Morrison and Roderick Wilson, in *Native Peoples: The Canadian Experience*, record estimates ranging from 4.5 million to 18 million.[3] These estimates are not unreasonably high, especially when looked at from the wider indigenous America's populations. J.M. Blaut in *The Colonizer's Model* reasons that in 1492, indigenous populations numbered "at least 50 million people and conceivably as many as 200 million," and that by the sixteenth century "perhaps three-quarters of the entire population of America was wiped out" largely by epidemics.[4] But even if such estimates are high, even if we would do what some early anthropologists like Kroeber did,[5] reducing the numbers by half without any methodological rationale, the remaining numbers are still staggeringly high. They would still indicate that indigenous peoples suffered and died in more than holocaustic proportions. In any case, the decimation of a people should not be qualified by their numbers. It is impossible to comprehend such annihilation, and equally impossible to find words adequate enough to express the horror of it, but such estimates should put into perspective how restrained Native peoples have been in their resistance. It should also put into perspective the ludicrousness of referring to North America as "wild and uninhabited"—plainly, someone and something de-peopled these lands!

Colonization as an historical event (or series of events) in Canada has now been amply documented by numerous scholars representing an intriguing mix of disciplines, and it is certainly being documented by Aboriginal scholars and writers. We know that Aboriginal peoples lost their balance of power in relation to Euro-Canadians. We can trace this loss not only to military invasion but also to attempted genocide, starvation, land theft, and structural changes over time in areas fundamental to cultural integrity. Colonial land theft in Canada is best understood in the study of what sociologist James Frideres calls "geographical incursion," as well as in the study of Aboriginal rights, treaties, the *Indian Act*, and constitutional law. While institutional invasion is less definable, it is possible to trace the Euro-Canadian colonial forces that have disempowered Aboriginal peoples in every area vital to their well-being. These forces implicate actual people who came as fur traders, missionaries, treaty and scrip commissioners, soldiers, colonial officials, police, land speculators, Indian agents, storekeepers, and even artists, travellers, and poets.

But the invasion is only the beginning of the colonization process. As the invasion deepens, the colonizer moves to protect and enhance his newly gained position of power. This is done in many ways, including "usurpation and replacement," as A.D. Fisher has put it[6]—or, from the colonizer's perspective, "peopling" the "empty" spaces, renaming the "natives" and (their) landscape, building strategic points of entry and defence (i.e., forts), and occupying strategic roles as (re)educators, employers, and, gradually, as legislators.[7] In some places, such as in Central America and the United States, brutal violence was exercised against original peoples, and this, in combination with deadly epidemics, sped up and collapsed the invasion and replacement process. Deadly epidemics also played a huge role in depopulating Native peoples in Canada; for this reason the Canadian government could for the most part bypass military action in its invasions of Native lands and resources. Epidemics facilitated Canada's institutional takeover, and because the invasion and power maintenance have been largely structural, the process has been slower. But because the aggression and destruction have been less visible, they have been all the more insidious, for, as Frideres says, the "ultimate consequence of colonization is to weaken the resistance of the colonized Aboriginals to the point at which they can be controlled."[8]

What makes this unhappy (and ongoing) Canadian story of control so slippery is that colonization is not a uniform movement, nor is it a movement that is only in the past. Succeeding generations from every culture group (generally, but not universally, moving east to west) across Canada have experienced different versions of invasions repetitively. For western Native peoples there have been at least three major periods and phases of colonization: pre-Confederation, consisting largely of epidemics, explorers, missionaries, fur traders, and expansionists; Confederation, which effectively ended Native independence through displacement and legislation; and the post-World War II era, which roared in modernization.

For Native people of Canada, the dispossession and the dying continues. The incursion is definitely not "of the past."[9] In fact, the grossest amount of destruction has been taking place since World War II.[10] Between 1940 and the 1990s, the Canadian government and society have been aggressively whipping Native peoples into "modernization," that is, encroaching or limiting their land-based ways while at the same time imposing urbanization and industrialization.[11] In addition, both the American and Canadian governments have treated northern Native lands as the last frontier. In Canada,

Native peoples continue to lose massive amounts of ecological space and resources to megaprojects to extract or produce hydroelectricity, lumber, gas and oil, and uranium and other minerals. Even in areas where First Nations or Inuit groups (excluding the Metis, whose land rights have been ignored) have succeeded in recovering or reclaiming land space, they are confronted with potential ecological and cultural disasters. What is left of Native lands is being threatened with sound and chemical pollution, foreign businesses, deforestation, and destruction of animals.[12] And now global warming. And what is left of an economically viable land-based lifestyle for many northern Native peoples is being threatened by animal rights activists.[13] The loss cannot be measured strictly in terms of square footage or annual income because Native peoples' relationship to the land is more than about commodities; threatening Native lands and resources is not only assailing Native livelihood, it is also further threatening coherent cultural systems and identities. What is culturally essential cannot be measured in monetary terms, though, of course, the importance of economy should not be underestimated. In other words, what White colonization of 500 years could not accomplish, modernization and industrialization is threatening to finish.

Such ongoing destruction and staged intrusions are still being rationalized as "progress" and "development," and the consequences are still nothing short of deadly. Not only do Native peoples continue to lose their lands and resources, arguably the very ground of their cultural beings, but they, as a result, continue to lose their lives in disturbing proportions.[14] The social consequences of colonization (both in material and intellectual terms) continue to assail Native communities. It is in this sense there is nothing "postcolonial" about the Native experience.

I have given some attention to establishing the Euro-Canadian subjugation of Aboriginal peoples because it is this, the destruction that subjugation has wreaked, that places Canadian Native peoples as the colonized. Colonization is not abstract; it is an experience.[15] Native persons have experienced invasion, dispossession, and objectification as nothing less than devastating. This devastation, which is at the heart of the colonial experience, informs early and contemporary Native writing.

This Canadian story spills over all the usual boundaries of geographies, eras, and cultures. The ways in which Native peoples have been overrun have led to the ways in which they have responded. Resistance is necessarily defensive, at least at first. Since Native peoples in Canada have been attacked through text and policy (and the two go hand in hand), they have used the written word to address their dislocation as well as their marginalization.

Exposition of the Invasive Process

I had a dream—but I did not believe my dream—that there would
be white men everywhere, overwhelming this land. Today I see it. I
love this land greatly, and what is still the Indian's I am resolved to
hold fast. For that I pray much.

—Thunderchild,
in *Voices of the Plains Cree* (1923)[16]

As soon as Native individuals could use the techniques of writing in the enemy's language, in this case, the English language, they immediately addressed
their colonial conditions. At the outset, the emphasis was, of course, on loss
of lands and resources. The earliest Native writers speak to the material loss
of space. Of landscape. Of homelands. The Mohawks, for example, suffered
land loss several times over. They were among the loyalists who were relocated
onto Mississauga land after America's declaration of independence. Once
relocated, the Mohawks then suffered shrinkage of land space as a result of
British Canadian imperial policies. On 10 December 1798, Loyalist Mohawk
Joseph Brant wrote a letter to Captain Green, obviously hoping for a positive
resolution concerning their new lands around the Grand River. Brant exposes
the multifarious ways British Canadian officials incurred on the Mohawk land
space around the Grand River area:

I presume that you are well acquainted with the long difficulties we
had concerning the lands on this river—these difficulties we had
not the least idea of when we first settled here, looking on them as
granted to us to be indisputably our own, other wise we would never
have accepted the lands, yet afterwards it seemed a little odd to us
that the writings Gov. Haldimand gave us after our settling on the
lands, was not so complete as the strong assurances and promises he
made us at first.[17]

There were other protests. In July 1847 Ojibway George Copway (or Kah-
ge-gah-bowh, as he was also known) addressed what he referred to in the
terminology of his times as "the Indian's hunting grounds." First he sets out
the Ojibway cultural ways of dealing with landholdings, uses, and responsibilities:

The hunting grounds of the Indians were secured by right, a law and
custom among themselves. No one was allowed to hunt on another's
land, without invitation or permission. If any person was found

trespassing on the ground of another, all his things were taken from him, except a handful of shot, powder sufficient to serve him in the going *straight* home.... If he were found a second time trespassing, all his things were taken away from him, except food sufficient to subsist on while going home. And should he still come a third time to trespass on the same, or another man's hunting grounds, his nation, or tribe, are then informed of it, who take up his case. If still he disobeys, he is banished from his tribe.[18]

These ways pre-existed the White man's ways. "Invasion" implies something and somebody exists prior to the invasion. Moreover, what exists does so in a certain, culturally coherent manner. In other words, what exists before the invasion, and what makes invasion "invasion" is precisely the fact that peoples and cultures original to the landspace existed. This may seem so obvious as to merit no comment, but in the context of colonial politics, the Native re-establishment of the Native's culture is (and becomes even more) crucial. It is crucial because it has been denied. The colonizer's denial of a pre-existing culture justified the dispossession. And dispossession there was. Copway details the Ojibway loss of lands in the early nineteenth century: "In the year 1818, 1,800,000 acres of land were surrendered to the British government." Rhetorically, Copway asks, "For how much, do you ask?" Then answers, "For $2,960 per annum! What *a great sum* for British generosity!" Copway, obviously dismayed and disgusted, hopes that with respect to what lands remain unsold, "the scales will be removed from the eyes of my poor countrymen, that they may see the robberies perpetrated upon them, before they surrender another foot of the territory."[19]

But dispossession and displacement were everywhere, and so was Native protest in the form of letters, petitions, and editorials. Shinguaconse (c. 1773–1854) of Garden River near Sault Ste. Marie, who fought with General Brock in the War of 1812, wrote an extraordinary letter to Lord Elgin in 1849.[20] Clearly furious with invader-re-settlers, Shinguaconse skillfully impeaches Whites with their mendacity, trickery, and betrayal:

When your white children first came into this country, they did not come shouting the war cry and seeking to wrest this land from us.... They sought our friendship, we became brothers. Their enemies were ours, at the time we were strong and powerful, while they were few and weak. But did we oppress them or wrong them? No! And they did not attempt to do what is now done, nor did they tell us that at some future day you would.

Father.

Time wore on and you have become a great people, whilst we have melted away like snow beneath an April sun; our strength is wasted, our countless warriors dead, our forests laid low, you have hounded us from every place as with a wand, you have swept away all our pleasant land, and like some giant foe you tell us "willing or unwilling, you must now go from amid these rocks and wastes, I want them now! I want them to make rich my white children, whilst you may shrink away to holes and caves like starving dogs to die!" Yes, Father, your white children have opened our very graves to tell the dead even they shall have no resting place.

Father.

Was it for this we first received you with the hand of friendship, and gave you the room whereupon to spread your blanket? Was it for this that we voluntarily became the children of our Great Mother the Queen? Was it for this we served England's sovereign so well and truly, that the blood of the red skin has moistened the dust of his own hunting grounds....

Father,

We begin to fear that those sweet words had not their birth in the heart, but they lived only in the tongue; they are like those beautiful trees under whose shadow it is pleasant for a time to repose and hope, but we cannot forever indulge in their graceful shade—they produce no fruit.

Father,

We are men like you, we have the limbs of men, we have the hearts of men and we feel and know that all this country is ours; even the weakest and most cowardly animals of the forest when hunted to extremity, though they feel destruction sure, will turn upon the hunter.

Father,

Drive us not to the madness of despair. We are told that you have laws which guard and protect the property of your white children, but you have made none to protect the rights of your red children. Perhaps you expected that the red skin could protect himself from the rapacity of his pale faced brother.[21]

But White conscience was shameless. As was their total disrespect of Native protest. No matter that Shinguaconse or Copway or any other indignant Native spoke in the indigenous tradition of metaphors or thundered in the manner of biblical prophets. The colonizer's march was largely dictated by their re-settling schemes, which they overlaid with ideology and covered up with double-dealings. The eastern Native resistance convention of tactically calling on White moral sense or White ignominy, or to common humanity, or to veiled threats—all of it fell on deaf ears as colonizing Euro-Canadians stole the east and then turned westward.

Perhaps it should come as no surprise that an eastern Native poet, one of the first officially recognized Native poets, came to the defence of her western colleagues. Born in 1862 to an English mother and a Mohawk father on the Six Nations Indian Reserve, Pauline Johnson was to become a famous poet who celebrated and defended Native people in her works. Though her defence was in some ways compromised, as I later show, she gained an international reputation as a champion of Native rights. Her collection of poems in *Flint and Feather* is an Aboriginal classic.[22]

Two poems in particular stand out as works protesting physical invasions that took place in her time. One poem addresses the military invasion that conventional historians have called the "Northwest Rebellion." The other poem defends a "cattle thief" (most likely a reference to Almighty Voice, the Cree man who was hunted and shot by the North West Mounted Police for killing a White man's cow to feed his starving family). In these two poems we find dramatic examples of resistance. In the poem "The Cattle Thief," Johnson is emotional and convincing in her defence of the starving Cree man she calls Eagle Chief. After the "English" shoot him down, Eagle Chief's daughter rushes to protect his body, and then harangues the English:

> You have cursed, and called him a Cattle Thief, though
> You robbed him first of bread…
> How have you paid us for our game? How paid us for
> our land?…
> When you pay for the land you live in, we'll pay you for
> the meat we eat.
> Give back our land and our country, give back our
> herds of game…
> And blame, if you dare, the hunger that drove him to
> be a thief.[23]

"A Cry from an Indian Wife" is an intense poem expressing the humanity of both White and Indian fighters, of White and Indian wives during a war.[24]

The context is the Riel Resistance, and even though Johnson clearly feels conflicted between the two sides, she supports the Indian finally on the basis of land rights. The poem begins with the Indian wife telling her husband

> Here is your Knife!....
> Twill drink the lifeblood of a soldier host.
> Go; rise and strike, no matter what the cost.
> Yet stay. Revolt not at the Union Jack.
> Nor raise Thy hand against this stripling pack
> They never think how they would feel today,
> If some great nation came from far away,
> Wrestling their country from their hapless braves,
> Given what they gave us—but wars and graves.
> Then go and strike for liberty and life,
> And bring back honour to your Indian wife.
> Your wife? Ah, what of that, who cares for me?
> Who pities my poor love and agony?....
> Who prays for vict'ry for the Indian scout?
> None—therefore take your tomahawk and go.
> My heart may break and burn into its core...
> Yet stay, my heart is not the only one
> That grieves the loss of husband and of son...
> Think of the pale-faced maiden on her knees...
> She never thinks of my wild aching breast
> Nor prays for your dark face...
> O! Coward self I hesitate no more;
> Go forth and win the glories of the war
> Go forth, nor bend to greed of white men's hands,
> By right, by birth, we Indians own these lands.

It is intriguing that Johnson, herself an eastern metis, refers only to Whites and Indians about a situation that principally involved the Metis of Red River. The issue of Metis loss of land space in western Canada is as much an issue about Aboriginal land rights as it is for other Native groups. Yet, for all the attention Riel has received in the Canadian canons, Metis loss of their homelands remains the least appreciated in the Canadian consciousness, and courts. This, despite Riel's exceptionally cogent explanation of the causes behind the Red River Metis resistance of 1869. In an article published in Montreal in 1874, Riel pointed out that, in the first instance, Canada began doing "public works in its name" two years before the North-West Territories was officially transferred. Further,

The arrival of the Canadian agents in the country was remarkable by the disdain which they affected for the authority of the company and for the original settlers. They attempted to seize the best properties of the Metis particularly at Oak Point.... They pretended that they had bought these properties from the Indians....

Canada committed another intrusion in the summer of 1869 by surveying the public and private lands around Fort Garry with a new system of measurement, thus disturbing, without any explanation, the established order and unscrupulously upsetting the original settlers in the peaceful and legal possession of their land.

The objections of the Hudson's Bay Company government were soon followed by those of the settlers who greatly objected to the fact that people thus suspected should open public roads and survey their (the settlers') own lands, in the name of a foreign government, and wit no guarantees.

At the same time, Mr. McDougall appeared on the frontier at Pembina.... He brought wit him a Council entirely composed of men whom we did not know. But his principal claim to our respect was that a considerable number of rifles were following him close behind.

...neither the English government nor the government of the Hudson's Bay Company had...spoke to us about Mr. McDougall.... Therefore, Mr. McDougall was an invader. We repulsed him on November 1, 1869....

As a result of all this, and since the Imperial authorities had seen fit to reprimand the cabinet at Ottawa, it has always seemed strange to the people of Assiniboia to hear themselves spoken of in official and other documents in Canada as a rebellious and misguided population, because we did not want to submit to the arbitrary procedures of the Canadian government.[25]

Of course, the Metis saga of land loss only got worse with time, as it did for all the other Aboriginal groups in Canada. Moving east to west, Euro-Canadians expanded, took up the space, and, through the manipulative powers of legislation, both strengthened and rationalized their displacement of Aboriginal peoples. In western Canada, Native peoples were sidelined and avoided for a long and lonely century (1870 to the 1970s) in which they remained largely silenced.[26] It is this era and experience that may appropriately be referred to as a time of voicelessness, in that Native peoples had no visible political or cultural representation in Canadian society. They served only as shadowy props in the morality plays of White Canadian cultural and political productions, scarcely noticed in the periphery of mainstream Canadian consciousness. It was as if they had no history, no cultures, no life worth mentioning.

It is a great loss to Canadian knowledge that, with the exception of Riel, western Native peoples were not able to tell us in their own written words the encounters and the facts of the invasion processes as these things happened to them. Oral tradition of this experience exists, of course, but it is not readily available. Nor was it received in the Canadian courts during the trials of Big Bear, Poundmaker, or Riel. These men gave their testimonies but they were not respected. Riel supplemented his testimonies and interviews with his own writing, but apparently nothing could dissuade the colonial intentions.

During the 1860s to the 1880s, the time when western Native (Indian and Metis) peoples lost their lands, lives, and independence, Riel was alone in his ability to express in writing Canada's displacement of Aboriginal peoples. Riel's style and resistance deserve greater attention than I can give here.[27] In many respects, he is an anomaly. Riel's mother language was Red River French, not Cree or Ojibway. At the tender age of fourteen, Riel was plucked from his home by a patronizing order of priests and placed in a foreign institution. His training in a Quebec seminary, coupled with his interest in law, as well as his experience in his people's liberation struggle, mark his style. He uses few metaphors, is formal, logical, direct, and factual in approach when addressing Confederation officers. He believed in the powers of Western reasoning. Yet, he struggled profoundly with matters of faith rather than reason. His mysticism and visionary religion and politics complicate our understanding of his resistance. Though he gave his life for Aboriginal rights, he was in many ways deeply colonized, especially in his general acceptance of Western ideas of civilization and savagery as well as French social and religious traditions. However, he did come to see the Roman Catholic Church and its priests, along with the invading anglophone easterners, as usurpers. It was his decolonizing and prophetic positioning that led to his death. Riel's "rebellion" anticipated Third World liberation militancy, but his heart, his spiritual poetics, and his lonely stand place him within gentler Native resistance traditions.

In western Canada there had not yet developed "a coterie" of Indian writers who could report in the language of English (but maintain an indigenous ethos) on an era that was extremely significant, even cataclysmic, in the lives of western Aboriginal peoples. The deaths of Almighty Voice, Big Bear, Poundmaker, and Riel, among thousands of other Native peoples who will remain nameless in Canadian history, are an indication of how devastating and disturbing this particular era was. As we know so plainly, for the most part we can only rely on the colonizer's powers of documentation and interpretation. Penny Petrone, in *Native Literature in Canada*, reports that between 1914 and 1969, there were a handful of residential school graduates who wrote essays or short biographies.[28] However, most of these individuals had difficulty finding avenues of publication. One voice from that era does stand out.

Saskatchwan-born Plains Cree Edward Ahenakew (1885–1961) produced an intriguing collection, *Voices of the Plains Cree*.[29] Ahenakew was an ordained Anglican deacon who spent many years teaching in mission schools. In 1918–1919, an epidemic of influenza devastated thousands of Native peoples throughout the far northwest. Deeply affected by this suffering, Ahenakew, at the age of thirty-five, entered medical school in Edmonton. Illness and finances forced him to leave his medical training, and, under the encouragement of his church, Ahenakew went to rest at Chief Thunderchild's reserve. It was there in 1923 that he began taking notes for *Voices of the Plains Cree*, but it was not until 1973, fifty years later, that the manuscript found publication under the editorship of Ruth Buck.

Voices of the Plains Cree is an ingeniously crafted resistance book, which combines *achimoowin* and *atowkehwin* through the voices of Chief Thunderchild and Ahenakew's literary creation "Old Keyam." In Part One we hear the voice of Thunderchild (1849–1927), who, as a young man, was a follower of Big Bear. In Cree and to a Cree audience, while a Cree man was taking notes (to translate to English), Thunderchild offers legends and history as he recounts the days of Cree independence, of buffalo hunting, Blackfoot fighting, and sun dancing. Thunderchild exudes sadness, outrage, and disbelief that within such a short span of time the spirited Cree had become exiles and prisoners of alien forces in their own lands. Losing freedom of worship was particularly "heart-rending." Thunderchild told of the effects on Fine Day's wife: "Fine Day is one who is not permitted to make the Sun Dance that he vowed, and the shock has stunned his wife, as though she had been shot."[30]

Perhaps because Ahenakew the missionary was not free to express directly his outrage that his lands were occupied and his people shattered, he devised Old Keyam. "Keyam" is a Cree word with many subtle shades of meaning. Depending on the context, *keyam* can connotate either a fatalistic resignation or a wise acceptance of things we cannot change. Ahenakew interpreted it as "I do not care," and explained, "Old Keyam had tried in his youth to fit himself into the new life; he had thought that he would conquer; and he had been defeated instead. If we listen to what he has to say, perhaps we may understand those like him, who know not what to do, and in their bewilderment and their hurt, seem not to care."[31]

Through Old Keyam, Ahenakew tried to understand Cree responses, which appeared disproportionately placid, given the staggering events that had overtaken his people. He could also address White injustices and express his own disillusionments with White culture. There was also a part of Old Keyam in Ahenakew, who had tried to "fit himself into the new life," but "had been defeated instead." He was a man in anguish, one who felt the desperations of his people yet remained committed to Christianity, the enemy's religion, as Thunderchild made clear. As it turned out, Ahenakew's Plains Cree voices were not to be heard until the 1970s, at the start of an era that swept in new generations of decolonizing Aboriginal voices who would begin to retell the Canadian story, and hopefully, soon, will also refill the pages of Canadian history.

As noted earlier, contemporary Native resistance literature begins with Harold Cardinal, whose opening statement in *The Unjust Society* challenges Canadian records and policies: "The history of Canada's Indians is a shameful chronicle of the white man's disinterest, his deliberate trampling of Indian rights and his repeated betrayal of our trust. Generations of Indians have grown up behind a buckskin curtain.... Now at a time when our fellow Canadians consider the promise of a Just Society, once more the Indians of Canada are betrayed by a programme which offers nothing better than cultural genocide."[32]

Taking the Canadian politicians and public by storm, Cardinal, the young Cree president of the Indian Association of Alberta, charged the government with a "thinly disguised programme of extermination through assimilation," only slightly modifying the famous American saying "The only good Indian is a dead Indian" to "The only good Indian is a non-Indian." Native people, Cardinal explained, "look back on generations of accumulated frustration under conditions which can only be described as colonial, brutal and tyrannical, and look to the future with the gravest of doubts." He continued:

> As an Indian writing about a situation I am living and experience in common with thousands of our people it is my hope that this book will open the eyes of the Canadian public to its shame. I intend to document the betrayals of our trust, to show step by step how a dictatorial bureaucracy has eroded our rights, atrophied our culture and robbed us of simple human dignity. I will expose the ignorance and bigotry that has impeded our progress, the eighty

years of educational neglect that have hobbled our young people for generations, the gutless politicians who have knowingly watched us sink in the quicksands of apathy and despair and have failed to extend a hand.

Cardinal spelled out what such an extension of hand could look like: "I challenge the Honorable Mr. Trudeau and the Honorable Mr. Chrétien to re-examine their unfortunate policy, to offer the Indians of Canada hope instead of despair, freedom instead of frustration, life in the Just Society instead of cultural annihilation." He criticized Canada's priorities by comparing Canada's preservation of whooping cranes, while neglecting and assimilating Indians: "It sometimes seems to Indians that Canada shows more interest in preserving its rare whooping cranes than its Indians. And Canada, the Indian notes, does not ask its cranes to become Canada geese. It just wants to preserve them as whooping cranes. Indians hold no grudge against the big, beautiful, nearly extinct birds, but we would like to know how they managed their deal."[33]

Since this watershed moment between the federal government and Status Indians in Canadian history, Aboriginal writers of many identities have continued the tradition of thunderous tellings of their historical and contemporary place in Canadian society. On the heels of Cardinal's ringing and furious challenge to Canadian society and government came a slight but steady stream of other writers, each of them articulating the multifarious places of invasion experienced by Native peoples.

It must be emphasized here that as we move from the early Native sources to contemporary Native writing, the themes and texture become more compli-cated. We are addressing not only layers and legacies of historical experiences, interpretations, and issues, but also contemporary facts of neo-colonialism as well as decolonization efforts. Many Native writers combine all these ways of responding. We are at once deconstructing and reconstructing. Our works are reinscribing historical and cultural records and at the same time protesting ongoing injustices and current social conditions. Needless to say, the multi-facetedness of contemporary Native response makes it extremely challenging to speak from it or for its members.

Devastating Consequences of Colonization

With invasion come the consequences. In addition to documenting the dis-possession, Native writers have, at the same time, addressed the devastating consequences that colonization has wrought, repeatedly, century after century. Thousands of human lives have been lost through the centuries and thousands more continue to suffer a host of socio-economic consequences.

One of the most immediate ramifications deriving from the Native people's loss of space and freedom was the loss or severe curtailment of using the land for hunting and other resources, the very basis of their cultural nourishment. Already in the 1798 letter by Joseph Brant, we see that the British Canadian assumption of Native lands was destroying the hunting possibilities for the Mohawks, and with it their political sovereignty and livelihood. In a letter to Captain Green, which revealed the many ways that the British Canadian government was pressuring the Mohawks, Brant explained:

> the movements of Gov. Simco in attempting to curtail our lands to one half of the River, and recollecting our deed from Gov. Haldimand to be unequal to his first promises caused us to make such a large sale at once that the matter might come to a point and we might know whether the land was ours or not—the next reason was that the lands all around us being given away to different people, some of them, those that had even been engaged in war against us we found it necessary to sell some land, that we might have an income, the hunting being entirely destroyed.—We now learn that the ministry never intended we should alienate the lands.[34]

Control of lands was clearly not in the hands of the Mohawks, just as it had not been in the hands of the Mississaugas, on whose lands the loyalist Mohawks now depended. In any event, to say that Native peoples lost their lands and resources is also to say that they lost cultural ground. For Native peoples, land was truly everything. Their very cultures and their very physical and economic existence depended on their use of lands and land-based resources. To Aboriginal peoples, land was a relationship, a relationship which was (and is) often expressed in kinship and spiritual terms. As renowned Cree-Metis architect Douglas Cardinal explains in *Of The Spirit* (1977): "We feel a great sorrow for the destruction of the land, for life springs from the earth. When the land is destroyed all those living on the land, are destroyed too and we, the people of the land, feel a sense of our own destruction."[35] As is finally beginning to be understood by some, Aboriginal concepts and therefore uses of land were fundamentally at variance from European concepts.[36]

Naturally, cultural differences are recalled to explain Aboriginal practices. However, this can become very problematic. So many explanations offered on Native-White relationships, particularly on the socio-economic disparities between these two groups, have revolved around stereotypical notions of "cultural differences." Such treatment of Native cultures has been full of assumptions, generalizations, and romanticization, with much of it resulting in oversimplified and essentialist trait-listing. It is in response to these rather layered ideas that I refer to *real* differences. The Aboriginal use and relationship to the land is one such *real* difference. It truly represents a cultural difference, and White treatment of these land issues did (and do) have an impact on Native peoples in ways White peoples have not understood, or have denied understanding. To dispossess Aboriginal peoples of their land was (and is) to disconnect them from the source of their original languages, world views, faiths, and, of course, from their economic well-being. Contrary to the stereotypes of "Indians" as aimless wanderers, Aboriginal peoples were (and are) profoundly rooted to their lands. Land was never just a legal or economic commodity that could be gouged, sold, enclosed, or replaced. Aboriginal peoples did not "just" lose land, which would be bad enough in itself, but they lost and continue to lose a way of life.

The material loss of lands has left an emotional and spiritual gash in the hearts of all Aboriginal peoples. It is significant, I believe, that in western Canada shortly after the Metis were defeated and the First Nations were herded onto reserves, some of the more well-known leaders died. Poundmaker and Big Bear, after having been jailed, died of broken hearts because they understood the import of losing lands and freedoms. I believe this can also be said of Riel. He was hanged, yes, but long before that day, I believe he had been dying of a broken heart. Politically beaten, exiled, spiritually and intellectually abandoned, it was his heart, not his mind (though, that too was impacted), that was torn. And I also believe that of all the Native peoples who have been dying since the Europeans began invading, a great majority of them have been dying from broken hearts. The death toll among Native peoples, particularly the gross rate of suicide among Native youth, cannot be explained entirely by cold, sociological facts.

Clearly, forced spatial displacement and subjugation ravage the human spirit. Geographical and legislative restrictions, powerlessness, and the growing depletion of their customary resources overtaxed the Native peoples. Their use (or abuse) of alcohol, for example, is best understood as a symptom of dispossession rather than as some cultural reflex to an alien item. As early as 1861, Native Methodist missionary Peter Jones reveals the Natives' confusion and despair in their usage of alcohol and directly links this with White incursion: "Oh, what an awful account at the day of judgement must the unprincipled white man give, who has been an agent of Satan in the extermination of the original proprietors of the American soil! Will not the blood of the red man be required at his hands, who, for paltry gain, has impaired the minds, corrupted the morals, and ruined the constitutions of a once hardy and numerous race?"[37]

And one of the primary reasons why Chief Crowfoot, the controversial Blackfoot leader of the 1870s, chose to sign Treaty 7—and to tolerate and humour the North West Mounted Police, Father Lacombe, and the Canadian Pacific Railway—was because his people were suffering desperately from deadly diseases, starvation, demoralization, confusion, and despair, even before they lost their lands through treaties and the *Indian Act*. Many expressed their desperation by turning to alcohol. Crowfoot thought he could best assist his people by the process of making treaties, a process familiar to him since treaty making has Aboriginal roots.[38] Treaties signified honour in the highest sense because treaties between Native peoples were based, obviously, on the spoken word. Peoples of oral traditions approached the words of treaties with utmost respect and ceremony. Peoples' honours literally depended on their word. Neither Crowfoot nor other Native negotiators could have anticipated such disregard for honour as seen in the Euro-Canadian exploitation through treaties.

The theme of Native people's confusion and despair runs through much of Native writing and cuts across centuries. Native missionaries, analysts, commentators, scholars, novelists, poets, playwrights—all in some way address the emotional costs of imperialism. Despair and violence run particularly strong in the earlier novels of Beatrice Culleton Mosionier and Lee Maracle. A similar theme runs in much of the autobiographies and poetry written by Native peoples.

Beatrice Culleton Mosionier's *In Search of April Raintree* deals with the disintegrating effects of colonization on a family.[39] The story follows two metis sisters who are, on one level, searching for reintegration of family selves, but on another, perhaps deeper level, searching for a positive Native identity. April is searching for her sister Cheryl, who had been taken away by Child and Family Services. Both sisters are searching for a positive self-image of their Indianness, for Cheryl, an image based apparently on the White man's romanticized invention of the "Indian." April's search for her sister is also a search for herself. Having been conditioned to be ashamed of her culture, April finds self-acceptance through her sister, but not before April's personal dignity and Cheryl's life are sacrificed.

But Cheryl too is searching. All along April thinks Cheryl is proud of her Native heritage. But what Cheryl was proud of was the romantic image she held about both Indians in the past and about her parents, whom she never knew. How else to explain Cheryl's rapid disintegration following her discovery that her father, "a gutter creature," as Culleton describes him, was a drunk in the slums? From here on, Cheryl takes us to the slums, to prostitution, to squalor, to despair. Cheryl finally takes her own life. The reader is left wondering whether she committed suicide because her idealized image of Indianness, an image that had kept her obviously fragile identity together, was blown apart, or because she blamed herself for the horrific attack against April, which, as the courts unravel, was meant for Cheryl, or because Cheryl could no longer cope with the poverty and hopelessness all around her, a hopelessness in which she and her friends lived in.

Squalor, slumming, male violence against Native women, demoralization and rage also run strong in most of Lee Maracle's earlier works, beginning with *I Am Woman* (1988). In *I Am Woman* Lee Maracle spares the reader nothing. Her style is unrestrained as she relentlessly juxtaposes the misery against the uncaring Canadian society and co-opted Native organizational leadership.

Frustration and anger are also apparent in much non-fiction writing, particularly from the social-protest era of the 1970s. However, this writing does not go into the details of despair as much as into the resistance to it. We write against despair. We write as an alternative to our own despair. And we write because we want to alleviate the conditions that make people live desperate lives.

I begin with Metis social analyst, scholar and writer Howard Adams, who in *Prison of Grass* (1975) and again in *A Tortured People: The Politics of Colonization* (1996), seethes with outrage and criticism that Native peoples continue to live in extreme poverty and powerlessness. His works combine scholarship (documenting and questioning racist historical sources) and social protest. Other social protest non-fiction writers of the 1970s, like Waubageshig, Wilfred Pelletier, George Manuel, and myself, were also challenging the racist constructions of the dominant narrative, as well as re-establishing the emotional and cultural basis of Native humanity. Although we were not as expressively "angry" as Adams, we also used a combination of documentation, facts of biography, and barbed wit to point to historical and current injustices in areas such as education, the media, the governments, lands, resources, and racism.

George Manuel reviewed how provincial and federal Native organizations pressed for land and resource rights in the face of British Columbia's obstinate refusal to honour Native land rights. Wilfred Pelletier recalled his "childhood village" as a model for networking and organizing. Waubageshig turned to Frantz Fanon, the Algerian psychiatrist turned revolutionary, in his exposition of colonization as experienced by Canada's Native peoples. Verna J. Kirkness and myself, among a number of others, provided alternatives to the racist constructions in Canadian school textbooks and classrooms.

Biographies and autobiographies also pointed to historical and contemporary injustices. Some Native writers, including Lee Maracle, Monture-Angus, and Keeshig-Tobias, argue that theory in Native writing comes not from the construction of the narrative but from the telling of the story itself. I have found that most Native autobiographies are not centrally about personal life events; rather, life events are recounted to make sense of what was a colonial experience not understood at the time such events or responses took place. In other words, life events are told to locate the story. For example, Maria Campbell begins in *Halfbreed* by situating her community against the backdrop of the "Northwest Rebellion" and the Canadian treatment of Halfbreed peoples. Campbell traces her community's struggles to the consequence and subsequent colonial forces surrounding it, forces such as landlessness, poverty, the police, the priests, and the prejudice of White people in town and in the school. Her own family was able to withstand some of these pressures until her mother died when Campbell was twelve years old. After this period, Campbell's life took on a nightmarish slide. Her heart-rending account of her early marriage, loss of her siblings to Child and Welfare bureaucracy, birth of her children, abuse by her husband, her own abuse of drugs, and suicidal depression, as well as her experiences with racism, exploded Canada's naive notions of being a caring and charitable country.

Significantly, Campbell highlights her great-grandmother Campbell, whom she affectionately called "Cheechum." Cheechum was a niece of Gabriel Dumont, and her whole family fought beside Riel and Dumont during the "Rebellion." Cheechum passed on stories of this event and of the people to Campbell. She believed that the land belonged to Indian and Halfbreed peoples, not to White "settlers"; she refused to be a Christian and she scorned offers of welfare and old-age pension. She made her living from hunting, trapping, and gardening. Cheechum "never accepted defeat at Batoche" and remained, in her own way, a resistance fighter throughout her life.[40]

Poets have expressed powerfully the drastic legacy of colonialism. Perhaps no one Native poet has treated more the theme of contemporary despair than Duncan Mercredi of Winnipeg. In a successive series of books of poetry published in the 1990s (*Spirit of the Wolf, Dreams of the Wolf in the City,* and *Wolf and Shadows*), Mercredi sets the "wolf" against "the rage of the city." He writes about the "Black Robe," about how "parking trucks on the block / circle endlessly / luring black and blue children," about smoke-filled bars where "brown" men and women [are] "dancing in the past / playing the blues / into back alleys / tripping over bodies wasted on city life." He writes too of leaving "the land of northern lights" and Kokum, about the forest and eagles against city lights, concrete, sirens and streets, about caskets and "the blues at midnight."[41]

In a poem called "dreams of the wolf in the city," the wolf "feels anguish" and "wolf runs as he feels the breath of diesel monsters / and the forest turns to concrete under his feet / and trails turn to back alleys."[42] Mercredi knows why the brown people from the forest now live in "needle tracks" with "scarred trees." In "Occupied Territories," Mercredi tells us of an old "warrior" facing "new enemies" in a "new battlefield" of "shadows" and "alleys" making him remember

> occupied territories
> old warrior stops
> he remembers his reason
> he fought to free occupied territories
> medals flash bombs explode.[43]

And, just as in war, there is death here; more, the death here of children is because of an internal war, the occupation of Native lands. This is as deadly to young men as war:

> (Vision of a child rope around his/her neck)
> here over there
> old warrior crouches in the alley
> occupied territories...
> (A rifle shot—forest goes silent—a young man falls)
> here over there...
> (A little body rises from beneath the water)
> here over there
> old warrior cries
> over there hero
> here what does he want
> occupied territories
> he had returned
> to occupied territories.[44]

The city as battlefield is a theme that runs through much of Native poetry. In 1977, Ojibway poet George Kenny also wrote about Native people's urban struggles. In the poem "Rubbie at Central Park," Kenny situates Winnipeg as a place where "thirty thousand Indians / find acceptance / with a 10 fl. oz bottle of rubbing / alcohol to start forgetting."[45] He continues,

the personnel man at the Bay
or any other employment office
took a look at clothes one didn't
have...
or maybe, just said to himself,
oh oh, a wino, look at his
scarred face
and said a sorry he didn't mean.[46]

What society has done with Native suffering grieves Jeannette Armstrong. In her poem "Death Mummer," she walks through Vancouver's "Thunderbird Park" and notes,

There are no Indians here
None
even in the million dollar museum
that so carefully preserves
their clothing, their cooking utensils
their food;
for taxpayers...
to rush their children by
There are some Indians
hanging around Kings hotel
and they are dead,
preserved in alcohol.
It would be neater though
to kill us all at once.[47]

But it isn't just society that gets Armstrong. She too feels implicated for having items that are used for museum pieces: "With blood-stained fingers / I remove my mask." But she "staggers under" the "clever mask" that she has "fashioned" for herself:

From the bones and skin
Of my dead tribe
And dipped in the fresh blood
Of my brothers and sisters
Scooped from old battle streets
Near hotels.[48]

Native resistance literature, then, is born on the bones and tears of suffering Native humanity. The suffering runs wide and deep and is not found merely in back alleys, barrooms, or poor houses. With piercing verse, Sarain Stump captured the "400 [500] year old pain": "and I had been killed a thousand times / Right at his feet / But he hadn't understood."[49]

Chapter Five

Native Writers Resist: Addressing Dehumanization

Native intellectuals and writers also suffer. Our vocations do not protect us either from dispossession, social inequality, poverty, or the daily indecencies of racism in stores and streets or in our places of play and work. Many, if not most of us, have direct connection to those people "preserved in alcohol," or those who beg, or those who are looking for their sisters, or those going to faraway places in order to hunt, get a job, or go to school. Or those people left behind to fend off village bullies. Or those whose blueberry hills have been stolen. In the words of Metis writer Marilyn Dumont: "Who knows what it's like to leave, to give up a piece of land? If you do, it might haunt you forever, follow you til you come back."[1]

Many of us "come back" to lands that no longer have earth. Many of us come back haunted from the war of words ringing in our heads. Many of us went to faraway places to fight the words—but wearing the uniform of the dispossessed, who knows us in these word-wielding places? As I have written, "I do my footnotes so well / nobody knows where I come from."[2] Our footnotes serve as reminders that colonial writing is about power and legitimization, and those who must live under its terms are like poet Duke Redbird's "Old woman in the field / bent low."[3] Yet as writers we are impelled to disturb any people who are sleeping. To be a Native intellectual is to wrestle with ideas, images, and words that attack our humanity. Textual debasement is a powerful weapon of colonialism and, much like material invasion, it has many faces, fronts, and forms. So does resistance to it.

Challenging Historical and Cultural Records: The Subtext of the Power Struggle

> They say that sometimes we cover our hair with feathers and wear masks when we dance. Yes, but a white man told me one day that the white people have also sometimes masquerade balls and white women have feathers on their bonnets and the white chiefs give prizes for those who imitate best, birds or animals. And this is all good when white men do it but very bad when Indians do the same thing.
>
> —Maquinna, 1896

Most, if not all, Native writers have in some way protested their dehumanization, refuting in particular the charge of savagery, which is at the heart of the colonial discourse. This discourse is a power struggle. From the earliest resistance writings, it is abundantly clear how deeply Native peoples were affected by the destructive effects of racist constructions. Surely at sites of contact, and certainly long before Native peoples were able to write, they addressed what they considered unjust, untrue, and hypocritical. For example, in 1896, Nootka leader Maquinna dictated a letter (for publication in a Victoria, BC, newspaper) to protest the 1894 *Indian Act* prohibition of the potlatch.[4] Such editorials, as well as translated speeches, debates, or petitions, are to be found regarding events that Native peoples were questioning, events such as land grabs, treaty signings, religious prohibitions, or residential schools.[5]

As soon as Native individuals learned the tools of Western literacy, they challenged, even retaliated against, the stereotypes and the name calling. And they fought the battle of words rather brilliantly at times, obviously taking their gloves off as required by racism. There are exceptional examples from the earliest Native writers.

Catherine Soneegoh Sutton (1823–1865), an Ojibway born near Credit River, Ontario, was a Native-rights activist of the mid-1800s. She spoke, wrote, and protested on behalf of Native peoples, especially concerning their land rights. She herself was embroiled in a land dispute against the Indian Department. She may have been one of the first Status Indian women to openly and officially resist her loss of land title due to marriage to a non-Indian. Of interest is a letter she wrote in response to a vicious editorial. The following is an excerpt from the editorial, c. 1864:

> On the shores of Goulais Bay Lake Superior... an Indian reserve was
> laid of a few years ago... some of the best land in the country and so
> situated as to block up the means of access to the entire regions lying
> in the rear of it and all this for about a dozen of the most wretched,
> squalid, miserable specimens of human nature that I have ever seen:
> indeed, a close inspection of, and a little acquaintance with, these
> creatures leads one to doubt whether they are human, but whether
> they are men or monkeys, it matters not now, the present adminis-
> tration have found means to extinguish their title.[6]

Sutton responded,

> I suppose the individual who published the above and Mr. Charles
> Linsey, the great Hearo who tried last fall to frighten the Manitoulin
> Indians out of their senses and their lands, are one and the same....
> I have frequently seen those Indians alluded to but I never took
> them for monkyes neither did I ever hear such a thing hinted at by
> the white people I think they were always, considered to be human
> beings, possessing living souls.... [W]hen I was in England... I saw
> a great many monkeys.... I observed there was one trait common
> to them all and a close inspection & a little acquaintance with the
> Editor of the Leader has led me to the conclusion that the same trait
> stands out prominently in his natural disposition.... I will tell you
> the trait which I observed so common to every variety of monkeys
> was an entire absence of humanity.

She continues, with tongue in cheek: "my english his so poor that I frequently have to consult Webster and I find the word extinguish means to
destroy to put an end to... our present administration can extinguish the red
man's title at pleasure, what hope is their for the remnant that are yet left....
I suppose Mr. Linsey will... go to manitoulin with soldiers to subdue the
Indians or monkeys as he calls them."[7]

In calling Indians "monkeys," the editorialist was no doubt reflecting the
scientific racism in vogue at that time. The editorial follows Canadian tradition in that it likens "Indians" to animals, which is simply another way of
saying they were savages. Being called savage has especially infuriated Native
peoples, as reflected in Sutton's response to this particular depiction. In fact,
it would be difficult to find any Native Canadian writing within the period
covered here that did not in some way respond to that image.

Naturally, the first response to being characterized as a savage or a non-
human is to simply say, "I am not a savage." In a contemporary verse titled,

"Prejudice (Or, In-laws)," the writer Constance Stevenson of Saskatchewan echoes a long tradition of objection, however defensive, even uncertain:

> I am of a different race,
> And I know it bothers you...
> Is it because I'm an Indian
> Or, in your terms, a savage?
> I never asked to be Indian,
> Nor am I am savage.[8]

That Native peoples have felt compelled to address the charge of savagery is an indication of the power such a charge carries. Comprehending this is central to understanding the colonial relationship between Whites and Natives. Jennings explains that words like "savagery" "evolved from centuries of conquest and have been created for the purposes of conquest rather than the purposes of knowledge. To call a man savage is to warrant his death and to leave him unknown and unmourned."[9] This understanding stands in rather sharp contrast to Canadian historian James Walker, who, despite pointing out how much the torturing techniques of White Quebecers of the 1600s resemble those of the Iroquois, virtually excuses the historical usage of the term savage: "Perhaps 'savage' was a meaningful word, when used with regard to Indians, for historians fifty years ago. Today that word has taken on connotations that are no longer acceptable."[10] But did this word—and the imagery that comes with the word—ever have acceptable connotations?

There have been attempts to disarm the word and usage of the word "savage," arguing, for instance, that in earlier points of contact Europeans simply meant "man of the woods" from the Latin word *silvaticus*. This, though, was not a neutral ethnological term; it carried all the conceptual weaponry of being unchristian, uncultivated, or undomesticated; in other words, wild and uncivilized. And the medieval meaning of *wild* was to be beast-like. Robert Berkhofer in *The White Man's Indian* traces the term "savage" to the German legend of the *Wilder Mann*. Such a wild man "was a hairy, naked, club-wielding child of nature who existed halfway between humanity and animality," one who lived "a life of bestial self-fulfilment, directed by instinct, and ignorant of God and morality.... strong of physique, lustful of women and degraded of origin."[11] The *Wilder Mann* was, in effect, Europe's caveman, a caveman that Europeans expected to find in their travels, and so they did. Europe's *Wilder Mann* became America's *savage*, in the sense that Europeans had preconceived and projected the legend onto indigenous peoples of the Americas. The French and English often referred to Native peoples of the North as *savage*, and curiously, Berkhofer postulates that "perhaps the denomination of these peoples as *sauvage* in French and *savage* [or *salvage*] in English seemed more appropriate," on the judgement that northern peoples presumably lacked "complex social and governmental organization," and so appeared to these explorers "wilder [than Aztec or Inca] Indians."[12] Berkhofer's comment here reflects his lack of specialization in northern Native peoples. This is also a case in point that attempting to contextualize what is in fact a racist ideology can appear to defend or legitimize what should, at the very least, be problematized. Why, I wonder, do scholars keep trying to defend the use of *savage* and related words (barbarian, heathen, pagan, infidel, etc.)—should we not confront and dispense with such loaded verbiage?

In any event, the word and the substance of the word are never acceptable, certainly not to Native peoples. In any context, civilization means being more "human," and savagery less than "human." Dickason, in *The Myth of the Savage*, notes that the French used the verb *humaniser* when referring to evangelizing Indians. "There was never any doubt," she asserts, "as to the meaning of *humaniser*: it signified the transformation of savages into Europeans."[13] Dickason argues that "the idea of savagery made it possible for Europe to bypass the complexity and integrity of New World societies, it also greatly eased the task of bringing about the acceptance and assimilation of new facts that did not accord with cherished beliefs."[14] She also contests the view that the French use of *sauvage* (*silvaticus*) in the sixteenth and seventeenth centuries simply meant "a man of the woods": "While shades of emphasis could and did vary from writer to writer, the general implication was always clear: to be savage meant to be living according to nature, in a manner 'closer to that of wild animals than to that of man.' The beast far outweighed the innocent."[15] To be called a savage, whether "man" or woman, it is to be deprived of humanness.

Native writers have felt keenly and understood exactly the political and polemical uses of such attacks. In the context of discussing the federal government's collusion with missionaries concerning residential schools, Harold Cardinal in *The Unjust Society* writes, "The unvarnished truth is that the missionaries of all Christian sects regarded the Indians as savages, heathens or something even worse."[16] Architect Douglas Cardinal states, "The immigrant culture tried to change our philosophy and destroy our spirit and pride by introducing an alien immigrant philosophy and religion that fostered inhumanity and forced on our minds the idea that we were savages."[17]

But being the brunt of name-calling calls for a response beyond the artifice of documentary tones. There are a number of interesting textual techniques Native writers have adopted or invented to impress the fact that Native peoples were and are not savages.

The majority of Native writers necessarily take an argumentative, stylistically contrapuntal approach in their refutation against the savage portrayal. For purposes of analysis, I begin with Native writers' *feelings* about being called savages. Their experience has been difficult, to say the least, but one made considerably more so by *seeing* graphic representations of "savage Indians." To such drastic dramatizations, these writers have responded in several different strategic directions, all of which we could place under the heading "We Are Not Savages." One stream takes a defensive stance by saying "we are civilized" and seeks to establish that Native peoples were civilized, that they had and have cultures. The other stream takes the offence by countering that it is the Whiteman, not Native people, who were or are the savages. This stream can further take other sub-directions: one simply uses White records to show that Whites were the savages (not in the ideological abstract civ/sav terms but in behaviour); the other takes a turn towards an idealized nativism in which Aboriginal culture represents a higher moral vision, and therefore a "better" culture.

Feeling the Savage: Dehumanization as an Experience

Again, colonization is not abstract, it is an experience. The outcome is loss and denigration. It cannot be restated enough that the characterization of Native peoples as savage has had a profoundly painful and destructive impact on Native peoples, an impact about which Native writers across historic periods have minced no words. This should come as no surprise to anyone who has an inkling about the power of images and the power of the dominant narrative. In the words of Metis scholar Joyce Green, "Power is sustained through popular culture without much critique simply because its very existence is deemed to legitimate it. Society for the most part, takes as given the way things are. Those who advance radical critiques of the way things are bear the onus of legitimating their critique of what most accept as common sense. And yet common sense can be popular misconception, mythology, or ideology that serves some at the expense of others."[18]

Jane Willis, author of *Geneish,* spent her growing years in residential schools in northern Quebec and Ontario in the 1950s and 1960s. In addition to recording horror stories about child labour, bad food, health problems, military-style discipline and regulations, and just plain meanness, Willis provides the intellectual connection between racism and its effects on an individual. The general theme of Willis's autobiography is how the school changed her from a self-confident, curious, and spontaneous child to one full of doubts, inhibitions, and fears:

For twelve years I was taught... to hate myself. I was made to feel untrustworthy, inferior, incapable and immoral. The barbarian in me I was told, had to be destroyed if I was to be saved. I was taught to feel nothing but shame for my "pagan savage" ancestors.... Because they were savages they did not have the right to defend their land and families. The white man... had a perfect right to kill whole tribes of Indians.... I was told I was intelligent, but not intelligent enough to think for myself. Only the white man could do that for me. Only he knew what was good for me.... When I had been stripped of all pride, self-respect, and self-confidence, I was told to make something of myself to show the whiteman that not all Indians were savages or stupid.... For twelve years I was brainwashed into believing that "Indian" was synonymous with "subhuman," "savage," "idiot," and "worthless." It took almost that long for me to regain my self-respect.[19]

Teaching Native children to feel racial shame and to hate themselves has not been confined to Status children in residential schools. What is perhaps less well-known, and requires repeating, is that Metis and non-Status Indian youth were also intellectually and emotionally (and corporeally) battered in public schools, and generally in Canadian society. Howard Adams and Maria Campbell have especially tackled the issue of racial shame. In the words of Howard Adams: "I knew that whites were looking at me through their racial stereotypes... it made me feel stripped of all humanity and decency, and left me with nothing but my Indianness, which at the time I did not value.... Not only did my sense of inferiority become inflamed, but I came to hate myself for the image I could see in their eyes. Everywhere white supremacy surrounded me. Even in solitary silence, I felt the word 'savage' deep in my soul."[20]

Maria Campbell also struggled with feelings of inferiority, shame, and self-hate that come with the society's racist association of Indianness and savagery. In *Halfbreed*, Campbell recounts how a combination of poverty and prejudice led her to feelings of shame. In school, White children "would tease and call 'Gophers, gophers, Road Allowance people eat gophers.'" Campbell goes on, "We fought back of course but we were terribly hurt and above all ashamed."[21] Throughout her years in school, Campbell, along with other Halfbreed children, continued to face racism. The depth of her shame came out at a school dance where White peers poked fun at her chaperone Sophie, an older Native woman. When a White girl asked if Sophie was Maria's mother, Campbell recalls, "Everyone started to snicker and I looked at her and said 'That old, ugly Indian?'" Campbell instantly felt remorseful: "I felt shame and hatred for her, myself and the people around me. I could almost see Cheechum standing beside me with a switch saying 'They make you hate what you are'"[22]

For a long, excruciating time, Campbell hated what she was, so much so that she rejected her childhood sweetheart's marriage proposal. She remembers "looking at him and saying 'Marry you? You've got to be joking! I'm going to do something more with my life besides make Halfbreeds.'" As a youngster, Campbell could not make sense of her confusion:

> I wanted to cry. I couldn't understand what was wrong with me. I loved Smokey and wanted to be with him forever, yet when I thought of him and marriage, I saw only shacks, kids, no food, and both of us fighting. I saw myself with my head down and Smokey looking like an old man, laughing only when he was drunk. I loved my people so much and missed them when I couldn't see them often. I felt alive when I went to their parties, and I overflowed with happiness when we would all sit down and share a meal, yet I hated all of it as much as I loved it.[23]

What was it that Maria Campbell dreamed about? What was it that drove her so far away from herself, her loved ones, and her community? Campbell, much like so many of us in our childhood years, was inculcated with what she and Howard Adams call the "White ideal" of success. Campbell points to a simple dream in explaining her "driving ambition." That dream was for her brothers and sisters to have a toothbrush, a bowl of fruit, a glass of milk and cookies, "and to talk about what they want to do. There will be no more mud shacks and they'll walk with their heads high and not be afraid."[24] Campbell's Cheechum understood the power of suggestive symbols. She "would look at her and see the toothbrushes, fruit and all those other symbols of white ideal of success and say sadly, 'you'll have them, my girl, you'll have them.'"[25] As her book reveals, Campbell paid a very high price to obtain some of those symbols.

In *Prison of Grass*, Howard Adams situates the Native's struggle with the White ideal in the broader context of colonization and oppression. As noted earlier, Adams argues that the Native who has "internalized" the colonizer's culture judges him- or herself against the standards, expectations, and stereotypes of the White ideal. Such a Native then aspires to achieve the colonizer's terms and materials of "success." This includes notions and standards of beauty. More, the colonizer stands as the standard of beauty.

As part of explaining how the White ideal works inside the colonized, Adams relates a personal story about a love affair. At the age of twenty-one, he fell in love with a White girl: "I had always known what ultimate beauty would be.... This blonde blue-eyed goddess matched my vision perfectly.... Because she was white, she automatically possessed beauty and virtue... when I did kiss her I was kissing white beauty, white dignity, and white civilization... Her love had baptized me in the stream of whiteness and led me to seek white success."[26] However, the romance did not last. It could not last, for, as Adams explains, "Her whiteness oppressed me. It crushed me into inferiority; it emphasized my Indianness." Adams then generalizes this condition to all Native people:

> Every native person has this inclination towards acceptance and success in white society. Because it operates subconsciously, it is not clearly understood at the conscious level. The supposed splendour of whiteness and ugliness of things non-white deeply affects native people in their thought and behaviour.... These flattering and pleasing myths reinforce the white man's so called superiority, but to native people they are degrading and destroy their esteem, confidence and pride.[27]

In *Halfbreed*, Campbell too provides powerful examples of how a people behave when they have lost their confidence and pride. She explains that it was not simply poverty that drove the people to shame and despair, it was lack of hope, which comes from oppressive dispossession. Speaking to the White audience, Campbell states: "you at least had dreams, you had a tomorrow. My parents and I never shared any aspirations for a future. I never saw my father talk to a white man unless he was drunk. I never saw him or any of our men walk with either heads held high before white people."[28]

Both Campbell and Adams eventually come to a new consciousness about their colonial conditions, particularly about how the colonized respond to oppressive racism. For Campbell, feelings of shame and confusion did not diminish until years later, after much personal disintegration, when she finally came to understand that her heartbreaking journey was all part of the colonization experience. She situates the Metis' defeat at Batoche as the original site that haunted her family and community.

The "savage" has generated much sense of shame, a theme not restricted to the protest literature of the 1970s. The Native confrontation with the "savage" continues in more recent writing of every genre. In a 1992 autobiographical essay, "Disadvantaged to Advantage," metis writer Ernie Louttit shares his experiences with racism growing up in Thorold, Ontario.[29] His family circumstances were such that his siblings looked White while he had the "dark hair, brown eyes and dark skin" he had "inherited" from his "natural father in my mother's first marriage." At the age of five, he was first made aware of his "difference" when his "blue-eyed Irish stepfather" roared at his mother to "get that little black bastard out of my sight." In his elementary school years, Louttit was the only "Indian" and often found himself taunted by other children: "Where's your bow and arrow, Geronimo? Where's your bow and arrow?" In an effort to help him, his brother used to say, "Don't let them call you that." As Louttit explains, "I do not think my brother meant to insult me but the meaning it conveyed was that it was bad to be Indian."[30] Louttit, like so many other Native writers, continued to experience racism in school at every turn. In high school his brother conveyed to him, "it was not a good thing to be seen with an Indian girl, much less date them." Louttit had a White girlfriend. However, "my white girlfriend's father insisted his daughter was degrading herself by dating a 'savage.'"[31]

Jeannette Armstrong's character Slash also faces youthful dating dilemmas produced by discrimination in the town school. Some of these experiences Slash could express (to a sympathetic priest), things such as dealing with the usual stereotypes (of tipis and feathers) and name-calling ("Injuns" and "full of lice"). But there "were some things," Slash says, "that we were too ashamed to even tell. Like all the white girls laughing at Tony when he asked one of them to dance at the sock-hop. He quit school after that. Also how none of the Indian girls ever got asked to dance at the sock-hops because us guys wouldn't dance with them because the white guys didn't."[32]

Seeing the Savage

Should anyone wonder still why the "savage" has caused us extreme aggravation, it is important to remember that most of us first met the savage visually, not only abstractly in print. Many of us first saw the savage Indian image in comic books, in school textbooks, and in movie theatres. It was my experience with the pictorial image as much as with written material that drove me to research and resistance. Graphic, colourful, larger-than-life presentations of the lurking, crouching, tomahawk-swinging, scalp-taking, painted, naked, howling savage (who was rumoured to be my forefather) left a profound and lasting imprint on me. And, as my subsequent research has confirmed, on so many other Native peoples as well.

A handful of Canadian Aboriginal educators and writers have produced critical works on the Indian image-making industry. Olive Patricia Dickason's *The Myth of the Savage* (1984) is an historical study of European myths and preconceptions that came with the colonial project and were projected onto Amerindians. *Fluffs and Feathers: An Exhibit on the Symbols of Indianness* (1992) by Mohawk author Deborah Doxtator, based on a museum/tourism project, is an excellent overview of stereotypic symbols associated with Indianness. Such productions have not been well understood as the resistance works that they, in fact, are. For example, in *Fluffs and Feathers*, Doxtator puts on display a racist poem published in 1895, a poem celebrating Bill Cody, a.k.a. Buffalo Bill, and, in effect, extolling civilization:

Bill Cody
(by an old comrade)

You bet I know him Pardner, he
ain't no circus fraud
He's Western born and Western
bred, if he has been abroad,
I knew him in the days way back,
beyond Missouri's flow.
When the country round was
nothing but a huge Wild Western
Show
When the injuns were as thick as
fleas, and the man who ventured
through
The sand hills of Nebraska had to
fight the hostile Sioux,
These were the times, I tell you;
and we all remember still
The Days when Cody was a
scout, and all the men knew Bill.[33]

Doxtator here is making a contrapuntal move—she is putting on display an artifact of White culture, much like museums have displayed Native articles. By treating this poem like a museum piece, a poem that sees "injuns" as fleas, Doxtator is documenting racism from a particular era. She is also exorcising the hate and the imagery. She points to the poem as a monument to remind us all what the nature of this discourse is about.

"We Are Not Savages, We Have Faces and Feelings"

There is no difference between us, under the skins, that any expert with a carving knife has ever discovered.... We are as well behaved as you and you would think so if you knew us better.

—Levi General (1873–1925)[34]

Indians cared, loved as passionately as other people.

—Basil Johnson[35]

To say we are human, namely, that we have faces and feelings, is to reconstruct our humanity. Chief Dan George goes to the heart—or faces—of this issue in his first collection *My Heart Soars*.[36] It is here that his prose and poetry, known for their gentleness, most evidently qualify as protest writing. Using the device of addressing various parties through prayers, lectures, and intimate conversations, Dan George simply unveils Native humanity. "They say we do not show our feelings. This is not so," he writes.[37] Dan George moves on to re-establish Native humanity by variously drawing on the "faces of my people." His words are heartbreaking, even when prosaic:

> Look at the faces of my people:
> You will find expressions of love and despair,
> hope and joy, sadness and desire, and all the
> human feelings that live in the hearts of people
> of all colours. Yet, the heart never knows
> the colour of the skin.[38]

Accompanying these poems are drawings of Native peoples by Helmut Hirnschall, many of them close-ups of faces: expressive faces, engaged faces, pondering faces, angry faces, tearful faces, sad faces, funny faces, baby faces, gentle faces, wrinkled faces, laughing and joyful faces. Faces uniquely human.

Ojibway writer George Kenny has also been particularly driven to put forward Native humanity, "as if Chaucer himself was kicking / him along, never letting him rest, / this indian dedicated to becoming / published."[39] Kenny was born in 1955 in Sioux Lookout, Ontario, and raised in Lac Seul Indian Reserve. Unlike in Ojibway artist Arthur Shilling's *Ojibway Dream*,[40] George Kenny's "people" are not always beautiful, but they are always consummately human in his slim collection of eighteen poems and eight short stories, *Indians Don't Cry*. In a short story of the same title, Kenny begins, "Indians don't cry. That's bullshit. Frank Littledeer cursed as tears streamed down."[41] The story is set in northwest Ontario. It is September, and Frank, an Ojibway man, just back from having seen his children flying off to residential school "some eighty miles away," comes home to an empty cabin echoing with pain and brokenness. There he reflects on his problems: drinking, unemployment, racism in town, retrieving his wife from town barrooms where "white men would call him names," finding his wife in bed with a White man, his raging reaction, his wife's leaving, his great loneliness. Kenny packs into a few pages some of the more personal devastating consequences of life lived on the margins. Obviously stung by racist othering, George Kenny ends his vignette, "Tomorrow would come.... In spite of the dry, racking sob that was rising in his throat, a grim smile played on Frank's lips as he remember how they had ridiculed him—Indians don't cry. That's a goddam lie."[42]

Unmistakably reacting to the stereotypes of the Main Street Indian (which were running rampant, especially from the 1950s to the 1970s), Kenny gives us a number of poems to remind us of the humanity of homeless people. In "Broken, I Knew a Man," Kenny writes,

> His soul was like the open pages of
> Layton's best works, always penned in truth,
> no matter how dirty or whiskey soaked....
> Today, I read in the local paper
> INDIAN KILLED BY FREIGHT TRAIN IN HUDSON
> and I wondered, who will be next
> to greet, broken, the summer sun.[43]

Kenny also provides the reader with emotional sketches of his family's cultural cohesion, hard work, beliefs, and achievements. He lets us feel the heartbreaks they experienced in residential schools and cities. His grief over the deaths of his parents informs some of the most moving poems.[44]

Purposefully, Kenny begins and ends his collection with poems that mock and confront age-old stereotypes. In "Rain Dance" he writes "as a modern Indian" who will "chant my songs / clap my hands / wriggle my hips / flash my feet," performing "for the crest-gleaming teeth / of the green-backed tourists."[45] In response to the nursery rhyme "One little, two little, three little / Indians," Kenny, uncharacteristically, wants to "slice that composer's neck / like a rabbit on snare wire, by its throat." In this poem, Kenny is one of the very few (indeed, so few as to be rare) Native writers to express militancy with visions of actual violence, to meet violation with violence. But even his desire to "slice" and to make the composer scream "child-like" is qualified with a moral and social purpose: "until he or she realized / that stupid song's driving my soul / into the ranks of AIM."[46] This gentle poet would go to the length of metaphorical violence so that the composer will be brought to a consciousness of what his or her words have done. If reconstructing our humanity sometimes appears as extreme romanticization or as provocative, it is in contrapuntal reaction to extreme dehumanization.

"We Were Not the Savages: We Were/Are Civilized"

Five hundred years of colonialism, and the colonizers still ponder whether we are peoples with lands. Five hundred years of colonialism and court judges still rule whether or not we are peoples with laws. And what of our cultures? They too have been ruled upon by others, determining whether we have a history, art, literature, or even an imagination.

—Loretta Todd, *Indigena*[47]

Another way of saying "I am not savage" is to say, as the late and respected Mi'kmaq poet Rita Joe has simply put it: "I am not / What they portray me / I am civilized."[48]

An associated image of the savage as unspeakably cruel is the savage without culture. And in the rather memorable précis provided by sixteenth-century French cosmographer Andre Thevet, Natives were, "a remarkably strange and savage people, without law, without religion, without any civility whatever, living like irrational beasts, as nature has produced them, eating roots, always naked, men as well as women."[49] The *Wilder Mann* rears its head—this is the savage with barely a language, with barely a human face. This is the creature of White wrath, "more savage than the animals around him," as Alexander Begg combusted.[50] Emphasizing the demerits of the colonized, as Memmi put it, has been a key element of "proof" that the colonizer has been rewarded by *his* merits (i.e. bootstraps).

The devaluation of Aboriginal cultures has generated a contrapuntal chorus of counterculture response. At the outset of the 1970s especially, Native speakers and writers were often cornered into the hapless role of apologists, having to explain and defend the Native way of life.[51] Although, with time, our explanations have turned to retorts or even silences, there are still vestiges of this defensive approach in our resistance that is inescapable. And, so, whether we re-establish the Trickster, recall our languages, outline our customs or political systems, all this is to say we are rational, we do have laws, faiths, governments and "civility": that is, we do have cultures, we are civilized.

Again the earliest Native writers led the way in addressing the colonial charge that "Indians" had an inferior culture, or no culture at all. Perhaps because they were in a most painful position of having to defend a culture that they had in parts rejected (evangelical Christianity demanded abandonment of indigenous cultures), Native missionaries—among them Peter Jones, George Copway, George Henry, Peter Jacobs, John Sunday, Allen Salt, Henry Steinhaur, and Henry Budd—were especially vocal on the subject, as Penny Petrone has established.[52] Petrone provides extensive biographical information along with some interesting anecdotes and commentaries about these men. They were placed in impossible situations, and how they dealt with these colonial/Christian/indigenous contradictions reveals an intersection of problems indicative of colonial pressures, and yet also anticipates decolonizing strategies. Not only did they defend their Christian faith and their Native cultures at once (at the time, this would have been received as heretical), but they also often criticized White society rather severely. Some had internalized cultural English standards, but many valourized Aboriginal cultures. Some, like George Copway, used Hiawathian prose (see Chapter 6) in their efforts to re-establish the beauty and validity of their cultures.

The drive to re-establish Aboriginal culture is particularly strong in nonfiction social commentaries of the 1970s. One of the first such books of the era is *Indians Without Tipis,* edited by D. Bruce Sealey and Verna J. Kirkness. Advertised as a "resource book," *Indians Without Tipis* is a compilation of essays and articles on the history and culture of Indians and Metis. The material is written by some of the earlier Manitoba Native educators and organizational leaders. The style is restrained, at times even apologetic. The editors introduce the section on culture by writing, "If one accepts as a working definition of the word culture as 'the sum total of the way in which people live' then a study of the cultures of native peoples would fill many volumes." But even here they qualify this, writing, "many will disagree with the approach and the content. The great value of the articles is that they give a viewpoint of Native people."[53]

Most Native writers, whether historians or poets, have felt compelled to emphasize the cultivated bases of Native cultures. It is with some significance that Rita Joe introduced some of her poems in her first collection *Poems of Rita Joe* (1978) with historical and cultural explanations. In a poem that "lament[s] forgotten skills" and notes that "regret stays" and "uncertainty returns to haunt / The native ways I abandoned," she explains, "Before the white man came, we had our own political, educational and economic way of life."[54] Normally understated and gracious, even Rita Joe calls for the death of words "that were written":

> So my children may see
> The glories of their forefathers
> And share the pride of history
>
> ...
>
> Our children read and hate
> The books offered—
> A written record of events
> By the white men.[55]

Native writers from the 1990s are no longer hesitant or apologetic about reclaiming their cultural heritage. In an article, "From Colonization to Repatriation," included in *Indigena*, Gloria Canmer Webster, who comes from the northwest coast people of the potlatches begins her Kwakiutl cultural re-counting with a classic phrase: "When the white people came, our ancestors were living as they had for centuries."[56] For centuries, her people had been living in the abundance of "unpolluted rivers and oceans," which provide everything else they needed: from cedar trees for houses, canoes, furniture and clothing, to roots, berries and game to supplement their diet." Cranmer Webster describes food preservation methods, all of which enabled her people to develop a rich artistic and ceremonial culture, including "carving masks and rattle, composing songs, performing dances, feasting, and telling myths and legends." Then, "together all of these activities ensured that each individual group enjoyed a healthy sense of identity."[57]

Reclaiming one's cultural heritage can take satirical tones too. In *Bear Bones and Feathers* (1994), in a series of Pope poems (or "da fadder poop," as it would be in Cree-ified English), the compelling Cree poet Louise Bernice Halfe desacrilizes "holy" history and not-so-holy behaviour. In a poem "Im So Sorry," Halfe mocks missionary misdeeds and arrogance:

I'm so sorry, the pope said
...
I didn't know the...
Blueberries, and sweetgrass
Were your offerings.
I wouldn't have taken your babies
And fed them wafers and wine.
I'm so sorry, I just thought
we could borrow land for a little
to plant our seeds...
...
I'm so sorry, I should have told
the settlers to quit their scalping,
selling hair at two bits for each Indian
I'm so sorry. I'm so sorry.[58]

Using a different medium, artist Joane Cardinal-Shubert also parodies "civilization." On the occasion of an art exhibit in Ottawa (and later in Calgary), the well-known contemporary visual artist (and sister to metis architect Douglas Cardinal) provides a typical "in a nutshell" explanatory response to cultural takeover: "It is only a hundred years since our ancestors lived in Tipis, hunted the buffalo, and invented beef jerky. It is only a hundred years and some since your ancestors herded us onto reserves, washed us with scrubbrushes and lye soap, and chopped our hair off, uniforming the children in religious residential schools in an attempt to knock out the savagery. Our ancestors were beaten for speaking their language.... It is only a hundred years and now we stand before you in this institution with our art work on the walls." With tongue in cheek, Cardinal-Schubert ends with a mocking question: "Now we are civilized, aren't we?"[59]

Cardinal-Schubert goes on to say that Native cultures pre-existed European arrival, and that because of racism, it took her a long time to like herself, to take a stand, and to be proud of her heritage. But to be proud of the Indian heritage means having to dispel the hounding myth of civilization/savagery; it means having to say we are *not* the savages.

"We Were Not the Savages, You Were"

Many Native writers move from a position of defence to that of offence in their counter-charges of savagery. Using metaphor, rhetoric, sarcasm, and parody, Native writers have challenged and redefined who and what is a savage. Sometimes their styles are reminiscent of Shakespeare's Anthony and Brutus sparring about honour and dishonour. Often, the writer sets up the argument by casting a line of doubt. In 1847, George Copway begins one of his paragraphs: "I have heard it said, that our forefathers were cruel to the forefathers of the whites." Copway questions the presumed Native cruelty by contextualizing (therefore humanizing, though quite apologetically) Native actions: "But was not this done through ignorance, or in self-defence?" He then returns the blame for whatever violence occurred: "Had your fathers adopted the plan of the great philanthropist, William Penn, neither fields, nor clubs, nor waters, would have been crimsoned with each other's blood." It is no accident that he likens White cruelty to animal behaviour, for one of the key features of White writing has been to compare Indians with animals: "The whitemen have been like the greedy lion, pouncing upon and devouring its prey. They have driven us from our nation, our homes, and possessions," and, using sharp sarcasm, Copway sallies: "and will, perhaps, soon compel us to scale the Rocky Mountains; and for aught I can tell, we may yet be driven to the Pacific Ocean, there to find our graves."[60]

In charging the White man with ungratefulness and betrayal, Copway asks, by way of ironic contrast, "Is it not well known that the Indians have a generous and magnanimous heart?" The question is rhetorical as he goes on to answer (in the context of the Governor of Massachusetts' having thanked Indians for their assistance): "I feel proud to mention in this connection, the names of a Pochahontus, Massasoit…Philip, Tecumseh…and a thousand of others" whose names "are an honour to the world." Copway again uses the rhetorical technique: "And what have we received since, in return? Is it for the deeds of a Pochahontus, a Massasoit…that we have been plundered and oppressed, and expelled from the hallowed graves of our ancestors?" Copway then turns back to casting doubt on stereotypes: "It is often said, that the Indians are *revengeful, cruel*, and *ungovernable.*" Again, Copway sallies: "Go to them with nothing but *the* BIBLE *in your hands* and LOVE *in your hearts*, and you may live with them in perfect safety."[61]

Pauline Johnson, too, counter-punches the colonial name-calling and imagery. She goes to battle for Native peoples much more directly in her poem "The Cattle Thief" (already referred to above). She not only defends the cattle thief but returns the shots, so to speak, with name-calling of her own. Johnson goes after the invaders, using and turning the knife of "the enemy's language." She even demonizes the "desperate English settlers" as the savages [cursing] "like a troop of demons" or [rushing] "like a pack of demons on the body." She assumes the English voice:

> 'Cut the fiend up into inches, throw his carcass on the plain
> Let the wolves eat the cursed Indian, he'd have
> Treated us the same'
> A dozen hands responded, a dozen knives gleamed
> High.[62]

Obviously aware that White writers often portrayed "Indians" as savage creatures who tortured and mutilated White bodies, Johnson is deliberate in her choice of words and imagery. Perhaps she had read Richardson's *Wacousta*, or Cooper's *The Last of the Mohicans*, or perhaps any number of captivity narratives or dime novels of her era. Her intent is apparent; she is returning and reversing the violation.

Most contemporary Native writers also turn the tables on the colonizer to point out White cruelty and contradictions; in effect, to point to White savagery. The following poem, "Savage Man" by Alfred Groulx, follows a well-established technique of setting Native "truth" against White betrayal and hypocrisy. The style is stark:

> You came to our land
> You called us savage man
> We greeted you with smiles
> You greeted us with lies…
> We shared with you this land

You demanded more than you needed
We sent our chiefs to sign treaties
You sent your armies to enforce them.…
We agree to learn your tongue
You took more, you took our voice…
We respected Mother Earth and her ways,
You cut off her limbs and scarred her face
We honoured your way of life
You robbed us of ours.[63]

Veteran Ojibway poet Duke Redbird uses a "warm" style to point to invader lies. Using the metaphor of an old woman, Redbird provides an image of White treachery against golden brown innocence and humanity in his poem "Old Woman." He first establishes the earth's energy and beauty:

Old woman, I know who you are.
I know this barren waste land
Upon which I stand
Was once a forest.
And you, old woman,

Had life and beauty,
Energy and passion,
Love and endurance,
Freedom and chatter with the gods…
But your body carried the burden
Of Sorrow, and the weight of treachery.

For others came, pale helpless souls.
And our arms encircled them.

Then, Redbird rhetorically asks,

Where are they now,
After they cut down your beloved forest,
And slaughtered your animal brothers,

And tore the wings from your bright birds,
And ground your mountains into dust?
Did they leave you anything at all.[64]

The brutal acts and devastating consequences of White invasion and dispossession are the stones used to throw savagery back to Whites. Scalping, for instance. This is not unexpected, because colonialist writers have traditionally used Indian scalping as one of the "final" proofs of Indian savagery. Native writers have turned the tables on this too.

In *Prison of Grass*, Adams quotes an elementary school textbook used in Saskatchewan in the 1970s, which smears Indians as warlike scalpers. He explains that "ideas like this continue to affect the attitudes of whites and Indians alike; many Indians in fact believe that their ancestors were totally savage and warlike."[65] "The truth is," Adams retorts, "scalping was done more frequently by whites than by Indians." Adams provides evidence of "White settlers" paying bounties for dead Indians "and scalps were actual proof of the deed." English newcomers were paid to bring in the scalps, and such actions were taken throughout the New England area. The French, too, participated in scalp taking: "In the competition over the Canadian fur trade, they offered the Micmac Indians a bounty for every scalp they took from the Beothuk of Newfoundland."[66] If scalping is one proof of savagery, then Whites too are savage. Amazingly, such an "equalizer" argument may still be lost on White audiences.

It is a point not lost on Mi'kmaq historian Daniel N. Paul. He emphatically denies in *We Were Not the Savages* (1993) that Mi'kmaqs took Beothuk scalps. Calling it "despicable propaganda," "false and malicious rumours" used by the British to "spread fear and hatred of the Micmac," Paul argues, "there is not one shred of evidence to support such allegations." Quite the contrary, "the extinction of the Beothuk was brought about by the brutal actions of Europeans involved in the fishery off Newfoundland and by the Inuit."[67] Not only were the Europeans largely responsible for Beothuk extinction, according to Paul, they were also responsible for the dispossession and decimation of the Mi'kmaq.

Significantly, Paul too turns to evidence of White scalping to indicate White savagery. In the context of massive depopulation suffered by the Mi'kmaq due to "genocide, diseases, starvation and war," the Mi'kmaq declared war on the British on 23 September 1749. In response, Lord Cornwallis proposed, in effect, a policy of extermination including a reward "for every Indian Mikmac taken, or killed." In Paul's words: "The horror contained in these words probably escaped the British. In their blind arrogance they could not see the unspeakable crime against humanity which they were about to commit."[68] Paul points to a proclamation of extinction issued by Lord Cornwallis on 2 October 1749. Parts of it read:

> Whereas… the Micmacs have of late in a most treacherous manner taken 20 of His Majesty's Subjects prisoners.…
>
> For those cause we… do hereby authorize and command all Officers Civil and Military, and all his Majesty's Subjects or others to annoy,

distress, take or destroy the Savage commonly called Micmac…and with the consent and advice of His Majexty's Council, *do promise a reward of ten Guineas for every Indian Micmac taken or killed, to be paid upon producing such Savage taken or his scalp* (as in the custom of America).[69]

We Were Not the Savages re-examines and reinscribes the Euro-Canadian colonizer narrative concerning the Euro-Canadian–Mi'kmaq encounter. In chapter after chapter, Paul marshals a relentless array of evidence from the colonizer records supporting his central thesis that the Mi'kmaq were largely a democratic and peaceful people who were brought to near extinction by European arrogance, dishonour, and brutality. Paul ends his revision with a classically rhetorical question/challenge: "You have now read a history of one of the American Aboriginal peoples, a people who gave their all to defend their home and country and fought courageously for survival. Based on what you now know, what is your honest judgement about *who were the barbarian savages* when the Europeans and Aboriginal Americans collided?"[70]

The theme of imperialist Whites lacking humanity runs from "sea to shining sea." In a poem, "History Lesson," Jeannette Armstrong uses powerful imagery from the stereotypes to express who the savages were in the early encounters between European and Aboriginal peoples:

> Out of the belly of Christopher's ship
> a mob bursts
> Running in all directions
> Pulling furs off animals
> Shooting buffalo
> Shooting each other…
> Pioneers and traders
> bring gifts
> Smallpox, Seagrams
> and Rice Krispies
> Civilization has reached
> The promised land.[71]

Armstrong also turns to oral tradition to impress the same point. In "This Is My Story," a not so subtle allegory, Armstrong imagines the return of Kyoti. The vision is that of Kyoti, an Okanagan legendary character with Trickster-like qualities, a character who likes to sleep long into the morning. But in her vision, Kyoti wakes up "from an unusually short nap" and, hoping to feast with the Salmon people, takes a walk "up Okanagon River which run into Columbia River... Kyoti had come up through there before. One time before that I know of."[72] And that time had been happy, joyful time when the Salmon people would gather and feast during the salmon run. But this time Kyoti "noticed a lot of new things," things like the landscape full of Swallow people, things like the Salmon people not knowing their Salmon language, things like new chiefs who were afraid to dismantle dams that would free up the salmon to run again. Armstrong writes,

> Kyoti had seen People in really had shape. They walked around with their minds hurt.... Their bodies were poisoned.... They thought they were Swallows, but couldn't figure out why the Swallows taunted and laughed at them.... They couldn't seem to see that the Swallows stole everything they could pick up for their houses, how they took over any place and shitted all over it, not caring....
>
> Kyoti could see... that them Swallows were still a Monster people. They were pretty tricky making themselves act like they were People but all the while, underneath, being really selfish Monsters that destroy People and things like rivers and mountains.[73]

By discovering that the Swallows were monsters, Kyoti finds once again a reason to wake up early: "It was time to change the Swallows from Monsters into something that didn't destroy things. Kyoti was Kyoti and that was the work Kyoti had to do." Obviously, Armstrong has turned the tables. The swallows are the savages, the salmons are the human people, and Kyoti (that is, Coyote?) has a humanizing (and civilizing) mission to fulfill.

We have come full circle. Whites have accused us of savagery; they convinced themselves that their descriptions, their actions, and their policies were justifiable, indeed, necessary, so that they could "civilize" us. But their very own records show that the drive for civilization was more professed than real, that what was real was the oppressive behaviour. And this behaviour and its effects on human beings and on the land were and remain anything but civil. Now we can write and reinscribe the documents, not only arguing we are civilized, but that we are more human and our higher moral Native ethics call us to civilize the Whites. This must be read as contrapuntal reply, not as an anthropological or spiritual "reality" or ontological truth.

Perhaps Douglas Cardinal in *Of the Spirit* speaks most bluntly to the Native's higher moral vision, which, as editor George Melnyk explains, consists of a "primitive" or "first" vision based on a cultural (natural, cultivating, tending), not "civilized" (anti-natural), understanding of life and land. The Indian sense of the land is both dynamic and encompassing. According to

Melnyk, "self-understanding comes not only from an image growth but from the immense organic being of the land." In Cardinal's vision, Melnyk continues, "life is holy, life is one, life is whole. This is not the phallic one of our culture. The oneness of Indian culture finds its symbolic expression in the circle, the native peoples' ultimate metaphor for totality."[74]

Cardinal makes clear in a style reminiscent of the earliest resistance writers, that this vision is morally superior to the "civilized" vision. Facetiously, Cardinal refers to White colonizers as guardians, then spells out their obvious contradictions in their actions: "These racists are the present guardians of our children, our future.... These guardians of our people, our children, these guardians of education, honour, justice, these guardians of the lands, the rivers, the air, these guardians of humanity, these guardians of the concept of the Great Spirit have shown by their actions that they are not fit guardians." Not only are they not fit guardians, they are not fit humans: "It is our belief that the atrocities perpetrated on our people were done by ignorant men who lacked the knowledge and insight to conduct themselves as human beings."[75]

Such declarations are not only contrapuntal devices, but are prophetic statements, sociological observations, and historical judgements. We will perhaps always be tempted to turn the tables; this may be the inevitable conclusion to experiencing dehumanization for half a millennium. This may be the supreme irony of history, that the colonizer's debris always rains on his umbrella, sooner or later. But Armstrong and Cardinal here are not just reversing roles, they are questioning the very tenets of Western civilization. This is, in part, why they compare European and indigenous behaviours. This is why Adams and Paul, among others, point to the glaring contradictions concerning scalping. How could a people so violent and cruel become the standard bearers of "civilization," and so arrogantly at that? Given the evidence of history, is this not a legitimate question?

Some here may suggest that this is simply "reverse racism," that reversing the old colonial civ/sav binary keeps us mired in colonialism and continues to rob both sides of our humanity. But there are profound differences between Native writers' calls to humanity and the 500 years of dehumanization to which indigenous peoples around the world have been subjected. In the first instance, as noted earlier, racism is a belief in one's "racial" or genetic superiority (usually assumed to be located in the brain). There is absolutely no indication that Native writers, and certainly not Armstrong nor Cardinal, have adopted any genetic argumentation in their discussions about human development. In all the Native material I have read, I have not found one piece that I could classify as racist. That Natives point to historically documented European (be they Spanish, Portuguese, Dutch, English, or French) inhumanity is an inevitable feature of the counter-discourse. But this does not make them racist. To suggest so is to attempt to discredit them and the weight of history and experience from which they speak. It is also to attempt to neutralize the indisputable history of global colonization. Memmi reminds us that the "colonized is not free to choose between being colonized or not being colonized."[76] To insist the colonized get out of the imposed binaries is largely to serve liberalist ideals or even postcolonial theory making, for it is not possible for the colonized to skip merrily over colonial fences. If they could, they would. Of course, we are all trying to scale these fortifications, but this is for our liberation, not for postcolonial privileging of theory.

Nor should the onus of moral behaviour always fall back on the colonized—that it does is a form of blaming the victim—for the issue is centrally about power. To the charge of "reverse racism," it must be emphasized that racism is a particular prejudice or ideology that legitimizes an unequal relationship. Native intellectuals still speak from a place of relative powerlessness. The bald reality of powerlessness stares at Native people everywhere they turn. What is clear is that as long as the dehumanization and the inequality exist, each new generation of Native writers will take up the mantle of rebalancing. Re-establishing Native humanity cannot be racist, ipso facto, and as fashionable as it may be to cry "reverse racism," it is nonetheless reactionary and implicates those accustomed to privilege.

Arguing that "we were not the savage, you were" can lead to what appears as primitivist romanticization. For example, ascribing higher moral properties to "natural" living against "civilized" living is reminiscent of Rousseau's *bon sauvage* of the eighteenth century. However, romanticization is neither simple nor necessarily positive. While it is true that Native cultures are based on an ethical and practical relationship to the land, romanticization also reflects the infantilization and naturalization of Native cultures (which in turn confuses stereotypic and real cultural differences), misrepresentation, internalization, and decolonization. It is virtually impossible to appreciate Native resistance discourse without having to deal with this confusing intersection of issues.

Chapter Six

An Intersection: Internalization, Difference, Criticism

I was born in Nature's wide domain! The trees were all that sheltered my infant limbs—the blue heavens all that covered me. I am one of Nature's children; I have always admired her; she shall be my glory; her features—her robes, and the wreath about her brow—the seasons—her stately oaks, and the evergreen—her hair, ringlets over the earth—all contribute to my enduring love for her; and wherever I see her, emotions of pleasure roll in my breast, and well and burst like waves on the shores of the ocean.... It is thought great to be born in palaces, surrounded with wealth—but to be born in Nature's wide domain is greater still.

I remember the tall trees, and the dark woods... where the little wren sang so melodiously after the going down of the sun in the west—the current of the broad river Trent—the skipping of the fish and the noise of the rapids a little above.... Is this dear spot, made green by tears of memory, any less enticing and hallowed than the palaces where princes are born? I would much more glory in this birthplace, with the broad canopy of heaven above me, and the giant arms of the forest trees for my shelter, than to be born in palaces of marble, studded with pillars of gold! Nature will be Nature still,

> while palaces shall decay and fall in ruins. Yes, Niagara will be Ni-
> agara a thousand years hence!
>
> —George Copway, 1851[1]

Reconstruction entails both deconstruction and romanticization. For Native academics, especially, because of the ideological complex of our dehumanization, we have woven our idealizations throughout our deconstructive argumentations. However, the fabric of our weaving is anything but simple. We carry the weight of "the colonizer's model of the world" (to borrow Blaut's phrase); in our case, specifically, we remain shadowed by the savage, both the noble and the ignoble. Our resistance is our reconstruction, which does remain textured with idealization and internalization.

A convolution of issues central to the relationships I have been here discussing emerges when we examine our reconstruction process. We find a fascinating and sometimes confusing mix of issues that braid together an array of stereotypes, notions of cultural differences, and problems of internalization. As I have emphasized, it is virtually impossible to understand or situate Native resistance writing without having some appreciation of what these issues are and how they glue together. The scope and magnitude of this sticky mix is such that it may never be possible to completely peel off the layers; nonetheless, we must explore their effects on us. In this and the next chapter I turn to some of those effects on us, effects that have considerably complicated our discourse.

Up to this point, I have treated Native writing in its broad sense, taking in history, biography, social commentaries, essays and so forth, as well as some fiction and poetry. In this and the next chapter I focus more on creative Native writing, particularly novels and poetry, which is usually considered "literary." However, and I re-emphasize, my examination of this literature is interdisciplinary rather than literary, per se. My interest is to shift the typological and ideological approaches that plague the study of Native peoples. But before we can trouble paradigms, we must sift through colonial debris, much of which sits in the hearts and minds of the colonized.

Internalization

The concept of internalization is not perfectly understood, for much of it appears to be an unconscious process. In previous chapters, I have emphasized its manifestation in the lives of Native writers in terms of their feelings about themselves as peoples subjected to social and ideational hatred based on their racial, cultural, and ethnic groupings as "Indians." Aboriginal and other non-Western intellectuals have long noted a dramatic and profound transformation in people who have been subjected to othering for a sustained amount of time. Clearly, over time, a complex relationship develops between the colonizer and the colonized. Both classic and more contemporary critics—from Fanon and Memmi to Edward Said and Ngugi wa Thiong'o—have convincingly shown that colonization produces a pervasive structural and psychological relationship between the colonizer and the colonized. Scholars studying Native peoples have been slow to ask what may be the most important question here: what happens to a people whose very essences have been soaked in stereotypes for half a millennium? My study of White and Native writing has been centrally concerned with the much maligned and misrepresented "Indian" because this construct has dramatically impugned Native peoples at every crucial place of their lives. At minimum, what we can learn from the Native experience is that words and images are not just words and images. They can pack a powerful punch.

We must come back to the savage, with its polarizing spectrum of images. We struggle mightily with these images, whether we are trying to debunk them, rehabilitate them or whether we are (unconsciously) internalizing them in our everyday lives or in our intellectual pursuits. As Puxley has pointed out, "A lengthy colonial experience not only deprives people of their right to define their experience authentically, but even deprives them of consciousness of such a right."[2] The internalization of the grotesque, ignoble savage is perhaps the most damaging. This savage leads us to a sense of shame (who wants to claim the hideous Magua, from *The Last of the Mohicans*, as a forefather?) and self-rejection, which then often leads to the rejection of what I call the "same-other."[3] By same-other, I mean that one's sense of racial shame is projected onto those of the same race or grouping, who are then unconsciously cast as other. Being ashamed of being "Indian" means being ashamed not only of oneself but also of other Indians. Many Native writers have had to deal with their own struggles of rejections of the same-other, due largely, to the impact of the White ideal; that is, the colonizer's standards such as beauty and status. We have already learned from Howard Adams, Maria Campbell, and others that this process is excruciating and disorienting because it makes us hate what and who we love. And we live shrouded in shame twice over: racial shame and, to the extent we may be conscious, shame about feeling ashamed.

Hatred of the same-other is particularly evident in some early missionary writing. In a letter sent to a Methodist paper, the *Christian Guardian*, in 1837, Ojibway missionary George Henry wrote, "Yes, Mr. Papermaker, if you had seen these Indians a few years ago, you would think they were the animals you called Ourang Outangs, for they appeared more like them than human beings; but since the Great Spirit has blessed them, they have good clothes; plates and dishes; window and bed curtains; knives and forks; chairs and tables."[4]

Eleven years later, apparently after his disillusionment with the church, this same man wrote among the most unflattering and ethnocentric assessments of European culture, assessments based on his tour of Europe as a performing Indian (sponsored by George Catlin, that famous American artist of the 1830s and '40s in search of the "vanishing Indian"). Henry compared Londoners to mosquitoes, "like musketoes in America in the summer season, so are the people in this city... in their number, and biting one another to get a living."[5] It is possible that Henry demonstrated both internalization and resistance at different times of his life, emphasizing one or the other or both, depending on his circumstances. If taken at face value, his letter screams, to use a popular postcolonial phraseology, "colonial mimicry"; his travel literature conveyed his more subversive mimicry. Dee Horne, in *Contemporary American Indian Writing*, describes these "two modes of mimicry": "In colonial mimicry, the mimic imitates to become like another while in subversive modes ... the mimic imitates to critique another. While the colonial mimic imitates colonizers in an effort to access, take on, their power, the subversive mimic engages in partial repetitions of colonial discourse to contest its authority."[6]

Individual Native responses to untenable colonial situations may not be as they appear. Our critical awareness about this process is embryonic. Moreover, it should not be assumed that the internalization process for Aboriginal persons is exactly the same as those truly (at least politically) postcolonial peoples who live in countries that have long regained political independence, and whose population was always numerically larger than the colonizer's. These are just some, but arguably huge, differences between and among postcolonials; obviously there are parallels to be made, but, equally, there are differences to be investigated—and no doubt theorized. Much more research is required before we can subsume all postcolonials under universalized theories.[7]

Many writers—in the period studied here—seem unaware (usually in parts, not in total) that they are projecting images, words, descriptions, or beliefs that have been imposed by European prejudices. Pauline Johnson provides among the most interesting examples of the colonized adopting or internalizing colonizer terms and images. From Johnson's collection *Flint and Feather*, we find some rather unsettling examples of negative internalization. Johnson was a staunch defender of Indian actions and rights, but she seems to have adopted much of the colonizer's language.

Two poems from *Flint and Feather,* "Ojistoh" and "As Red Men Die," indicate the troubling extent to which Johnson had internalized White stereotypes of "Indians." One suspects what readings had inspired these poems. She was, undoubtedly, schooled in exploration literature, missionary writings, captivity narratives, and dime novels, literature considered fashionable in her era. "Ojistoh" is a story of a Mohawk woman who was captured by the Huron as an act of revenge against her husband. Johnson writes,

> they hated him, those Huron braves,
> Him who had flung their warriors into graves
> Him who had crushed them underneath his heel,
> Whose arm was iron, whose heart was steel
> To all—save me, Ojistoh, chosen wife.[8]

In their hate, the Hurons "with subtle witchcraft" and cowardice ("Their hearts grew weak as women at his name") "councilled long" how to avenge their dead, and came upon a scheme to strike him where "His pride was highest, and his fame most fair" by seizing her. After a gallant struggle, Ojistoh is flung "on their pony's back" and tied to her captor, whom she despises. As they neared the Huron home fires, Ojistoh stereotypically draws on her feminine—and savage—wiles, that of sensual treachery:

> I smiled, and laid my cheek against his back
> "loose thou my hands" I said…
> Forget we now that thou and I are foes.
> I like thee well, and wish to clasp thee close.

Predictably, the foolish Huron "cut the cords" and she "wound" her arms "about his tawny waist," and then her hand

> crept up the buckskin of her belt
> His knife hilt in my burning palm I felt
> One hand caressed his cheek, the other drew
> the weapon softly…
> And—buried in his back his scalping knife.[9]

Then she was free and rode home joyfully and madly back to her "Mohawk, and my home."

"As Red Men Die" is again an unabashedly ethnocentric glorification of her people, the Mohawks, at the expense of the despised Huron. The poem tells of an unflinchingly courageous Mohawk who mocks the hated Huron, even to his torturous death at the burning stake. In wording and imagery, "As Red Men Die" could have been inspired by a combination of the *Jesuit*

Relations and *Wacousta*:

> Captive! Is there a hell to him like this?
> A taunt more galling than the Huron's hiss?
> He—proud and scornful, he—who laughed at law,
> He—scion of the deadly Iroquois,
> He—the bloodthirsty, the—the Mohawk chief.[10]

The Huron captors then taunt the Mohawk to either "Walk o'er the bed of fire" or "*with the women rest thee here?*" [emphasis in original]. To such baiting, the Mohawk's "eyes flash like an eagle's / Like a god he stands / Prepare the fire!" he scornfully demands. The poem's ending triggers images from *The Last of the Mohicans*:

> He knoweth not what this same jeering band
> Will bite the dust—will lick the Mohawk's hand;
> Will kneel and cower at the Mohawk's feet;
> Will shrink when Mohawk war drums wildly beat.
> His death will be avenged with hideous hate
> By Iroquois, swift to annihilate
> His vile detested captors…
> Not thinking, soon that reeking, red and raw,
> Their scalps will deck the belts of Iroquois…
> Up the long trail of fire he boating goes,
> Dancing a war dance to defy his foes.
> His flesh is scorched, his muscles burn and shrink,
> But still he dances to death's awful brink.
> The eagle plume that crests his haughty head
> Will *never* droop until his heart be dead…
> His voice that leaps to Happier Hunting Grounds
> One savage yell—
>   Then Loyal to his race
> He bends to death—but *never* disgrace.[11]

One wonders why Johnson borrowed this language so extensively. It may, in part, be that she took to poetic licence, or that given the political climate, she had little choice but to latch onto popular stereotypes to gain an audience. I would like to think she engaged in subversive mimicry, but I do not think these are sufficient explanations. Were no other words or tropes available to her in her era? Could she not have created a different language? Or, at the very least, avoided it? She surely must have felt conflicted—and indeed she did, as her poem "A Cry From an Indian Wife" so clearly indicates—because her defence of Native humanity is unmistakable. That she used such hate literature is disturbing and speaks to her educational background, her largely English upbringing in a Mohawk community with Loyalist traditions, and her own mixed loyalties. And, most of all, it speaks to the power of the dominant narrative on Canadian audiences and writers, Native and non-Native alike. But again, words or performances are not necessarily as they appear.

Johnson appropriates colonial phrases such as "red-skin," "wild," "tomahawk," "hapless brave," "hissing," and so forth, both to internalize but also to resist. In "A Cry From an Indian Wife," Johnson begins with Hiawathian grandeur: "My Forest Brave, my Red-skin love, farewell." To go with this colonial-soothing verse, she donned "Indian princess" regalia during her performances. Modelling after Hiawatha, or Pocahontas, may seem benign. But the fact is, Johnson had little choice in her dramatic readings. Though British Canadian audiences adored Johnson, they soon demanded that she entertain them not just with her romantic "Red-skin," verses but also her "red cloak, buckskin and a bearclaw necklace."[12] In order for her to have an audience, she had to acquiesce to dominant requirements that Indians, if alive, must be noble, stereotypically so. Johnson in real life was an elegant Halfbreed "lady" who wore Victorian gowns as easily as she navigated Mohawk streams in her beloved canoe. She was a proud, determined, and highly gifted woman whose artistic freedom was largely determined by the colonial forces of her times. To what extent she capitalized on prevailing images (for she was certainly aware of them) or to what extent she was victim of them remains a question.

Other creative Native individuals have suffered various consequences under the travails of the noble savage. Those individuals who refuse to submit to stereotypical performances may, among other things, lose their audience. I recall, in the very early 1970s, a University of Alberta audience giving Chief Dan George a standing ovation but booing then well-known activist Kahn-Tineta Horn.

But beyond its ill effects on individuals, the noble savage construct presents a number of other complications for the Native community. Chief Dan George, for example, gained great popularity because his bearing reflected, unmistakably, the noble savage. To this day, long after his passing, he leaves us wondering how we should read his acting or his poetic prose, along with his long, flowing grey hair, chiselled cheekbones, and soft undemanding voice, complete with a dignified bearing reminiscent of that self-ennobling English impostor Grey Owl.[13] Ironically, the age-old notion of the Vanishing Indian (a variation of the noble savage) was perhaps best expressed by George in his famous elegy "My Very Good Dear Friends." His words rang out: "for I was born a thousand years ago... born in a culture of bows and arrows. But within the span of half a lifetime I was flung across the ages to the culture of the atom bomb.... And from bows and arrows to atom bombs is a distance far beyond a flight to the moon.... For a few brief years I knew my people when we lived the old life.... But we were living on the dying energy of a dying culture."[14]

It seems fitting that Chief Dan George played the role of David Joe, father to Rita Joe in Ryga's *Ecstasy of Rita Joe*. Hailed as Canada's centennial play, *The Ecstasy of Rita Joe* presents Indian culture as belonging to the past, a culture that cannot "make it" in White society. Confronted by Jaime, the frustrated, volatile, and city-hungry suitor to his daughter, David Joe, Ryga's symbol of the "authentic" Indian, can only whimper, "I know nothing... only the old stories."[15] Native peoples, it seems, are so culturally "old" as to be irrelevant, so that upon contact with the modern (a.k.a., civilized, superior, new, progressive) world, they become disoriented, living in a dream or trance, like Rita and her father. Incapable of living a culturally efficacious life either in the city or on the reserve, the two young people, Rita Joe and Jaime, who represent the future of Native society, meet horrible deaths. In other words, they vanish. And the old man with his old stories is left in a state of sorrow and reminiscence. It is just a matter of time before he too will vanish.

The Vanishing Indian is a quintessentially colonial desire and expectation. In Canada, an assortment of artists, travellers, missionaries, officials, soldiers, poets, novelists, and anthropologists "all agreed that Indians were disappearing." The "imminent disappearance of the Indian," writes Daniel Francis in *The Imaginary Indian*, "was an article of faith among Canadians until well into the twentieth century."[16] Canadian (or White American) interest in Indians was fed in large part by this expectation. As Berkhofer put it, "Most romantic of all was the impression of the Indian as rapidly passing away before the onslaught of civilization."[17] Various artists of the 1800s built their reputations on capturing "a record of their [Indian] culture before it died away."[18] Photographer Edward Curtis traversed the length and breadth of North America in his mission to "present Indians as they existed before the whiteman came."[19] Curtis, along with other well-known artists such as George Catlin or Paul Kane, doctored his pictures to convey what they became famous for, an Indian "unspoiled" by White culture.

In the early nineteenth-century United States, the Vanishing Indian spawned a particular version of the noble savage, as cultural nationalists revived and romanticized legendary Indian figures such as Pocahontas. This noble savage was quite different from the European primitivist construction in that Americans created it only after they had, for the most part, destroyed Native American peoples' cultures. For Americans, their noble savage was not a critic of society (as it was for Rousseau and Voltaire) so much as it was cultural appropriation for their art. Their savage was noble only because he was "safely dead and historically past."[20] Berkhofer situates Henry Wadsworth Longfellow's *The Song of Hiawatha* within this American tradition.

Despite centuries of expecting the "Indian" to vanish, the Indian has not. Both the theme and real Native peoples seem to have equally stubborn resilience. But the "Indian" continues to be generalized and symbolized as one monolithic stone-age culture, a culture of the past, the only pure expression of Indianness, the only "authentic" Indian. It is here that the more subtle literary device in the form of the more pleasing Hiawatha comes in—the Vanishing Indian hands over its work to Hiawatha and Hiawatha becomes the "authentic" Indian. But "authenticity" exacts a deadly price. If the Indian did not vanish physically, he had to remain moribund culturally. A noble savage could exist only in a timeless vacuum. In effect, Indians could have no fluidity, no agency in their culture(s); therefore, they could have no histories. They can only have "traditions," which are always placed and treated as "prehistoric" or "traits." In many ways, the as-required shape-shifting vanishing Indian/Hiawatha/noble savage construct is a form of intellectual genocide in that it absolutely disallows Native cultural change. While Westerners have marched on with the confidence of an assumed dynamic and progressive culture, they have invented a Native whose culture is fixed and outside of time. Hence, many colonial references to "Indian" qualities of timelessness or prehistoricism. So, the moment the Native steps out of timelessness, he or she is deemed assimilated, that is, non-Indian. The colonizer niftily confuses the issue between cultural change or agency and "assimilation" (note it is always a one-way street), and so sets up the Native as immutably and antithetically unprogressive. As Francis explains, "Indians were defined in relation to the past and in contradistinction to White society. To the degree that they changed, they were perceived to become less Indian."[21] Thus, Native society has been ossified and relegated to a prehistoric natural world, and Native characters are merely caricatures.

Consigning the Indian to an unchanging primitive world has deep European roots. In the context of trying to make sense of the New World and its colonial discoveries and behaviours, a minority of European thinkers (spanning the Renaissance, Englightenment, and Romantic periods) idealized the noble savage of the Americas. Whether it was Montaigne and Las Casas in the 1500s, or Voltaire and Rousseau in the 1700s, the "positive" treatment of the New World man was centrally about the Old World man. New-found indigenous peoples around the world provided an enormous spurt of intellectual growth for Europeans. The North American Indian, among them, invigorated the European mind. As a critic of European society, the culturally "raw" Indian was dichotomized from the Old World overgrown with conventions. If Europe had too many rules, the Indian had none. If Europe burdened its people with its lords and its propertied classes, the Indian had no kings or property over which to oppress the masses. If the church was corrupt, the Indian had only his primeval forest in which to commune. Berkhofer points out that while there were variations in emphasis at different periods, European ideas regarding the noble savage remained largely the same. It was thought that human freedom was inherent in the raw state of nature. What was human-made was artificial and untrue, what was "unspoiled" and (thought to be) natural as found in earliest "primitive man" was inherently good. Finding such a world promised a new social order for Europeans. The European idea of the noble savage was abstract; it was meant as a tool for social criticism. The ennobling of the Indian was almost accidental, and Native peoples as human beings were largely inconsequential to European (and later White American) concerns. Intellectual idealization was one thing, understanding or acceptance of real Native life was quite another matter. Berkhofer makes this clear: not only did the American Indian take "a minor position in comparison to other exotic peoples in the Noble Savage convention," but "no philosopher or *litterateur* intended for his fellow citizens to adopt the lifestyles of the savages, noble or otherwise. Critical though the *philosphes* and authors may have been of European civilization, they merely wanted to reform it, not abandon it for the actual life of savagery they so often praised."[22] Ethnocentrism is a powerful force—Berkhofer seems to accept a "life of savagery" exists.

Concerning White American uses of the noble savage, Berkhofer writes that while the "noble Indian deserved White pity for his condition and his passing," his way of life "no less than that of the ignoble savage demanded censure according to the scale of progress and the passage of history."[23] Idealizing the Indian's presumed natural world appears, at first glance, to be positive, as in the usage of the *bon sauvage* in primitivist criticism of European conventions. However, upon closer inspection, there are serious historical, cultural, and sociological problems with such a presentation. Being used as the colonizer's social conscience or the vehicle for playing Indian, but left behind as irrelevant to modern culture, carries chilling implications.

E.T. Seton's "Red Man" is a perfect example. An outspoken critic of America's burgeoning industrialization in the early twentieth century, Seton offered the Indian as a social conscience of the times. Seton was most sincere, even arguing that the red man's spiritually based culture was superior to the White man's materially based one. He admired and respected the Indian he constructed. However, Seton's nature-loving Indian came complete with buckskin, headdresses, canoes, bows and arrows, tipis, and Indian villages—

the beginnings of the Boy Scout and Girl Guide movements. Not surprisingly, such a caricatured Indian had nothing meaningful to say to modern America and was left behind along with Seton.[24] One might argue that Seton was not that irrelevant, as his ideas and programs were developed into the Boy Scouts and Girl Guides programs that White Canadian children still attend. I believe these are meaningful to White Canadians in that they can appropriate "Indian" identity without ever having to consider colonial history. However, the Indian remains shelved as a handy cultural curio, best if lagging behind a few centuries.

For the Native community, the image of the noble savage carries social, political, and intellectual consequences. Hanging on to Hiawatha in the face of everyday reality may paralyze and disorient contemporary youth, for how must they reconcile the repulsive, scalping savage with the gentle, generous, intuitively all-knowing Hiawatha in a postmodern society? Kateri Damm observes that "Indianness can be erased when the reality of Indigenous life confronts the fiction of the Indigenous stereotypes."[25] And as if all this is not enough, Native peoples must contend with non-Native Canadians who often express confusion or disappointment, even anger, when they must reconcile their stereotypic expectations with reality. Real Native peoples are measured against the noble savage. A number of Native humorists have, in fact, built their counter-discourse around satirical treatment of this experience (e.g., Basil Johnston, Emma Lee Warrior, Drew Hayden Taylor, Margo Kane, etc.).

But, as I have noted earlier, White disappointment can have more serious political implications. Daniel Francis recounts the poet Charles Mair's surprise at Treaty 8 negotiations in 1899 to find "commonplace men smoking briar-roots" instead of "the picturesque Red Man."[26] In the words of Mair, secretary to the Halfbreed Scrip Commission for northern Alberta: "there presented itself a body of respectable-looking men, as well dressed and evidently quite as independent in their feelings as any like number of average pioneers in the East.... One was prepared, in this wild region of forest, to behold some savage types of men; indeed, I craved to renew the vanished scenes of old. But alas! One beheld, instead, men with well-washed unpainted faces, and combed and common hair; men in suits of ordinary store-clothes, and even some with 'boiled' if not laundered shirts. One felt disappointed, even defrauded."[27]

Had Mair and his colleagues in the colonial offices in Ottawa expected to see what he, in fact, saw, common men similar to himself, might the outcome from treaties and Halfbreed scrips been entirely different? There is no doubt that Mair—or Mackenzie, Butler, McLean, Paul Kane, Edward Curtis, and numerous others at each epoch of contact—were expressing disappointment that they had not encountered the exotic savage they had been taught to imagine.

True, the noble savage has imbued our writers and even some scholars with a tradition of idealism. This in itself is not necessarily negative, but its influence on our reconstructions is evident. Native peoples have had to punctuate cultural differences to counter the portrayal of themselves as uncultured, unregulated savages. In this process of defending and repositioning, we have, inevitably perhaps, utopianized our culture(s). The noble savage has been an ideal image—and tool—for this pursuit. Again, this process has not necessarily been conscious; the enduring image has been there for us to internalize. Or to use as fodder for our art or research.

Writers and poets of different eras have not only drawn from romanticized images to shore up arguments that we were not savages. We have, perhaps irresistibly, built our inventions around them too. Perhaps more than any other writer, Duke Redbird has turned the Hiawathian vision of the pre-colonial Native into an art form. In fact, it became his signature poetry. Redbird's poetry, especially his early work, is replete with primitivist yearnings for his "moccasins" to have walked along "giant forest trees," for his hands to have "fondled the spotted fawn," or his eyes to have beheld "the golden rainbow of the north."[28] In the tradition of primitivism, Redbird often juxtaposes what is artificial with what is natural. In "I Am the Redman," Redbird poses as the "son of the forest, mountain and lake" or as "Son of the tree, hill and stream" and immediately—and contrapuntally—retorts after such lines, "What use have I of asphalt?" or "What use have I of china and crystal / What use have I of diamonds and gold?" Redbird ends this poem by not only challenging one of European's key posts of civilization, Christianity, but by submitting that the "white brother" can only be saved by "the red man's" nature-based spirituality.

> I am the redman
> Son of the earth and water and sky...
> What use have I of nylon and plastic?
> What use have I of your religion?
> Think you these be holy and sacred
> That I should kneel in awe?
> I am the redman
> I look at you white brother
> And I say to you
> Save not me from sin and evil,
> Save yourself.[29]

But there is much here other than primitivist yearning. There is, of course, resistance. And romanticism. And appealing poetry. But for Redbird I believe there is also a genuine philosophical declaration about the intrinsic value of cultures that respect the environment. And the fact that multimedia poet and activist Redbird (born as Gary Richardson, a metis of Ojibway and Irish parentage and a member of the Saugeen First Nation in Ontario) was fostered by a White middle-class urban family for many years seems to have influenced his vision for uncontaminated natural beauty and his criticism of the superfluous in White culture.

Native romanticism is more than an imitation of European primitivism. In the following poem from *My Heart Soars*, Chief Dan George uses words and imagery that might evoke a Hiawathian vision, yet he too is expressing something much deeper than a glorified version of his cultural background:

> I have known you
> when your forests were mine,
> when they gave me my meat
> and clothing
> I have known you
> in your streams
> and rivers
> where your fish flashed
> and danced in the sun,
> where the waters said come,
> come and eat of my abundance.
> I have known you
> in the freedom of our winds.
> And my spirit,
> like the winds,
> once roamed
> your good lands.[30]

At first glance, one might think Chief Dan George is also simply a romanticist in the tradition of Longfellow. His golden and graceful world does sparkle with gleaming streams and sun. Yet George, like most Native romantics, cannot be so easily dismissed. Though he too expresses gentle intimacy with nature, his pensive style is his way of talking back. Take, for example, another poem in which he indicates the pain of "no longer" having the beauty or agency of his culture:

> No longer
> can I give you a handful of berries as a gift,

> no longer
> are the roots I dig used as medicine,
> no longer
> can I sing a song to please the salmon,
> no longer
> does the pipe I smoke make others sit
> with me in friendship
> no longer
> does anyone want to walk with me to the
> blue mountain to pray,
> no longer
> does the deer trust my footsteps.[31]

Some might describe this poem as mere nostalgia or lament, but George is actually re-establishing the value of his world. He is, like Copway before him, staking out his culture as equal as (if not better than) the civilizer's. Like most Native romantics, he is using romanticization as a technique of resistance. Take, as another example, the following poem ("poem #10") by Rita Joe. Both in intent and content, this poem is even more reminiscent of Copway's "wide domain," which opened this chapter. By juxtaposing the glories of lands, seas, rivers, and scenery against "monuments and scrolls" (or, in the case of Copway, marbled palaces), the poet is both romantic and resistant:

> Aye! No monuments,
> No literature,
> No scrolls or canvas-drawn pictures
> Relate the wonders of our yesterday.
>
> How frustrated the searchings
> Of the educators.
> Let them find
> Land name
> Titles of seas,
>
> Rivers;
> Wipe them not from memory,
> These are our monuments.[32]

Rita Joe in *Poems of Rita Joe* places Mi'kmaq text alongside the English; by so doing she is also repositioning her culture as original and equal to the colonialists'. But there is another intriguing theme that runs through these works, and that is the theme of cultural tenacity. Rita Joe turns directly to "scholars"—scholars because they are the keepers of history and knowledge—

to remind them they will "find our art / in names and scenery / Betrothed to the Indian / since time began."[33] Similarly, Copway associates his universe with the sheltering forests. He points, defiantly, to the enduring qualities of Native culture: "Nature will be Nature still, while palaces shall decay and fall in ruins." "Yes," Copway exults, "Niagara will be Niagara a thousand years hence!"[34] And even though Chief Dan George can no longer give away berries, roots, or salmon, these body/spirit-nourishing essentials will remain. And through them the Natives' "bones," in Louise Halfe's profoundest sense, that is, of Native presence on this land,[35] will never vanish. However, a massive material portion of the Natives' lands did and continues to vanish. Even the most generous and optimistic of romantics "are bent low," in the poetic words of Redbird, with grief.

The noble savage has engendered tension between romance and reality. First, it is important to recall that some White Canadians in high places of power have contested Native peoples' claims to land as mere expressions of the noble savage. Doxtator, in *Fluffs and Feathers*, reminds us that Supreme Court of British Columbia's Chief Justice Allan McEachern, in his 1991 ruling against the Gitksan and Wet'suwet'en, discounted their testimonies regarding their close relationship to the land as nothing more than romanticization.[36] This is the very same judge (and case cited earlier) who also accused the Native claimants of being too brutish to have appreciated notions of delineated territories. Too savage or too noble—Aboriginal peoples cannot win. Even though his ruling was later overturned, it is frightening to what contradictions colonialists will go to entrench their material benefits.

However, it is the purview and craft of writers, even if colonized, to take poetic licence with words and metaphors. And just because they demonstrate, in style or in vision, a Hiawathian penchant, it does not in any way suggest that the *real* Natives' relationships to their lands are imaginary. The Native writers who use romantic tropes are also reflecting *real* aspects of their cultures (or desires for that culture as only peoples dispossessed or exiled within their own countries can desire), that is, attachments to their lands and land-based lifestyles. George Copway, Rita Joe, Chief Dan George—all are mourning the loss of their land-based cultures of which they had the privilege of experiencing. Those who did not have the experience of growing up on the land mourn the absence of such an experience and may tend to idealize both nature and Native peoples. The form and contents of their romanticism do raise important issues concerning the complexities of our identities and writing, but it cannot undermine the Native reclamation of lands. Many of us, myself included, did grow up in land-based *real* cultures—cultures which have suffered due to agricultural or urban encroachments and resource extractions (not to be confused with human development). Life is truly different when lived off and by the land and its resources. It was not from a place of pure fantasy that my favourite Marvel comic book was Longfellow's *Hiawatha* when I was a child. I could relate to the forest scenes as well as to the shape- and space-shifting mythical animals, characters, and ghosts. I also recognized words like *Nokomis*. In fact, of all the comics and schoolbooks I read then this comic-book version of the Hiawatha story was the only thing I could relate to!

Internalization of European-originated romantic traditions does present interesting challenges for us, even in scholarship. It bears on Native scholars as we seek to theorize our histories and identities for contemporary times. George Sioui, in *For An Amerindian Autohistory*, takes quite an unusual approach. Sioui, an historian of Huron heritage, argues that French romanticist Louis Armand Lahontan was not inventing but in fact explaining Native world views. That is, the noble savage was not constructed out of thin French air, it was founded on Native cultures. Sioui argues that historians must "rehabilitate" friendly European sources to get back to the "circle of life," that is, to Native social and moral ethics.[37] But more, he argues, such sources were based on objective assessments of Native thinking and values, and these values are very much extant. For this reason, Sioui believes historians must incorporate the "vigour of the Amerindian conscience" in their works, they must turn to Native traditions (and traditionalists) and to Native people for a "proper understanding" of Native history.[38] Sioui refers to this as "Amerindian autohistory." He explains, "if no fair or satisfactory historical evaluation seems to have come from the outside (heterohistory), the only remaining source is autovision or autohistory."[39]

It is true that Native ethics and epistemologies were grounded in a moral understanding of the human relationship to the universe (all of which is difficult to translate into English). But Sioui's thesis is at times obscure, especially when he turns to the issue of historical methodology. For example, it is not at all clear whether he is espousing a division of labour between White and Native (or Huron?) historians when he argues that Amerindian history "should be based on a delimitation and recognition of its ideological territory and its particular philosophy."[40] The thesis is most clear as an idealized vision: "The goal of Amerindian autohistory is to assist history in its duty to repair the damage it has traditionally caused to the integrity of Amerindian cultures."[41]

Sioui's proposal is appealing; particularly, his call for "an ethical approach to history." Nor can I argue with his reasoning that "all written data that have been used by the dominant society so far to 'write the history of the Amerindian' should be revised and reinterpreted."[42] But I have difficulty with his idealization of what he calls his "ideological portrait of Amerindians," especially to the extent the portrait resembles the noble savage. I have difficulty with the use of the noble savage, whether the symbol was constructed by Europeans or Natives, as some kind of final authority on the Native "moral code." Also, Sioui's movement between the era of Lahontan and that of contemporary Native elders requires some imagination. Sioui does make an interesting, if not optimistic, argument for a "rehabilitation" of friendly European sources, which should be applied to historiography. After all, unfriendly sources have long been applied, why not friendly ones? Still, as we reconstruct our histories, must we again go back to Adario, the seventeeth-century Tionontati chief, or to Hiawatha?

There is tremendous pressure today for all Native artists and intellectuals to produce works expressly and manifestly different from the dominant culture. In a continuing attempt to find a culture unspoiled by contact, difference has been fetishized, so much so that a notion of the authentic necessarily different (or alternative) native is very much in vogue. This puts Aboriginal peoples in an untenable situation: we are wrapped in stereotypes and yet are generally expected to exude "uncontaminated" indigenity. We are expected not only to produce "authentic" material (notice the pressure for Native scholars to do "traditional epistemologies," now "Indigenous Knowledge", to validate any and all research through "elders," to hire staff in Native Studies through the blessings of "the community"—whoever or whatever that is—or to write poetry in syllabics), but even to look authentically different![43] In this respect, very little has changed since the days of Pauline Johnson. Marilyn Dumont chides against universalizing "one experience of nativeness and calls for attention to "a multiplicity of experiences out there that go on being ignored because they do not fit a popular understanding of culture, but which have to be expressed because their denial by the image making machine is another kind of colonialism."[44]

Authenticity, Cultural Difference, and the Noble Savage

There is a deep, convoluted, and abiding connection between notions of Native cultural difference and the noble savage. To go back to the land issue, our intimate connection to the landscape and its ecology did and does make a difference in our world views and arrangement of knowledge. Native peoples' relationship to the land is different from capitalistic and legal notions of use and occupancy of land. As noted earlier, anthropologist Robin Ridington provides evidence that suggests the difference is much more profound than has been appreciated. Of course, this is what Native intellectuals have long been impressing. Jeannette Armstrong has perhaps said it best; in an essay "Land Speaking," she simply offers, like a gift to us:

> As I understand it from my Okanagan ancestors, language was given to us by the land we live within ... I have heard elders explain that the language changed as we moved and spread over the land through time. My own father told me that it was the land that changed the language because there is special knowledge in each different place. All my elders say it is land that holds all knowledge of life and death and is a constant teacher...We survived and thrived by listening intently to its teachings—to its language—and then inventing human words to retell its stories to our succeeding generations. It is the land that speaks.[45]

As one who grew up with Cree and with the land, I think I "know" this land. As Metis from northern Alberta, my family does not legally own the land I grew up on, but the land, if it belongs to anyone, belongs to my Plains Cree-Metis ancestors and family. My bones have known this land long before Alberta was born. My younger brother has lovingly tended to this land since the passing of our parents. There is a blueberry patch there that I especially love; when I go there I experience that particular land; I hear it speaking with the luminosity of blueberries in September sun embraced in sunlit green of gently waving poplar leaves. And I remember too why bears and panthers still prowl through my dreams. The land feeds us, sings to us, gives us light—but it also steals us away from this earth. The land does teach us about life and death. This is all true; this is not poetic waxing. This is the romantic tradition I speak of; it is based from the land speaking, to reiterate Jeannette Armstrong's language. The Ojibway too settled on lands that gave off light. Richard Wagamese's "quality of light" in his novels comes from his Ojibway lands. But (and alas), to come back to bald English: it is not just about living off the land; it is about a whole way of perceiving, practising, and connecting language, land, knowledge, skill, and spirituality, and human-nature relationships from our land-based cosmologies. If "cultural difference" has any meaning, it lies here.

But now it is a difference that has obviously been compounded by dispossession and repeated geographical and cultural dislocations. Even so, land remains central to Aboriginal ethos, even to those who are distanced from it. Here, some might interject that Whites too love their lands. There is no question they do. We would not here be discussing dispossession otherwise.

Of course, people love land (or home) in myriad ways. But "love" is not just about attitudes and sentiments, it is about who ends up with the actual land mass with its enormous resources. Further, *how* we understand and approach this difference is made complex by prevailing uses of the noble savage, uses that have confused both Native and non-Native peoples.

It is a layered and vicious circle. The stereotype holds that Indians were primitive, and, as such, their cultures were infantile and fixed, or frozen in time or outside time. The underlying assumption and the logical outcome of ossifying Native society is that if Native people change, the Indian will vanish! Seen this way, an archiving mentality becomes crucial. This is partly why museums have gone so far as to collect and display skeletal remains of the Native dead. For the colonized Native world, "archiving" (meant poetically here) is reflected in the sacralization of the old and anyone who represents the past. Such sacralizing is born from and leads back to the conclusion that only old people know anything "real" or "authentic" about Native culture. Authenticity has been virtually restricted to "elders" and "traditions." There is nothing intrinsically wrong with culture-building elders or tradition. The issue is how these concepts get stereotyped and how they get played out in real-life circumstances, such as in government policies, legislation, education, or health, or in our textbooks and theatres. The point to authenticity and cultural difference is that Native identity has been consigned forever to the past. Hence, much confusion and some division in our ranks. Besides the horrifying genocidal implications of being mummified, we have become entrenched in new ways as the Other by the uncomprehending, the very thing we have fought to overcome.

And, when taken to extremes, cultural romanticization can lead to fundamentalism, even jingoism.[46] This, in turn, can lead right to where the colonizers would want us to remain: benign stereotypes. Internalizing the noble savage makes us even more benign. Can the noble savage have a revolution? Is the noble savage even allowed to resist? It might be that romanticism (especially when mixed with essentialist spirituality and nativism) blocks a consciousness required for decolonization and material resistance. Howard Adams, who wrote much on the "ossification of native society," insists that Aboriginal peoples dispel stereotypes and "destroy all encrustations of colonial mentality that repress them."[47]

Authenticity demands we be "different," but if our difference is defined outside ourselves, be it legislatively or socially imposed, or if our difference is restricted to the prehistoric past, such a difference is not ours! Whose interest does it serve that we be different? Are we that different? More to the point, why should we be different (in that colonial sense)? Surely, after 500 years, we might have significant cultural similarities. James Axtell, Jack Weatherford, and Francis Jennings, among others, have noted the significant cultural exchange that took place between Europeans and indigenous peoples—something indigenous peoples have known all along. There is also the problem of restricting Aboriginal rights to cultural difference or tradition. Courts have already tried to restrict land claims to "traditional use" of resources. What if we were not different but still original to this land?[48] What is the colonizer's agenda for keeping us different? We must here recall Memmi's observation: "Colonial racism is built from three major ideological components: one, the gulf between the culture of the colonialist and the colonized; two, the exploitation of these differences for the benefit of the colonialist; three, the use of these supposed differences as standards of absolute fact."[49]

In this context, cultural difference is a veiled way of pandering to "racial difference." Since the idea and language of racial difference is no longer considered academically or politically respectable, the economics of adopting the cultural difference vocabulary is apparent. It also affords the colonizer the room to exploit Native culture(s) for economic, entertainment and even spiritual purposes, which serve as the basis for real estate, Hollywood, tourism, the New Age, art and literature (of any genre), and even, to a large extent, scholarship. And it affords the colonized to talk back and to manoeuvre.

Cultural Difference and Criticism

Colonization has produced this vicious circle. By disempowering and dehumanizing Native peoples, it has put them in a reactive and resistance situation. Idealization is a reflection of internalizing the colonizer's images and standards, but it is just as often a resistance declaration. What is even more interesting, not all romanticism is without foundation. Native peoples do have romantic traditions indigenous to themselves. Further, and more recently, the Native emphasis on cultural difference reflects a strategic decolonizing response to the problem of Western intellectual dominance, particularly to the problem of "the universal." As Ashcroft, Griffiths, and Tiffin explain,

> The idea of "post-colonial literary theory" emerges from the inability
> of European theory to deal adequately with the complexities and
> varied cultural provenance of post-colonial writing. European theo-
> ries themselves emerge from particular cultural traditions which
> are hidden by false notions of "the universal." Theories of style
> and genre, assumptions about the universal features of language,
> epistemologies and value systems are all radically questioned by
> the practices of post-colonial writing. Post-colonial theory has

produced from the need to address this different practice. Indigenous theories have developed to accommodate the differences within the various cultural traditions as well as the desire to describe in a comparative way the features shared across those traditions.[50]

Native peoples, in particular, have developed (and are still developing) a profile of "difference," especially emphasizing the beautiful natural land and lifestyle, languages, values, spirituality, holistic world views, egalitarian organizational structures, and even a different sense of time and space. It is here that many cultural diagrams in tabulated form are constructed. Well-intentioned charts comparing Native and White values have become popular in a wide variety of settings including social work, education, medical, and legal communities.[51] From this comes the monolithic Indian whose cardboard culture can be unfolded something akin to a DNA structure through which White and "Red" cultural traits are contrasted. Whites are materialistic, Reds spiritual; Whites are linear, Reds circular; Whites are individualistic, Reds tribal. Whites are patriarchal, Reds blur with "Mother Earth." Is this not some modification of the civ/sav construct? Such dichotomization of cultural difference is one small step away from racializing difference. In colonial discourse, racial or genetic notions are often veiled as cultural. Moreover, such binary essentialisms leads us back to the very stereotypes from which they come, the very stereotypes we are resisting. The influence of these constructs is evident in our works and responses, much of it being presented in terms of "tradition" or simply reduced into one blurried "Native culture."

What is of particular interest to me is where and how cultural differences have been worked out by both Native and non-Native literary writers and critics. Native writers have naturally been in the process of "seeking a critical center," as phrased by Native American critic Kimberly M. Blaeser.[52] However, in our efforts to define our centre, we can see the pull of colonialist definitions. Here, too, has been emerging a profile of Native culture (as if there is only one) as "tribal" (the term used in the United States) or "collective" (the Canadian term), featuring themes of tradition, Trickster, land, mother, and the circle. These presumed features are typically juxtaposed against Western culture, itself catalogued as individualistic, commercial, progressive, patriarchal, and linear. Perhaps some of this is unavoidable as most of us—Native and non-Native, critic or writer—have had to work within these headings. And some of it may even be true. But many of the assumptions have been treated as, in the words of Memmi, "absolute truth." In fact, they present us with interesting sets of problems, especially as have been treated under cultural studies.

"Cultural studies," an argumentative and burgeoning phenomenon in literary studies that has emphasized cultural differences, was meant to free the colonized from Western hegemonies, both in cultural and critical modes.[53] With respect to Native peoples, applying "cultural studies" to Native literary works poses problems similar to that of applying "cross-cultural" methodologies in historical works. I am thinking of the neo-cross-cultural approach adopted by Native specialist geographers, anthropologists, and historians from about the 1960s to the 1980s (see, for example, the work of A.G. Bailey, Cornelius Jaenen, Bruce Trigger, Jennifer Brown, Sylvia Van Kirk). This approach tended to qualify most data, be it theoretical or descriptive, with anthropological explanations and microscopic examination. Scholars working within this approach tended to frame all things Native in typical terms of "cultural differences" or "traditions." Compared to earlier racist material, this was, of course, a much-improved approach to Native history. And with greater awareness, there is greater improvement. But I doubt that these scholars were thinking of a Native readership. The fact is, ethnological descriptions often have a distancing effect between the describer and the described. The manner of delivering what I call "cultural tidbits," such as providing excessive detail on the most ordinary occurrences, or applying functionalist interpretation to the smallest item or gesture, objectifies the people or thing described. This process results in othering the very people the researcher is trying to make understandable to his or her audience.

Obviously, audience reception depends on the audience. The Native audience finds ethnological objectification irritating and alienating. Deborah Doxtator in *Fluffs and Feathers* finds that "Indians are perceived to have culture, not history," and "'Culture' can be presented as anonymous, almost divorced completely from real human beings. In contrast, Whites are taken to have history, and 'History' involves the actions of actual named individuals." It is not "unusual," she explains, for museums to "focus on presenting ethnographic 'pre-contact', 'Native culture' in ways that are perceived inappropriate for displaying Canadian history."[54] Not all ethnological studies or displays fall into the distancing mode, but many do. Because Native peoples are often approached as cultural entities vastly and mysteriously different from Whites, there is a tendency to treat both Aboriginal history and contemporary cultural productions only or largely as ethnological expressions. To Doxtator, academic disciplines "still have great difficulty accepting Indian art, history, literature, music and technology as art, history, music and technology without first placing it in an anthropological context."[55]

This leads us to the question of what constitutes literature, as opposed to, say, anthropology. And it takes us to the question of how Native writing should be reviewed or analyzed. Naturally, culture is always with us and in us; but ethnology and ideology have so pervaded literary criticism that the human personality has been forgotten, especially in the study of Native fiction. I am arguing for "common humanity" here. There is, obviously, tension between keeping a wary eye on Western universalization, on the one hand, and, on the other hand, applying ethnology ("cultural difference") to what is discernibly human in Native literary presentations.

Apparently reflecting on this matter of common humanity vis-à-vis cultural difference, Victor J. Ramraj, editor of *Concert of Voices: An Anthology of World Writing in English*, prefaces the anthology with this explanation:

> despite historical and cultural specificities (the focus of cross-cultural and multicultural studies), commonalities and affinities exist among these writings and between writings on both sides of the hegemonic divide.

> The colonial-imperial, marginal-central binary informs much of the writings of this linguistic community but it is not the exclusive or overriding preoccupation of the writers. They do not confine themselves to political and ideological issues or subsume beneath them other geneses and dimensions or experiences of love, ambition, resentment, envy, generosity, anger, and the range of responses that make humans human. To do this would be to simplify and falsify their complex lives. Moreover, to trace all experiences to hegemonic politics is to deny individuals and communities agency and responsibility for their own fates.[56]

In the case of Native literary works, I am arguing for the common sense to recognize the almost infinite range of human experience and expression. Consideration of the cultural context to any work is of course basic, no less so in the treatment of Native writing. But should not a literary review concern itself primarily with the psychology or individuality of Native characters, rather than, say, viewing Native feelings or behaviour as evidence of some cultural reflex? Critics reach for cultural explanations in works or themes that may not necessitate anthropological assistance. Reviewers are often in search of some generalized cultural pattern or pathos when they could be interested in uniqueness. Because of the overwhelming history of misrepresentation, *it is particularly crucial that what is unique about a Native person or persons is recognized*. In other words, the focus on presumed cultural differences between the Native and the re-settler has much potential to lose sight of Natives as not only uniquely human individuals within and among each other, but also as culturally (and in many other ways) different from each other. Relegating Native literature to ethnological and political analysis (or to trauma and healing studies, as is now becoming vogue) can keep us continuously unidimensional and on the margins. And othered. These are not the only options available to us as writers and critics.

However, before I can move on here, I need to bring in the other critical tool that has been used with respect to treating Native writing, a tool I have myself employed, but one that can also produce generalizations. Linked closely to cultural studies is the new awareness by Canadian literary specialists that, yes, along with cultural awareness, historical awareness is also important. Since the 1980s those specializing in (or making forays into) Native writing have acknowledged the influence and role of colonization in Aboriginal history and culture. This, in itself, has been an important recognition by writers and critics alike, but again, political interpretations have tended to submerge literary concerns and individual uniqueness. Similar in consequence to the ethnological typecastings, these ideologically driven political readings produce a lumping effect. Once again, "natives" (or Indigenes, or Aboriginals) are generalized as a mass, and "mass-ness" is a sore subject, one may say, to Native peoples.

Native writers, after all, are attempting to undo more than 500 years of caricatures by replacing the stereotypes with "real" human personalities. But it is impossible to deal with anything human without reference to culture or historical experience. It should go without saying that Aboriginal cultures are, of course, real, and they are in many fundamental respects (but not totally) different from Western culture(s). Native peoples carry within them centuries of cultural ethos, and, to the extent that they are alive and relate to each other, they have living cultures. Peter Puxley makes this same point in the context of Dene development by defining culture as "what people do together," encompassing a "total" range of expressions that define their political, linguistic, and cultural place in Canada.[57] Aboriginal peoples' cultures are real; they do not have to be "different" (especially visibly or ceremonially) to know this. Inescapably, Native writers, like all other writers, have to contextualize their cultural and political lives. Clearly, the issue is not whether we should refer to our cultures, or histories, or our contemporary lives, the issue is *how* this is done and, equally, how this is *received* and addressed.

The Problem of Audience

On the issue of audience, Native writers are confronted with a double-headed problem. Neither the White nor the Native audience has yet received Native writers and intellectuals in adequate ways. Marlene Nourbese Philips writes, "no work is in any full practical sense produced unless it is also received."[58] In many important ways, Native writers are without an audience. If White audiences have misunderstood and stereotyped us, Native audiences have been virtually non-existent. Although there has been noticeable and positive movement on these issues on both sides, the White audience is still considerably undereducated with respect to the key issues of Native cultures and political realities. For example, even when Native productions are (or could be) free of stereotypes, non-Native audiences may not, or cannot, catch the nuances, languages, specific cultural symbols, myths, or legends in many Native works. And this is so, not because we are so "remarkably" different that the "normal" reader cannot fathom us, or because the White reader is ill-intentioned, but because this readership is systemically miseducated about who contemporary Native peoples are. Concerning political facts, while there is a growing appreciation of the Native political experience, audiences, especially that of Euro-Canadians, may not yet or ever fully appreciate or accept the socio-political and cultural ramifications of acknowledging colonial consequences that implicate them.

The Native audience is also largely uneducated, but about different things. In the first instance, phonetic literacy in the English language is still an issue for Native peoples. Among the consequences of our alienation from the dominant Canadian educational system are the gaps in our knowledge about Western culture, especially the more esoteric aspects, such as the organization of history, the rise and fall of ideologies, philosophies, or schools of criticism. Conceptualizing and focussing on "great" men is quite alien to the majority of Native peoples (as I am sure it is for other Canadians too). So are literary events. Only a minority of Native people busy themselves with such "uneveryday" concerns. The large Native attendance at the annual Aboriginal Achievement Awards is exceptional. In any event, going to hear poets and other writers is still unfamiliar to many Native peoples for both cultural and economic reasons. In a certain sense, all Canadian writers face the problem of finding an audience, but all the more so for Native writers. As may be appreciated, factors such as these present special challenges for Native intellectuals and artists. While we are growing as a community, we are still small. And we are still getting acquainted with each other.

But happily, some things have changed with respect to our intellectual and personal engagements with each other since Harmut Lutz's interviews with eighteen Native writers in the 1991 book, *Contemporary Challenges: Coversations with Canadian Native Authors.* The Native academics, cultural critics, poets, and novelists Lutz interviewed were reluctant to notice each other. Only in response to his prodding did the interviewees refer to other Native writers, and those who did tended to go over the same authors (e.g.,

Jeannette Armstrong, Maria Campbell, Tomson Highway, Lee Maracle) and issues (e.g., appropriation, storytelling, oral traditions) that non-Native critics had highlighted. Some even admitted they were not familiar with Native literature, and some were not familiar with even the "big" names in Native literature. And no one made any evaluative comments about the aesthetic quality of Native works.

Today, there are a growing number of Aboriginal literary scholars, critics, and writers whose works have generated intellectual excitement and critical respect from both Aboriginal and non-Aboriginal thinkers. Yet Native intellectuals still face an uphill battle on a number of fronts. Largely due to scarcity in emotional and material resources, both personal and collective, we have not built effective or sustained means of communicating, publishing, advocating, or conferring. The work that has been done is considerable and, in general, quite stunning, but it remains specialized and, in the scheme of things, small.

Is there any basis of dialogue other than the usual havens of cultural and political representations? The overpowering, grinding dominance of the colonial machine constantly puts us (all of us) in a reactive situation. It might be understandable that some people would confuse stereotyped cultural difference as decolonization. Laura Groening in *Old Woman Speaks* confirms that even the best-intentioned Canadian writers continue to fall into formulated portrayals and characterizations. She, too, directs critics to turn to Aboriginal writers for direction. As I argue in the next chapter, it is possible to critically read Native works, taking into consideration their respective cultural and political contexts without compromising their humanity, that is, those aspects such as individuality that make us uniquely human.

I began this chapter with questions about our reconstruction. I end with one of the clearest descriptions of what this entails, at least for the potlatch peoples of the northwest coast who had encounters with "White people" such as Captain Vancouver, Edward Curtis, Franz Boas, and the infamous potlatch-hating Indian agent William Halliday. In a lovely overview of her people's experience, "From Colonization to Repatriation," Gloria Cranmer Webster addresses "some criticism" that potlatches today are not like they were "in the old days." But "how could they be?" she asks, then sets out to explain such changes as financing and record keeping, arguing that, in each case, the people have found a way to maintain continuity:

> There is no longer the system of loans with which to finance a potlatch. As the old people say, "Now, a man just puts his hand in his own pockets to pay for it." Today, we write out names and dances, because there are no longer recordkeepers as there were in the old days who

could keep all this information in their minds. We videotape potlatches these days.... If a culture is alive, it does not remain static.
Ours is definitely alive and changes as the times require.

We do not have a word for repatriation in the Kwak'wala language.
The closest we come to it is the word *u'mista*, which describes the
return of people taken captive in raids. It also means the return
of something important. We are working towards the *u'mista* of
much that was lost to us. The return of the potlatch collection is one
u'mista. The renewed interest among younger people in learning
about their cultural history is a kind of *u'mista*. The creation of a
new ceremonial gear to replace that held by museums is yet another
u'mista. We are taking back, from many sources, information about
our culture and our history, to help us rebuild our world which was
almost shattered during the bad times. Our aim is the complete
u'mista or repatriation of everything we lost when our world was
turned upside down, as our old people say. The *u'mista* of our lands
is part of our goal and there is some urgency to it.... While the
white people celebrate Columbus's five hundredth anniversary, we
celebrate our survival in spite of everything that has happened to us
since the water people first came to this continent.[59]

Native peoples in real life are going about reconstructing their lives and
communities, pushing paradigms long before we can write our novels and poems, or our dissertations. This process is infinitely more subtle and interesting
than any caricatures, tropes, allegories, arguments, dogmas, or speculations
we theorists may try to sort out.

Chapter Seven

Native Writers Reconstruct: Pushing Paradigms

Wake up. All the shadows are gone. There is daylight, even in the
swamps. The blue jays are laughing.... Laughing at the humans who
don't know the sun is up and it's a new day.

—Jeannette Armstrong,
Whispering in Shadows[1]

Situating Aboriginal articulation, or, as I prefer, talk-back, within postcolonial
intellectual development has proven useful, but since much of postcolonial
discourse centres on issues of culture and politics, these conceptual tools have
their own limitations. Among the issues that have come under scrutiny are
the excessive use of postmodern philosophy in literary criticism, universalization of cultural diversity, and poststructuralist deconstructions that threaten
indigenous identities. Furthermore, postcolonial criticism is charged with
treating indigenous writers and themes within dominantly Western modes
and countries. How then might we break through the seeming impasses of
Western cultural dominance?

We must keep sight of our principal task, which is the humanization of
Native peoples. This is more of a challenge than we may at first imagine be-
cause Native history and cultures have for so long been encased in stereotypes.
How do we deal with *real* Native cultures and political actions, indispensable

to human agency, without resorting to ethnological or political pigeon-holing? Or to any other sort of neo-master narrative?

And on whom does the task of deconstruction and reconstruction fall? I believe this task must be shared by all Canadians, by all intellectuals, Native and non-Native alike. Of course, we will come at this from a number of different perspectives, but the common goal must be the dislodging of racist material and the continuing development of works that promote Native decolonization. And it must be done in every field and area of study, though perhaps such a task might be most effective through literary means. As one who has taught both Native and White history and literature for more than three decades, I have certainly observed that students and other audiences (both Native and non-Native) respond to creative literature more openly than to history or theoretical discourses. For all its potential abuses, literature may still offer the best avenue through which we can convey Native humanity. I must be an optimist.

In this chapter I turn to Native literary expression in two novels in order to explore further how we might come to understand the "humanization" of Native characters. We come back to the question: what does make us human? To such a fundamental question I hope that no one ever thinks there are pure or ultimate answers to be found, be they Western or non-Western, theological or theoretical. Nonetheless, given the massive Native response to dehumanization that rings out across the centuries, this is a question particularly significant in the context of this study.

Both *Slash* (1985) by Jeannette Armstrong and *Honour the Sun* (1987) by Ruby Slipperjack have received substantial, though uneven, critical attention. Almost every academic who does Native literary criticism has pored over one or both of these novels.[2] Not surprisingly, there is considerable overlapping of analysis and argumentations—many of them extraordinarily perceptive and intellectually vibrant—and any new treatment runs the risk of redundancy. I revisit these novels *not* for the sake of literary criticism per se, but to show the intersection of issues and problems that confront us in the study of Native resistance discourse.

These two novels approach virtually everything differently, and their differences bring to relief many of the issues discussed in the previous chapters. Interestingly, *Slash* has received wider critical (particularly postcolonial and feminist)[3] attention than *Honour the Sun*, even though *Honour the Sun* is quintessentially female-centred in comparison to *Slash*.

Jeannette Armstrong is an internationally renowned writer and activist educated both in the ways of her Okanagan linguistic and cultural heritage and in Western schooling and culture. Perhaps best known for *Slash*, her first novel, Armstrong has published a second novel, *Whispering in Shadows*, co-edited anthologies, and written poetry, children's literature, social criticism, and instructional material. She is founder and director of the En'owkin International School of Writing and Visual Arts in Penticton, British Columbia. She is a frequent lecturer in literary, educational, and environmentalist circles, and continues to be an active advocate of indigenous rights. She always greets other Native writers and orators with open arms. Her soft-spoken ways belie her tough and unrelenting criticism of Western colonial history, culture, and literature.

Ruby Slipperjack is an Ojibway woman from Ontario who is obviously well versed in Ojibway ways of the Canadian Shield as well as in the Canadian mainstream system of schooling. In addition to *Honour the Sun*, Slipperjack has subsequently published four books, *Silent Words*, *Weesquachak and the Lost Ones*, *Little Voice*, and *Dog Tracks*. She is a visual artist, as well. Approachable and generous of spirit, Slipperjack prefers to stay out of political forays but sees and says much through her gentle and perceptive sense of humour. She completed her doctoral studies in (Native) education and literature and is chair of the Department of Indigenous Learning at Lakehead University.

There are many significant differences between these two writers. They come from very different languages, cultures, and geographical regions of Canada. Naturally, their differences are reflected in their works. Their main characters, Armstrong's Slash and Slipperjack's Owl, provide us with two quite dissimilar presentations of what, in the final analysis, is a common colonial experience.

Tommy Kelasket, or Slash, begins his journey in his close-knit Okanagan home in British Columbia. He grows up on a ranch in a well-integrated, functioning, caring home where parents work hard and take care of their children. Okanagan culture and language provide the ground of Slash's being. Everyone who is important to him speaks the original language, recites Okanagan myths and legends, stays connected to the land in the original ways, and eats home-cooked meals made in the original recipes.

Slash is a relatively happy boy until he goes to the town school. It is here that his safe and harmonious world slowly unravels as he is confronted with an alien language, colonial history, and everyday racism from his White classmates and teachers.[4] Slash cannot make sense of his world; he looks at Jimmy, his boyhood friend and cousin, who has aspired to gain White middle-class status. He is not impressed (nor, in the end, is Jimmy). On the other hand, he cannot integrate his early childhood life (or "traditions," as some would be tempted to say) with town life. Nothing that his parents or old Prac-wa, the apparent elder of his community, taught him can help him out in his new tough world.

Tommy, at the age of eighteen, gets his nickname Slash as a result of a violent incident during one of his alcohol-dazed bouts. For this he is imprisoned. Interestingly, it is in prison he meets Mardi, a young activist who directs him towards political involvement.[5] Slash joins her, moving from sit-in to sit-in across the United States and Canada. Slash, however, finds no peace here, and after Mardi dies (political assassination is intimated), Slash slides into a roller-coaster world of drinking and again finds himself in prison. Again, it is in prison that Slash finds another alternative, this time Native traditions.[6]

Towards the end of the novel, Slash finally figures things out—at least for himself. Tired of political rhetoric that never seems to make any changes, tired of his hateful feelings and confusion, and just plain tired, Slash goes back home to find himself, this time to stay. Though much had changed while he had been gone (his parents also succumb to a bout of drinking after his brother dies, but regain their composure after his father suffers a heart attack), Slash finds calm in Native spirituality, and in a family of his own. He and his wife, though, come to very different conclusions about political differences within the Status Indian community. He chooses to stay home and use his language and his land while his wife continues to attend meetings on the repatriation of the Canadian constitution. The novel abruptly ends on a jarring note of personal despair (his young wife dies in a car crash en route to a political rally—which can be taken to mean that roads to ideology lead to death) with a hazy intimation of promise for the future through his little son.

Honour the Sun is told through the eyes of Owl, a ten-year-old girl who records her life with a series of seasonal journal entries beginning in "Summer 1962" when she is ten and ending in "Summer 1968" when she is sixteen and leaving home and community. More than three-quarters of the novel is given to Owl's perspective as a ten-year-old. Owl's community is a small Ojibway (non-Status and non-reserve) village somewhere along the CNR rail line cutting through the Canadian Shield in northern Ontario. Her home, located near a lake and close to the railroad, is a cabin full of lively children (siblings, cousins, half-siblings) overseen by her somewhat gruff but kind and capable mother. On one level, there is a sense of the ordinary throughout, as can be gleaned from some of the titles of her journal entries: Blueberry Days, Ordinary Days, Camping, Gathering Firewood, Spring Time, Dog Days, Just Tagging Along, or Christmas at Home. And just as the titles suggest, much of the book is given to the everyday events as experienced by the preteen girl.[7] Such events include being teased by her boy cousins, being tricked into chewing snuff, the excitement of going to school for the first time, affection for their dog Rocky, affection for her family, sibling rivalry, and so forth. When recording these, Slipperjack writes with a wonderful sense of humour and warmth. There is a constant sense of adventure and delight in Owl's childhood days.

Yet there is nothing "ordinary" about Owl's life when compared to, say, a middle-class White girl growing up in a Canadian town or city. Among other things, Owl practically lives outdoors. Her family's life generally revolves around the outdoors whether playing, working, or travelling. Indeed, Owl and her family often canoe to an island where the family goes "camping," that is, practise their land-based way of life that includes picking berries and fishing. And sadly, sometimes hiding. This island becomes a source of her family's' sustenance as well as sanctuary from those end-of-the-month drinking sprees that bring out the violence and pain in her community.[8]

The two characters, both young, share in their frustration concerning the environment around them, an environment that closes in on them and over which they, as youngsters, have no control. But there are significant differences in the treatment of these two characters. For one thing, the surroundings are different. What closes in on Slash is the encounter with the world outside, the school, the town, the federal and even internal politics. Slash responds by unravelling, hitting rock bottom, then eventually comes home to his land, his family, his spirituality. What closes in on Owl is her own home and community, specifically the aptly named John Bull, a village predator who shoots innocent pets and bursts in on Owl's family and mother in the middle of the night.[9] And as Owl grows up into her teens, boys her age bewilder her and make her claustrophobic. As does her mother's capitulation to drinking, a capitulation that leaves Owl angry, frightened, and lonely.[10] Owl, resolving to be free of drunks, grabby guys, and physical intimidation, finds in residential schooling an avenue of escape from an intolerable homelife and community. Rather than a valorization of residential schools, her choice is an indictment of what colonization has wrought—to so unglue communities and fragment families, forcing the young to run—even to such unholy places as residential schools. It is not clear whether Owl knows how painful the experience of residential school could be, but for her this is the only way out. She does come back, but, unlike Slash, she does not stay. She does, though, intimate that the values her mother taught her, the value of "honouring the sun," that is, the gift of life, every morning, no matter how drastic and desperate the night, will stay with her no matter where she travels.[11]

There are other important differences between these novels. Coming from opposite ends of the country's geography and landscape, with unrelated linguistic families and cultures, the two characters obviously experience and respond to their worlds quite uniquely. And, of course, the authors have very distinct styles of writing and aesthetics. *Slash* is rather full of Slash's inner chatter and academic-sounding lectures on the various causes and consequences of colonization. There is virtually no humour in this work, nor is there much, if any, sense of innocence. Owl's journal entries and her numerous adventures full of funny twists make *Honour the Sun* a most readable novel. Even through the darkest moments there is a lilt that does not go away until Owl's mother starts drinking.[12] One does wonder, though, whether this is meant to show Owl's innocence or is reflective of Slipperjack's own innocence.

While Owl's individuality stands out, Slipperjack does in fact provide numerous clues as to Owl's cultural background. But the matter-of-factness with which she presents the story is, I think, the crux of her unstereotypical style. It allows the humanness of the character to develop without compromising the context. The context is there for anyone to see. There is her playground: the landscape of the Canadian Shield; there is her land-based life: the blueberry picking, the fishing, and the many resource capabilities of her family; there is her social organization: her mother the matriarch, the extended family; there are the myths, the language, the humour (in Ojibway, as Owl notes in one brief acknowledgement). And there are the clues of colonization: the alcohol, the railroad, the church, the day school on the reserve and the residential school far away, the hospital far away, the male violence. And yes, there are the cultural differences implied between Native and White communities, such as when the children think the White teacher had "lost it" by bringing a spruce tree into the classroom—and watch with astonishment and some delight as the teacher transforms it into a glittering Christmas tree.[13] Apparently, a Christmas tree was alien to Owl's cultural background, but just as obviously, and perhaps more significantly, Ojibway children, like all children, can find delight and wonder in Christmas glitter. In other words, acknowledgement of cultural differences cannot preclude appreciation of our humanity, however "common" it may be.

But is there not also a sense of naïvité here? Slipperjack does point to cultural and political differences, but never in terms of resistance or conflict, always in terms of simple fact. Can we rest with that? Perhaps Lutz is considering this when he suggests to Slipperjack that she, despite her claim that she [does not] "go to stridently political books that come with an open message, or preach," was in fact political, especially in her "strong statement about violence against women and children."[14] To this, Slipperjack answers, quite unguardedly opening herself up to postcolonial overconcern about essentialism: "Well, it says, 'this is how I feel… this is what is happening around me' and 'this is how I am reacting'…. This is where it stops. I cannot tell you why this and this and that happens; you figure it out yourself." Slipperjack goes on to suggest that she uses the theme of the child to create a common ground of experience: "The child has memory of creation.... That is one thing we all have in common, and I think that is one way that we can all communicate.... We all have that one thread that connects us all to creation."[15]

Armstrong, on the other hand, explains to Lutz that she "wanted a tool to use in education" in order to deal with a particularly significant historical period. But she did not want to restrict her writing to historical documentation, she wanted to go "beyond that" to convey "the feeling of what happened during that militancy period," especially "the spirit of the people, and the rise, and the groundswelling and *how* that occurred, what the people were feeling, what they dreamed, and what their pain and joy were at the time."[16] Accordingly, Armstrong created in Slash a composite character through what is, in effect, an historical novel.

However, Armstrong, aware that *Slash* has received criticism for its lack of character development, explains that she "couldn't isolate the character and keep the character in isolation from the development of the events in the community, and the whole of the people. And I know! I took creative writing, so I know what I should have been doing, but I know what I couldn't do and make the story for my people."[17]

Armstrong explains she had to convey Slash's "connectedness to his family, his friends, his people, and to the outer world always entered in.... More than Slash as a person." She continues,

> The character development of the people around him, the pieces of character that come in and to, are all part of his character development.... And looking at it from my point of view as a writer, it can't be any other way! With Native people it can't be any other way. That's how we are as a people.... And if I hadn't presented it that way in the novel, it wouldn't have been readable for our people, or it wouldn't have been real or truthful. Because as I was saying it's difficult for us to look at things in a separate way. Everything is part of something else. Everything is a part of a continuum of other things, a whole.... The characters I presented are all parts of that whole.[18]

Armstrong does concede that she, as a young writer, could not do both—feature an individual and a community at the same time: "Maybe, perhaps, later on, when I'm a more mature writer, I may be able to do that."[19]

Of course *Slash* quickly became one of the key Native works that critics adopted as the standard-bearers for an Aboriginal ethic. As discussed earlier, a cultural profiling of "Native literature" began to develop around themes of land, mother, collective, circle, Trickster, tradition, and so forth. These themes, lovely on their own, were not only oversimplified but swiftly became the markers by which other Native works could be judged. Inevitably, there were debates and controversies. It was undoubtedly from such a context that novelist and critic Thomas King, in his introduction to *All My Relations*, cautioned against using the idea of the authentic Indian as a new yardstick by which to judge other Native works:

> There is, I think, the assumption that contemporary Indians will write about Indians. At the same time, there is danger that if we do not centre our literature on Indians, our work might be seen as inauthentic. Authenticity can be a slippery and limiting term when applied to Native literature for it suggests cultural and political boundaries past which we should not let our writing wander. And, if we wish to stay within these boundaries, we must not only write about Indian people and Indian culture, we must also deal with the concepts of 'Indian-ness', a nebulous term that implies a set of expectations that are used to mark out that which is Indian and that which is not.[20]

Ironically, this cautionary remark itself became the standard by which writers and critics could defend their intellectual locations, especially if crossing perceived boundaries. *All My Relations* was published in 1990; since then, the literary critical scene for Aboriginal literatures has virtually been revolutionized. However, the ideological cultural portrait lingers. I chose to discuss *Slash* and *Honour The Sun* not in search of any cultural authentication but for two critical reasons: to direct our attention to some possible new ways to read Aboriginal works and most especially to foreground our humanity.

Aboriginal Basis for Contemporary Criticism

As far as the literary concerns of humanization go, I favour *Honour the Sun*. I like the character development of Owl. But from an historical perspective and as an exposition of the colonial experience, I favour *Slash*, even though it lacks in character development. However, the point of this exercise is that my assessment is not determined solely by Western standards of criticism or universalist notions of what constitutes humanity. It is not just Westerners or the Western canons that can measure the aesthetic value of art, literature, narrative, or character development! For a number of reasons in a *real* sense authentic to my Plains Cree-Metis cultural background, I can appreciate character development, among other literary ploys and tropes. I can only speak from my cultural moorings but I believe that other Native critics approach literature with more than one set of critical tools. This is probably particularly true for those who grew up with Native languages and/or land-based cultures.

In the Cree language and awareness, we can make clear distinctions between different essences and qualities of things. It is still important to emphasize this point because one of the more common traits ascribed to Natives is their egalitarianism; from this it is often assumed Natives live in some sort of an amorphous collective consciousness. But our worlds and world views are not a unified set of spiritualities and equalities. In Cree we are provided with all sorts of information that helps us develop our sensibilities and intellects, that provides us with moral and aesthetic values, and that prepares us to appreciate literary studies—even in a different language and mode. And I, of course, grew up with the character of characters, the always interesting cultural teaser, the psycho-prophetic Wehsehkehcha, who today is largely reduced to the Western understanding of "Trickster." But Wehsehkehcha was much much more than a trickster, as both Canadian and American Native writers and critics keep explaining.[21]

Owl, incidentally, may have grown up with Nanabozho, a character akin to the Cree's Nanabush, or more properly in our dialect Nehnapush—a twin of sorts to Wehsehkehcha, but we do not know, as the author does not convey this to us. In any case, Slipperjack provides us with a memorable girl whose culture is obviously unique (and, yes, in a number of significant ways "different" from the Canadian mainstream), but she does not go into any torturous ethnological explanation. Owl is a northern child, clearly Native, as we can see in her lifestyle and language, but she remains convincing as a child, even if somewhat precocious. Her humanity is never compromised, nor is her culture.

Armstrong does not indulge in cultural mystification, or ethnological lessons either. Though she points to the central importance of Okanagan myths and legends, language, elders, spirituality, and land, Slash's humanity is certainly not obscured by cultural concerns. Instead, Armstrong raises a lot of issues (often in the form of questions by Slash) concerning culture and the meaning of tradition and spirituality in the context of a world made more complex with colonial time. Still, Slash as an individual is compromised in the interests of politics, certainly in the interests of the collective. But this point is intentional. Jeannette Armstrong is rebuilding culture.

There are issues critics have not investigated. For example, what about the cultural differences between Native intellectuals? My own reading of *Slash* raises questions, not only about the bases from which we may appraise Native writing (often cast as Western versus Aboriginal), but also about cultural differences among Native peoples. To what extent does my Plains Cree-Metis background influence my reading of other Native works? There is also the possibility my response is entirely personal. For example, might I be drawn to Owl as a character because I too grew up by the railroad tracks in a small northern hamlet, and I too loved our dogs, (I have never forgotten Diamond, Sport, Rex). Perhaps I responded to Owl for the same reason I respond to Maria Campbell's ghost stories in *Halfbreed*, and again to her *Stories of the Road Allowance People*—because I can relate!

My own Aboriginally based Metis identity is not "nebulous." I did grow up in a culture that valued community, spirituality, land, kin, and the mother. If my background is read superficially or with a "stereotypic eye," it might appear to confirm popular generalizations about Native culture, and I may be expected to exhibit certain traits and beliefs. However, if "known" or "read" beyond those expectations, one would find my primary socialization as socially vibrant, intricate, cultivated, culturally framed but uncongealed. Individuality, there, could be encouraged without compromising community values. To repeat what should be obvious, but often is not, we were and are multidimensional. We were not expected to be carbon copies of each other or even to submit our individual selves to the collective. It was not taken for granted that the collective always and necessarily represented what was best for each of us—we were not a religious cult! Nor were we always caring to each other. Most of us can recall relatives (who were also often neighbours) who were simply irritating, and some to be avoided. In what meaningful ways, then, can we idealize "all our relations"?

We were most assuredly "human," and how best to know this but by our uniqueness. Individual dreams were encouraged, and people were given nicknames based on their personalities or events significant to them. Nor were we without a spirit of competitiveness. After all, the Cree and the Metis were movers when it came to business acuity and cultural exchange, as exemplified in fur trade history. It is true we shared our resources, and held a very special and unique relationship with the land, and loved our families, but it is equally true that we were as human as anybody else. Slash may be stilted as a character, but I wept when he wept, which was whenever he was leaving home or coming back. And I cried with Owl when her dog was brutally shot by the village bully.

Not to undermine the gravity of our colonial history, but I do think, at some place of common humanity in all of us, colonization cannot explain everything about who we were or who we are today. We are human, colonization or no colonization. This, of course, begs for much greater treatment than I can give it here, but perhaps my interest in literature lies here: that through the truth value of fiction we may more freely explore our humanity in its fuller spectrum than has been possible under the constraints of certain categorizations or academic disciplines, theories or oppositional politics.

I am not an anthropologist and I don't wish to serve as some informant for cultural studies or for studies of "difference." Nor do I wish my observations and experience to be taken as representative of the collective. Suffice it to say, my mother culture not only permits me to be a strong individualist, but it also trained me to appreciate uniqueness, and prepared me to translate my culture's gifts to new aesthetics, contexts, and places. I try to do in English what my *Nokom* and my beloved *Ama* (and *Bapa*) could do in Cree. To me, none of this is remarkable, as some earlier ethnographers would have it, it just is. Not however, as an ontological condition but that I was fortunate enough to be so nurtured.

We need to make distinctions between voluntary and forced change, between agency and victimization, and between different ethnicities within the Native populations. My own family and community were open to natural (as opposed to forcible) change, though this is, of course, made considerably complex by colonial forces, many we cannot measure. While there is no question but that colonization arrested (or ossified) Aboriginal cultural development, clearly it did not kill it. If humans can find an interstitial space from which to make agency possible, they will. And we have. Even in places where our communities as such no longer exist, individuals exist and they carry to amazing degrees the ethos and nuances of their cultural selves. And it is individuals, not cultures (in that abstract sense), that live and change. Change is as much my birthright as is my gender. I am a contemporary modern woman and I am informed by more than one era, one culture, one language, one perspective, or one tradition. This is more than postcolonial "hybridity," it is my culture. The genius of cultural portability must be as much mine as anyone else's. I do not submit to the expectation that my early childhood and cultural background must be the only factors to be considered for the rest of my (writing or academic) life. Needless to say, my primary socialization imbues my life and will remain with me, but it is not the only influence in my life.

That I did grow up in Cree-Metis society in my primary years, of course, points to *real* differences in my cultural upbringing, compared with a Westerner's cultural upbringing. Or an Okanagan's. It also raises another important question: what about those Native writers who did not grow up with a Native language? Or those who did not grow up in a land-based culture? Both these questions are becoming more crucial with time. Most Native languages are in danger of becoming extinct. Only Cree, Ojibway, and Inuktitut "appear to have the best chances of survival."[22] Moreover, 40 to 60 percent of Native people live in urban centres.[23] Writers emerging from these communities face an even more difficult task as they seek to develop an Aboriginally based critical centre. Perhaps they are even more vulnerable to idealization than those of us who are privileged to have grown up in indigenously based lifestyles. Native intellectuals do have a rich romantic tradition, but it is clear not all romanticization in Native writing is made from the same stuff. Further, it may become increasingly alien for younger, strictly urban generations to relate to cultural signs and practices that have normally depended on land-based knowledges. However, we cannot submit to any ossification. Obviously, and as I have just suggested, we are challenged to revise ideas of cultural change and continuity if we hope to step out of Hiawatha's shadow. Native peoples are living lives as Natives in a contemporary world. It behooves writers and literary critics to locate this reality. And in fact, most Aboriginal authors have long been presenting such a reality, a location not always appreciated by reviewers.

Many questions remain concerning the meaning and application of an Aboriginal basis (or bases) for criticism. I believe some intellectual directions will change as the quality of Aboriginal writing and, in tandem, criticism, grows even more nuanced with time. And while there are yet Native writers who do not write primarily for recreational or aesthetic purposes—there are those writing for the love of words. Contemporary Native literature is rich, diverse, complex, and textured. Of course, this does not mean these works are without a subtext of resistance, given the political conditions in this country.

Reinventing Ourselves in Resistance

Resistance discourse, though, must be thought of in a different way. To expand on an earlier point, we cannot keep giving all the power to Westerners by submitting to the popular and canonical thought that all things literary or all concerns about the individual or about character development emanate from Western culture. Nor can we (nor should we) "return to the past," that is, to pre-Columbian nativism, anymore than we should surrender to post-Columbian stereotypes. To acquiesce to either of these colonial markers is to subordinate ourselves to the colonizer's model of the world—the doctrine that Europe's rise to world dominance is due to some "internal" and "autonomous" quality of race and culture, that the world derives its progress from the diffusion of European civilization.[24] In other words, we cannot accept that human progress begins and ends with European culture. Because it does not.

Frantz Fanon argued for a "new native," a native who had to find his (or her) way, a way that was "neither tribal nor western."[25] Fanon was, of course, thinking of the inevitability of reinvention, of mobilizing human creativity.

I believe we must reinvent ourselves, our country, our Americas, our world. By reinvention, I do not mean refabrication or myth-making; I mean, among other things, throwing off the weight of antiquity, and, by doing so, offering new possibilities for reconstruction. Quite frankly, I think most of us, both European and indigenous peoples, were reinvented at the site of our encounters.[26] Europeans and their North American descendants have yet to acknowledge this. Native peoples have had to deal with it by virtue of our political circumstances. But, of course, each new generation is called to reinvent. First Nations and Metis writers and scholars have been reinventing and will continue to do so with each new generation. We see this already in our newer and younger writers such as Gregory Scofield, Richard Van Camp, Randy Lundy, Eden Robinson, Warren Cariou, and Joseph Boyden.

We can look to changes in Afro-American imagery and literature for an inspiring example of reinvention. Afro-Americans have also been excessively dehumanized, both politically and textually, and, as Toni Morrison has shown, the struggles continue.[27] There are, to be sure, many differences between the Afro-American and Native Canadian experiences. But I have been struck by the powerfully human presence of Afro-Americans in popular culture, which I can only envy and which, I am sure, prepared the White House for the Obamas. Whether I read or watch Alex Haley's *Roots*, Alice Walker's *The Color Purple*, or Maya Angelou's *I Know Why the Caged Bird Sings*, I see the cultural and political contexts, but primarily, I see people, I see individuals. I see characters. I react to these individuals. I don't have to part the seas of abstract collectivities, be they negative or romanticized, trip over anthropologists or typologies, before I can appreciate Black humanity. (The same, or course, would hold true for White humanity.) Neither cultural nor political concerns obscure this humanity. I hunger for such a change in the presentation of Native individuals and characters and cultures in Canadian productions.

But this book is about talk-back, or resistance discourse, by Aboriginal writers. Resistance literature does not in any way preclude emotion or psychology. Indeed, the very fact and essence of resistance is our humanity. We resist dehumanization because we are human. And, I emphasize, our resistance may not, need not, be beautiful, for dehumanization is not a thing of beauty. Our expressions may most certainly be angry, even "bitter," but that is for us to determine. As long as there remains injustice, there will be anger. In fact, I am surprised when Native writers say they are not angry. The colonial experience is damaging and damage produces anger. When subdued peoples are voicing the injustice, no one has the right to tell such peoples how to hurt or how to explore their pain. By reinventing, I do not mean skimming or glossing over the grounds either of the colonizer's records or of our resistance. I am not one to advance any false sweetening of our colonial experience, or for that matter, of ourselves. We cannot, we must not, etherealize our colonized history or our colonized condition in the name of beauty, faith or even desire for "healing." The important thing is an awakening, an inspired vision, a global hunger for human freedoms and dignity. Decolonization has to mean something beyond a collective rage or reversion to clichés. It is crucial not only to destroy colonial constructs, but to restore our humanity, and the heart of that humanity is moral agency through thought and emotion.

In summary, then, it is an inherent part of Aboriginal worlds to frame human experience as more than some collective reflex, thereby providing Native writers an indigenous literary theory specific to their experience in North America. Harlow writes, "the theory of resistance literature is in its politics."[28] The theory in Native writing is to be found in the complex combination of our colonial and contemporary experiences, along with our respective indigenous poetics. An Aboriginal basis for criticism cannot be typological, it must be human-centred and fluid. I prefer to treat our theories, knowledges, or quests as trends and tasks in motion rather than as traits and cultural grids. Jeannette Armstrong, in her article "The disempowerment of First North American Native Peoples and Empowerment Through Their Writing," directs us to Aboriginal ethics of "peace and co-operation," which she believes "transcend violence and aggression." She sets "principles of co-operation... which shall endure" as the new standards for change and for criticism.[29]

These reflections perhaps pave the way towards finding standards of criticism authentic to the Native experience(s): that one resists not primarily for impersonal ideologies, or even for nationalisms, but for the advancement of what makes us human. Ultimately, it is to Native writers we must turn for illumination on Native humanity.

Arthur Shilling dedicated his art and poetry to portraying "the beauty of my people."[30] He wrote exquisitely, "When I paint, I feel like I'm still at the beginning, excited at the next bend in the river. Frightened and scared. I can hear the beauty, smell it like sweetgrass burning, the sound of my people. Their cries mix in with my paint and propel my brush. What else could bring reds and blues so clear, such as I have never seen before."[31]

It is here now that we make a turn, that we look at "the next bend in the river" of Native resistance. Already in 1997, Anishinabe novelist Richard Wagamese indicated in *Quality of Light* that there was an infinite quality of (more) colour and light to come. He opens this novel (about a Native boy and a White boy who must deal with identity constructions):

We are born into a world of light. Every motion of our lives, every memory, is coloured by the degree of its intensity or shaded by the weight of its absence. I believe the happy times are lit by an ebullient incandescence—the pure white light of joy—and that the sadder times are bathed in swatches of purple, moving into pearl gray. When we find ourselves against the hushed palette of evening, searching the sky for one single band of light, we're filtering the spectrum of our lives. We're looking through the magic prism of memory, letting our comforts, questions or woundings lead us—emotional voyageurs portaging a need called yearning. Because it's not the memories themselves we seek to reclaim, but rather the opportunity to surround ourselves with the quality of light that lives there.

The muted grays of storm clouds breaking might take you back to the hollowness you found in a long good-bye. The electric blue in a morning horizon might awaken in you again that melancholic ache you carried when you discovered love. Or you lay on a hillside in the high sky heat of summer, the red behind your eyelids making you so warm and safe and peaceful. It's like the scarlet a part of you remembers through the skin of your mother's belly when you, your life and the universe was all fluid, warmth and motion.[32]

It is tempting to end here, at this site of inspiration, with all this colour and luminosity. But of course, even in these words our suffering is intimated, and we are called to the task of reconstruction. It calls us to challenge colonial imaginings. Lest we forget, Jeannette Armstrong reminds us that the "bloody sword" of colonization "has been to hack out the spirit of all the beautiful cultures encountered, leaving in its wake a death toll unrivalled in recorded history. This is what happened and continues to happen.[33]

Yet, the human spirit is resilient in its elasticity and its boundless optimism for a better tomorrow. Even amidst devastations of wartime proportions, humans create life and art.[34] It is the stuff of resistance to reinvent and to recreate. However, my attention here to art, beauty, and creativity, usually the province of literary concerns, should not in any way detract from this fact: we are a colonized people who must resist any and all expressions of dehumanization. Then without false consciousness we reinvent ourselves, much as our ancestors from many roads have always done.

Decolonizing Postcolonials

Hees not just dah stealing dats bad you know.
All dough dats bad enough.
Dah real bad ting is your kids and all your grandchildren
Dey don got no good stories about you if you're a teef.

—Maria Campell[1]

Native writers representing a cross-section of eras and peoples have poi-gnantly recorded how difficult it is to grow up Native in a country that has institutionalized "hatred of the Other."[2] To be Native and to read White literature is to be placed in a war zone of images and feelings. To be Native and to read White literature is to walk a long journey of alienation. In response to the war of words against us, we Native writers and scholars have drawn on our various languages, legends, narratives, or footnotes to dismantle stereotypes, upset conventions, and invent new genres. We have especially questioned the misrepresentation of Native peoples and cultures in historical, ethnographic, literary, and popular productions. In this process of revisiting, we have sought to establish our own humanity by a wide variety of means, including reinscribing historical and cultural records, turning to facts of biography, foregrounding human qualities and emotions as individuals through fiction, poetry, and drama, or by using voice in scholarship.

We have shown that the presentation of us as stone-age savages in immoral combat against progressive, righteous civilization—or as I prefer, civilages—has been a construction of the colonizer. We have also shown that this construction is not benign, it has had and continues to have profound consequences for Native peoples. The civ/sav ideology has indeed generated, on one hand, provocations for Native scholars and artists, and, on the other, a fathomless intellectual and recreational play box for the colonizer society. Native writers are, and, indeed, have long been "talking back" to "the imperial centre."[3] They are and have been retelling the Canadian story because it is their stories that have been erased, falsified, slandered, or stolen.

As Native peoples, we have lived under the shadows of the colonizer since Columbus (or Champlain) and cohorts put their medieval notions and political interests to pen. Throughout these chapters I have directed my attention to some of those colonial shadows that have both haunted and inspired our own expressions. The shadows remain colossal, both in their magnitude and in their impact on us all, and we, the decolonizing, continue to struggle against them. We face a monumental task in our efforts. Reconstruction has begun, but it will not come easily or quickly.

But this task is not reserved only for Native peoples. The onus to deconstruct and to rebuild cannot fall solely on the colonized. The responsibility to clean up colonial debris, whether in popular culture, historiography or in matters literary, lies first with the colonizer. Colonizer sons and daughters need, even more than us, to dismantle their colonial constructs. Some colonialists choose to harden and to entrench themselves into the spaces fortified by their forefathers.

I, along with my Native colleagues, am taking our contrapuntal space by, among other ways, redefining our positions in Canadian life. Invariably, this may cause discomfort, puzzlement, or even anger for some readers. I have, rather methodically, been "pulling out their fenceposts of civilization / one by one / calling names in Cree / bringing down their mooneow hills / in English too."[4] I can hear the remonstrations: "how then shall we respond?"

Jeanne Perreault, English professor at the University of Calgary, counsels her colleagues against retreat or silence. As co-editor of a 1994 special issue of *Ariel* devoted to Native literature, Perreault writes, "critical obtuseness... is not appropriate at this moment.... Rather than retreating into silence or withdrawal, bringing an informed consciousness about one's position can be useful for both literary critic and general reader." Mainstream historians too would find much value were they to engage in greater introspection than they are normally trained to do. Perreault advises that, "what readers and writers need to do is to discern from within the critical material… what values are held and how they are expressed."[5]

Another way is to learn from Native writers—and Native theorists—how to read their literatures and their methodologies. Lynette Hunter, professor of twentieth-century literature and culture suggests as much in her treatment of marginalized Canadian women in *Outsider Notes*. She advocates "the risks of personal vulnerability necessary to committed engagement," and observes that although she "cannot meet the text on the writer's ground," she can "listen." As an outsider listening, she can "participate in the conversation and begin to discuss the issues even though [her] reading may be embarrassing."[6] Her notes indicate Hunter listens sensibly and intelligently. W.H. New, in a discerning editorial to the 1990 *Canadian Literature* special issue on Native writing, provides some thoughts on why people may not be willing to hear: "Sometimes people are willing to listen only to those voices that confirm the conventions they already know. The unfamiliar makes them fear. Or makes them condescend. Neither fear nor condescension encourages listening. And no one who does not listen learns to hear."[7] New chooses to treat the discourse between Euro-Canadian and Native writers as "a series of opportunities to begin listening" because "boundaries are processes of interaction as much as they are lines of demarcation." He cautions that if Native writers "are not recognized for the creativity of the differences they bring to bear on cultural perception, margins also have a way of making the centre irrelevant, and of speaking on their own."[8]

Canadians might begin their listening by recognizing the import of Native resistance. Hearing the resistance challenges Western epistemological and canonical assumptions and practices. It should go without saying that scholarship must be vigorous and honest and more cooperative across disciplines. The point is that changes required of us entail much more than "crossing borders," genres, or cultures; it is much more than making accommodations here and there. It is even more than adding in the "peoples without history," to borrow Eric Wolf's title. Far more revolutionary is Blaut's criticism of Western cultural tenets presented as the hub of the human wheel out of which emanate all things progressive in culture and intellect, as it acts in colonization.[9] Blaut's challenge is that scholars abandon "the colonizer's model of the world."

The implications for Canadians are that they must abandon pervasive and prevailing assumptions that Western—in particular, historical and literary—productions are scientifically impartial treatises on the human condition and that the Native "voice" is "bitter" and biased, or innately inferior.[10] For re-settler nationalist historians, this means letting go of the colonial bedposts of thought and language: the civ/sav canopy with its underlying Eurocentrisim that continues to perpetuate colonialism. It means revisiting and, in many cases, abandoning old heroes. It means looking beyond presumed empirical sets of beliefs in order to see other data heretofore obscured by blinding Eurocentric subjectivism.

Scholars must set aside old presuppositions or paradigms, however deeply embedded they are in the Canadian psyche. This means, at the very least, works like *Wacousta* should be dissected, even excised, instead of being accorded Gothic proportions, as they commonly are in the Canadian literary tradition. All archival and subsequent historiographic and critical works should be reinvestigated. There is a dangerous tendency to tolerate, if not perpetuate, racism in scholarship in the guise of contextualizing narrative and history or cross-cultural understanding. *Wacousta* is not just another story; neither are Ralph Connor's Mountie stories, nor is much of imperialist writing. Exploration literature is not just another genre. The dominant Western narrative is not just another culture.

Obviously, I am not merely advancing an interdisciplinary or cross-cultural approach; I am advancing the de-imperialization of scholarship, which, of course, demands a complex combination of radical changes. Besides deconstructing colonial frameworks, the advancement of Aboriginal knowledges is essential,[11] as is the understanding of the critical spaces from which Aboriginal intellectuals are employing resistance strategies. Harlow emphasizes that an intellectual struggle against colonization is "no less crucial than the armed struggle."[12] As we have seen, the discursive battle has been axial to Canadian Native peoples' struggle. Here I finish an argument with which I began this book: Native use of "facts of biography" is a counter-discourse to emphasize a point made by the earliest Native writers; namely, that we are not savages, we have cultures. This is why we write about our places of birth, our landscapes, our grandmothers and grandfathers, our parents, our kin, our networks, our social regulations, our livelihoods, our use of resources, our foods, our ways of organizing, our faiths and ceremonies, our technologies, our music, our languages, our arts, and our stories. These attentions are pivotal to our strategies. They are not to be dismissed as anecdotal, confessional or advocacy biases but are offered to address colonization in academia, most especially, to personalize the depersonalized "Indian."

Throughout these chapters, I have made a point of acknowledging that change has taken place in the intellectual treatment of Aboriginal peoples, but the extent and nature of this change requires further qualification. While there has obviously been a marked improvement since the 1970s, more so since the 1990s, this has taken place mostly by those specializing in areas relevant to Native peoples and issues. There is no question that these specialists are using more Native material—or using material about Natives more carefully—in their works.[13] Many are also engaging Native individuals or communities in their research.[14]

There has also been an impressive development of critical writing and theorizing by Aboriginal writers, educators, and scholars from many different disciplines. In literary circles, formidable critics such as Jeannette Armstrong, Thomas King, and Lee Maracle are making international indentations in this area. However, many of the rest of us have not yet made significant inroads into some postcolonial circles of theorizing. But whether we are invited to conferences or cited in academic papers, I have not been entirely happy with how our works are being read. While our cultural and personal data are clearly and repetitively appreciated, our theoretical contributions are not substantially treated. There remains excessive reference to our "traditions," or to our personal or colonial "experience," and these are further generalized or re-translated. What I find missing are our research, critical constructions, interrogations, and ideas. I declared at the outset that Native writing and scholarship contains much anti-colonial theory, or at least much theoretical possibility. But our ideas or models and methodologies, which challenge how things are normally done, are only beginning to be discovered, not discerned. More often, non-Native scholars are taking our works as points of departure for the development of their own theories; in some ways I understand that this is one of the pressures academics live with. Still, those who use us—especially in fields outside Aboriginal literatures—are not really incorporating Native intellectual challenges into their discussions.

Of course, there are different theories about how we theorize, and there are also conflicting theories among us, but we do theorize. But it appears that we may still be considered more as storytelling peoples or cultural or victim /trauma informants, not contemporary theorists and intellectuals (not that these categories are necessarily exclusive of each other). This may, in part, explain why we are not usually included in international postcolonial discourse, even though the boundaries of resistance literature have broadened. No doubt, the lateness (we have been actively writing and teaching since the 1970s) and shape of our inclusion in this discourse probably reflect a number of different factors, among them ignorance about our existence, which may be due, in part, to the international tendency to pay little attention to Canadians in general. Then there is the convoluted mix of English and philosophy in the theories associated with postcolonial studies, which requires specialization that the majority of Aboriginal readers and for that matter, other "ordinary" Canadians, cannot access.

As White and Native Canadians, we also find ourselves in the awkward position of competing for space and acknowledgement. It appears that White Canadian literature has been the officially accepted representative of postcolonial literatures, even if White Canadian writers themselves do not always feel their works have received adequate recognition. Ashcroft, Griffiths, and Tiffin are aware of "indigenous populations" that have been invaded by "settler colonies" and provide Australia as a case in point of "contradictions which emerge" where "Aboriginal writing provides an excellent example of a dominated literature, while that of White Australia has characteristics of a dominating one in relation to it. Yet, Australian literature is dominated in turn by a relationship with Britain and with English literature." While *The Empire Writes Back* is sprinkled with references to indigenous populations, overall, the authors do not pursue the literary relationship between White colonizer and Native colonized except to say such a study would be "fascinating."[15]

In the *Post-Colonial Studies Reader*, however, Ashcroft, Griffiths, and Triffin do pursue such "fascinating" studies. The place of various indigenous peoples vis-à-vis White "invader settlers" is given special consideration. However, while several White Canadian writers and critics (Margery Fee, Terry Goldie, Linda Hutcheon) address the relationship between Native and White Canadians, no Native writers or scholars are included. A number of other White Canadian writers (Robert Kroetsch, Dennis Lee, Diana Brydon) concern themselves with their struggles vis-à-vis British colonialism. "Fascinating" it is. I find it unacceptable in a postcolonial reader, especially one published in the 1990s, that Natives are represented only through White Canadians. Perhaps it is here that we can most fully receive Greg Young-Ing's thought-provoking argument that even the most supportive White academics who treat Native issues have "the effect of ultimately blocking-out the Aboriginal Voice."[16]

Lynette Hunter in *Outsider Notes* provides a thoughtful and cogent reading on marginalization. "By marginalized," Hunter explains, "I understand those people who have difficulty of access of participating in the modes of communication that carry power and authority in their society."[17] Although more writers and scholars situate Canada's origins and development as imperialist, none are as qualified to convey the colonial experience as are the colonized. Nor is it fruitful to lock into a debate as to whether it is Natives or Whites who ought to be the official "postcolonialists."[18] We may all be postcolonialists, but we are not all placed on the same rung of privileges in the vertical mosaic of Canada. Native intellectuals are keenly aware of their placement.

Here, I must emphasize that while there may be numerous thematic similarities between what White colonial re-settlers experienced vis-à-vis the British Empire and what Native original settlers experienced vis-à-vis British Canada, the two cannot be conflated. They are not all the same. In fact, in some critical ways, the two are diametrically opposed. In other words, while on a literary level White Canadians can play with themes like place, landscape, and identity,[19] however poignant, they cannot compare their privileged, indeed, dominant, positions with Aboriginal peoples whose places have been stolen, whose landscapes have been bulldozed, and whose identities have been irreparably disturbed.

White Canadian historians and writers must come to terms with their powerful colonizer positions. Daniel Francis has explained,

> Canadians are conflicted in their attitudes toward Indians.... And we will continue to be so long as the Indian remains imaginary. Non-Native Canadians can hardly hope to work out a successful relationship with Native people who exist largely in fantasy. Chief Thunderthud did not prepare us to be equal partners with Native people.... The distance between fantasy and reality, is the distance between Indian and Native. It is also the distance non-Native Canadians must travel before we can come to terms with the imaginary Indian, which means coming to terms with ourselves as North Americans.[20]

I would qualify Francis's last statement. What White Canadians need to come to terms with is not so much their North American selves, but their colonialist selves. And of course, there are scholars who self-reflectively take an ethical and sensitive "positionality": Renate Eigenbrod writes, "If, as Euro-Canadian critics, we want to approach literature by Aboriginal authors in a fair manner, we have to rid ourselves of preconceived notions of linear and dualistic thinking and be open to complexities and indeterminacies.... we have to come to terms with our complicity in the colonization of the peoples and find the courage to let this literature be unsettling."[21]

But some scholars may live in the illusion that they not only understand "Natives," but that somehow, by their postcolonial powers of analysis, they have neutralized the colonial experience. No one—White or Native, however brilliant or even decolonizing—should ever assume to understand the whole of this experience, much less believe the alienation and the othering is over. For many reasons Native writers and scholars have made apparent, neither the political nor the textual devastations are over.

We are all challenged to keep decolonizing as we seek to de-imperialize the Western voice. As my own consciousness continues to be altered, I continue to revisit my own perceptions and my sources. For example, even during this project, I have changed my treatment of Fanon and Memmi. I find their male-dominant voices, among other things, limited and limiting. While Fanon and Memmi provide powerful and original insights concerning colonization, application of their analysis (and Fanon's ideas on radical violence) can only go so far for Aboriginal peoples in Canada. We remain seriously out-muscled in our own country. But that is only the most obvious difference. There are other fundamental differences, including a Native ethic of tolerance and a strong regard for individuality (not to be confused with individual*ism)* that does not easily turn to ideology or collective political violence. I do think that the recent turn to an Aboriginal "aesthetic of healing"[22] is, in part, an effort to translate Native ideas or world views to a "language" accessible to most today. It is an effort to bridge conceptual gaps. I would though make some caution-ary remarks. As constructive as "healing aesthetics" may sound, we must be careful not to squeeze the life out of Native literature by making it serve, yet again, another utilitarian function. Poets, playwrights, and novelists, among others, must also write for the love of words. Healing is fast becoming the new cultural marker by which we define or judge Aboriginal literature.

In any event, even if our aesthetics allowed us to completely adopt Fanon or Memmi's thinking, we would end up in another kind of air-tight para-digm. Their words and models emerge from another era under very different geographical, political, and cultural circumstances. Not that we cannot make comparisons, for some emerge with eerie familiarity. I have been struck by the degree to which I can relate my experiences and research with those of Fanon's and Memmi's. They are, of course, not the last or final word on colonization, for, as is obvious in postcolonial ruminations, there are ever new and stimu-lating analyses of colonization today.

Native Canadian scholars and writers have been troubling the colonizer, which, I believe, is largely why our writings have been received with reticence, some defensiveness, or even incomprehension. In Canada, we are the uncom-fortable mirrors to the White Canadian identity. Not only are we painting "the beauty of our people," as Arthur Shilling put it, we are also painting the colo-nizing face. However, to date, our portraitures have been largely restricted to political and constitutional arenas and commentaries, and, to a lesser extent, to our creative writing. I look forward to more substantial treatment of the colonizer personality and psyche, which has yet to appear in some substance in our poetry, novels, and plays.[23] On a more transcendent note, I would like to see greater treatment of the colonizer—or oppressor—in us all.

The Aboriginal bases (note the pluralization) for contemporary criticism is in process of development. This is an area rich in intellectual challenge, in large part because it is a multidimensional intersection of many roads, many worlds, many stereotypes. In my concern for fluidity in criticism, I do not mean to discount the Aboriginal intellectual search for the kind of "critical centre" that Native American critic Kimberly Blaeser mentions in her thoughtful essay "Native Literature: Seeking a Critical Center."[24] Much remains to be explored, not only in our portraits of the colonizer, but in our portraits of ourselves. We must treat Native history and writing in all its dimensions, complexity, and even contradictions. Dismantling paradigms and stereotypes will require developing new critical languages and approaches. With time and experience and dialogue, it will become easier to crystallize (in the sense of clarity, not hardening) our bases of knowledge, expression and research.

For Native intellectuals, the challenge is to maintain our cultural integrity without resorting to romanticism, fundamentalism, or nativism. How shall "I" say I am human and at the same time different without resorting to stereotypes or to a return to the past? How shall I say I am different and yet the same as a human? And how shall we claim and develop our literatures and intellects unique to us without having always to juxtapose them against Western portrayals and canonization? Or without always preoccupying ourselves with the colonizer's yearnings for primitivistic authenticity. We are individual and cultural selves-in-process. Gaile McGregor, in *The Wacousta Syndrome*, invokes W.L. Morton's history lesson: "the only real victories are the victories over defeat... what is important is not to have triumphed, but to have endured."[25] Perhaps, but Native peoples have had about enough of enduring; we are moving to take our places in Canadian society as socially and culturally vibrant intellectuals and artists without the colonial burdens of misrepresentations and marginalization.

Clearly, we have begun, though much dethroning remains to be done. The politics of narrative as determined by those in power no longer totally overshadow our discourse, but it still definitely shadows it. I suspect we will resist until Canada "heals" itself from the Nero complex, until we the indigenous are no longer the Other in our own lands.

I finish, then, from my poem "Long Way from Home," which in many ways is the foundation of thought, imagination, and resistance in this book:

Oh I did my footnotes so well
nobody knows where I come from
I've walked these hallways

with them a long time now
and still they don't see
the earth gives eyes
injustice gives rage
now I'm standing here
prehistoric designer jeans and all
pulling out their fenceposts of civilization
one by one
calling names in Cree
bringing down their mooneow hills
in English too
this is home now.[26]

Notes

Introduction

1   Joyce Green, "Exploring Identity and Citizenship: Aboriginal Women, Bill C-31 and the Sawridge Case" (PhD diss., University of Alberta, 1997), 26. Identity and Citizenship…(Diss: University of Alberta, 1997), 26.

2   Gerald McMaster and Lee-Ann Martin, Introduction, *Indigena: Contemporary Native Perspectives*, eds. Gerald McMaster and Lee-Ann Martin (Vancouver: Douglas and McIntyre, 1992).

3   Albert Memmi, *The Colonizer and the Colonized* (Boston: Beacon Press, 1957), 54–55.

4   Edward Said, *Orientalism* (London: Routledge and Kegan Paul, 1978), 22.

5   Olive Dickason, *The Myth of the Savage and the Beginnings of French Colonialism in the Americas*, Edmonton: University of Alberta Press, 1984), 273.

6   Vitoria's defence is often cited in the context of origins of the theory of Aboriginal rights. See, for example, Peter A. Cumming and Neil H. Mickenberg, *Native Rights in Canada* (Toronto: General Publishing, 1970).

7   Dickason, *Myth*, 193.

8   Robert Berkhofer, *The White Man's Indian* (New York: Random House, 1978).

9   Daniel Francis, *The Imaginary Indian: The Image of the Indian in Canadian Culture* (Vancouver: Arsenal Pulp Press, 1992), 224.

10 For a good overview of the development of Metis identity, see Jacqueline Peterson and Jennifer S.H. Brown, eds., *The New Peoples: Being and Becoming Metis in North America* (Winnipeg: University of Manitoba Press, 1985).

11 Frantz Fanon, *The Wretched of the Earth* (New York: Grove Press, 1963).

12 J.M. Blaut, *The Colonizer's Model of the World: Geographical Diffusionism and Eurocentric History* (New York and London: Guilford Press, 1993).

13 Alice Lee, "lesson", in *Writing the Circle: Native Women of Western Canada*, eds. Jeanne Perreault and Sylvia Vance (Edmonton: NeWest Publishers, 1990), 160.

14 Lenore Keeshig-Tobias, "Trickster Beyond 1992: Our Relationship," in *Indigena*, ed. McMaster and Martin, 101–112.

15 Ibid., 103.

16 Ibid., 101.

17 Terry Goldie, *Fear and Temptation: The Image of the Indigene in Canadian, Australian, and New Zealand Literatures* (Kingston: McGill-Queen's University Press, 1989), 6.

18 Ibid.

19 As more non-White immigrants come to Canada, we may expect to see more tension between these immigrants and Native peoples. Non-White immigrants arrive with preconceived notions about "Indians" because they too have seen Hollywood movies. Further, Native peoples experience a new level of displacement when they see immigrants getting educational and job opportunities—for example, the English as a Second Language programs—that are not as readily available to them. Urban Native peoples especially struggle with these issues.

20 Berkhofer, *White Man's Indian*, 55.

21 Memmi, *Colonizer and the Colonized*, 74.

22 See Bruce R. Morrison and C. Roderick Wilson, *Native Peoples: The Canadian Experience*, 2nd ed. (Toronto: McClelland and Stewart, 1995), esp. 13–66, for such anthropological details; see also Olive Dickason, *Canada's First Nations: A History of Founding Peoples from Earliest Times* (Toronto: McClelland and Stewart, 1992), 20–85.

23 James S. Frideres, *Aboriginal Peoples in Canada: Contemporary Conflicts* (Scarborough: Prentice Hall Allyn and Bacon Canada, 1998), 22.

24 Quoted from a letter written to Lord Elgin, Governor General of Montreal, as quoted in Penny Petrone, *Native Literature in Canada* (Toronto: Oxford University Press, 1990), 64. It has normally been assumed that the early custom of addressing Whites as "father" indicates infantilization. However, Olive Dickason suggests that this may reflect a cultural custom of respect, not authority (Dickason, *Canada's First Nations*, 16).

25 Joyce Green, "Exploring Identity and Citizenship", 24. Green here is, in part, quoting from George Manuel and Michael Posluns, *The Fourth World* (Toronto: Collier, 1974).

26 Bill Ashcroft, Gareth Griffiths, and Helen Tiffin, "Introduction," in *The Empire Writes Back: Theory and Practice in Post-Colonial Literature*, Bill Ashcroft, Gareth Griffiths, and Helen Tiffin, eds. (New York: Routledge, 1989), 7.

27 I owe this phrase to Jacqueline Peterson, "Many Roads to Red River: Metis Genesis in the Great Lakes Region, 1680–1815," in *The New Peoples*, ed. Peterson and Brown, 37–72.

28 Barbara Harlow, *Resistance Literature* (New York: Methuen, 1987), 4.

29 With respect to Native accounts, the words "narrative" and "tales" have been used interchangeably, which is a technique for undermining the Native experience. Only recently has the literary meaning of the word "narrative" been applied to Native writing.

30 Quoted in Renate Eigenbrod, "Can 'The Subaltern' Be Read? The Role of the Critic in Postcolonial Studies," *Acolit* 2 (1996): 100.

31 Arun Mukherjee, *Oppositional Aesthetics: Readings from a Hyphenated Space* (Toronto: TSAR, 1994), xiii.

32 Penny Petrone, "Indian Literature," in *Oxford Companion to Canadian Literature*, ed. William Toye (Oxford University Press, 1983), 383–388.

33 There are some excellent reviews of Widdowson and Howard on the Internet. See, for example, Taiaiake Alfred, "Redressing Racist Academics, Or, Put Your Clothes Back On, Please!" (Jan. 16, 2009). Original available at http://www.taiaiake.com/

34 In an article "What Dick Pound said was really dumb—also true" (Oct. 25, 2008) Margaret Wente from *The Globe and Mail* defended Vancouver Olympics committee member, and Chancellor at McGill University, Dick Pound's racist comments to *La Presse*, comparing pre-European Canada as "a land of savages" to China as a 5000 year-old civilization.

Chapter One

1 For a beginning discussion of Native "voice" in response to the notion of Native "voicelessness" in literature (and society), see Emma LaRocque, "Preface," in *Writing the Circle*, ed. Perreault and Vance, xv–xxx.

2 Emma LaRoque, *Defeathering The Indian*. Agincourt: Book Society of Canada, 1975.

3 Harlow, *Resistance Literature*, xvi.

4 Ibid., xvii.

5 Harlow also traces the problematic term "Third World," noting that it "seems to possess more rhetorical power than precision." Ibid., 4.

6 Writing in English is not the only kind of literacy. Peter Kulchyski in *Like the Sound of a Drum* (Winnipeg: University of Manitoba Press, 2005) makes compelling observations that particular inscriptions on the Pangnirtung landscape, "marks perhaps on one level a written response, the construction of a different sort of text" (189). See also Drew Mildon, "A Bad Connection: First Nations Oral Histories in the Canadian Courts," in *Aboriginal Oral Traditions*, ed. by Renée Hulan and Renate Eigenbrod (Halifax: Fernwood Publishing, 2008).

7 For an adequate summary of Native people's experience of the Canadian school system, see Frideres, *Aboriginal Peoples in Canada*, 148–168. Frideres presents figures indicating that about 60 percent of Native students do not complete high school.

8 Memmi, *Colonizer and the Colonized*, 106–109.

9 George Copway, in *An Anthology of Canadian Native Literature in English*, ed. Daniel David Moses and Terry Goldie (Toronto: Oxford University Press, 1992), 19.

10 Chief Dan George, *My Heart Soars* (Saanichton: Hancock House, 1974), 85.

11 *Royal Commission on Aboriginal Peoples Report* (Ottawa: Minister of Supply and Services, 1996).

12 George Clutesi emphasizes this point by setting the whole statement in an unnumbered page at the beginning of his book, *Potlatch* (Sidney, BC: Grays, 1969).

13 Catherine Soneegoh Sutton, quoted from a letter written to the editor of *The Leader* in 1864; as quoted in Petrone, *Native Literature in Canada* (Toronto: Oxford University Press, 1990), 65-68.

14 Patricia Monture-Angus, *Thunder in my Soul: A Mohawk Woman Speaks* (Halifax: Fernwood, 1995), 11.

15 Basil Johnston, "One Generation from Extinction," in *Native Writers and Canadian Writing: Canadian Literature Special Issue*, ed. W.H. New (Vancouver: University of British Columbia Press, 1990), 10–15.

16 Robin Ridington, "Cultures in Conflict: Problems in Discourse," in *Native Writers and Canadian Writing*, ed. W.H. New, 277.

17 See also Robin Ridington, "Technology, World View, and Adaptive Strategy in a Northern Hunting Society," in *The Native Imprint: The Contribution of First Peoples to Canada's Character*, ed. Olive P. Dickason (Edmonton: Athabasca University Press, 1995), 103–117.

18 I explore a complex of pedagogical and epistemological issues concerning the translation of land-based cultures into our classrooms in Emma LaRocque, "From the Land to the Classroom: Broadening Epistemology," in *Pushing the Margins*, ed. Jill Oaks, Rick Riewe, Marlyn Bennett, and Brenda Chisholm (Winnipeg: Native Studies Press, 2001), 62-75.

19 Janice Acoose, *Iskwewak: Kah' Ki Yaw Ni Wahkomakanak* (Toronto: Women's Press, 1995), 12.

20 Ibid.

21 This phrase is original to Harjo and is the title of an anthology, co-edited with Gloria Bird. Joy Harjo and Gloria Bird, eds., *Reinventing the Enemy's Language: Contemporary Native Women's Writings of North America* (New York: W.W. Norton, 1997).

22 Howard Adams, *Prison of Grass* (Toronto: General Publishing, 1975).

23 Some of the classic Afro-American statements on this include James Baldwin, *Notes of a Native Son* (Boston: Beacon Press, 1949), Malcolm X, *Malcolm X Speaks: Selected Speeches and Statements*, ed. George Breitman (New York: Grove Press, 1965), and Alex Haley, *Roots* (New York: Bantam Books, 1977).

24 Ashcroft, Griffiths, and Tiffin, "Introduction," *Empire Writes Back*, 2.

25 Ibid.

26 Peter Hitchcock, *Dialogics of the Oppressed* (Minneapolis: University of Minnesota Press, 1993), 4.

27 Harlow, *Resistance Literature*, 11.

28 Harlow, *Resistance Literature*, xvii.

29 Petrone, *Native Literature in Canada*. German scholar Hartmut Lutz has also produced a number of works detailing various writings by Native peoples. See also LaRocque, "Preface," in Writing the Circle, and Renee Hulan, ed., *Native North America: Critical and Cultural Perspectives* (Toronto: ECW Press, 1999).

30 My discussion of the civ/sav dichotomy was first published in "The Metis in English Canadian Literature," *Canadian Journal of Native Studies* 3, 1 (1983): 85–94.

31 S.R. Mealing, ed., *The Jesuit Relations and Allied Documents: A Selection, 1632–73* (Toronto: McClelland and Stewart, 1965), 44.

32 Parker Duchemin, "'A Parcel of Whelps': Alexander Mackenzie among the Indians,"

in *Native Writers and Canadian Writing*, ed. W.H. New (Vancouver, University of British Columbia Press, 1990)53-54.

33 Dickason, Canada's First Nations, 60.

34 Native resistance is amply recorded in fur trade journals: see Arthur J. Ray and Donald Freeman, *Give Us Good Measure* (Toronto: University of Toronto Press, 1977); Lewis O. Saum, *The Fur Trade and the Indian* (Seattle: The University of Washington Press, 1965).

35 Petrone, *Native Literature in Canada*, 35.

36 Jeannette Armstrong, ed., *Looking at the Words of our People: First Nations Analysis of Literature* (Penticton: Theytus Books, 1993).

37 Armand Garnet Ruffo, ed., *(Ad)dressing Our Words: Aboriginal Perspectives on Aboriginal Literatures* (Penticton: Theytus Books, 2001); Renate Eigenbrod and Jo-Ann Episkenew, eds. *Creating Community: A Roundtable on Canadian Aboriginal Literature* (Brandon University: Bearpaw Publishing, 2002); Renée Hulan and Renate Eigenbrod, eds. *Aboriginal Oral Traditions* (Halifax and Winnipeg: Fernwood Publishing, 2008).

38 Parts of this discussion have been presented in LaRocque, "Preface," in *Writing the Circle*, and "The Colonization of a Native Woman Scholar," in *Women of the First Nations: Power, Wisdom and Strength*, ed. Christine Miller and Patricia Chuchryk (Winnipeg: University of Manitoba Press, 1997), 11–18.

39 Mukherjee, *Oppositional Aesthetics*, xiii.

40 Barbara Christian, "The Race for Theory," in *Post-Colonial Studies Reader*, ed. Ashcroft, Griffiths, and Tiffin, 457.

41 Ibid., 459

42 Ibid.

43 Ibid., 457.

44 Historian Doug Sprague essentially charges Metis historian and critic Howard Adams with "advocacy history," although he also implicates "academic historians" of same—as if Metis cannot be academic historians! See Doug Sprague, *Canada and the Metis, 1869–1885* (Waterloo: Wilfrid Laurier University Press, 1988), 13 n. 19.

45 Russell Ferguson, "Introduction: Invisible Center," in *Out There: Marginalisation and Contemporary Cultures* (New York: The New Museum of Contemporary Art, 1990), 11.

46 Duchemin, "'A Parcel of Whelps,'" 63.

47 Kathleen Rockhill, "The Chaos of Subjectivity in the Ordered Halls of Academe," *Canadian Woman Studies* 8, 4 (1987): 12.

48 In some dialects, it can also refer to "people of four directions."

49 Jeanne Perreault, in *Writing Selves: Contemporary Feminist Autography* (Minneapolis: University of Minnesota Press, 1995), writes that feminist writers and theorists "of all races, sexualities and classes" (1) have been "grappling with modes of expression that evade the familiar narrative of life events" (3), and out of this " a new kind of subjectivity is evolving" (4). In the process of writing "self-in-the-making," concepts such as subjectivity, agency, and self are being reframed. See also, Leslie Brown and Susan Strega, eds., *Research as Resistance: Critical, Indigenous, and Anti-Oppressive Approaches* (Toronto: Canadian Scholars' Press, 2005).

50 Hitchcock, *Dialogics*, xi.

51 Harlow, *Resistance Literature*, 3.

52 Jules Michelet, *History of the French Revolution*, ed. Gordon Wright (Chicago: University of Chicago Press, 1967), xv.

53 Said, *Orientalism*, 9.

54 Ibid., 10.

55 For an insightful commentary on the Aboriginal writers' use of orality in their written works, see Renate Eigenbrod, "The Oral in the Written: A Literature Between Two Cultures," *Canadian Journal of Native Studies* 15, 1 (1995): 89–102. The question, though, is this: does the use of orality in writing reflect an in-between-ness, or is it more a reflection of an ongoing-ness, that is, recreating and reinventing a language and literature from Aboriginal poetics?

56 Janice Williamson, *Sounding Differences: Conversations with Seventeen Canadian Women Writers* (Toronto: University of Toronto Press, 1993).

57 Harlow, *Resistance Literature*, 4.

58 Edward Said, *The World, The Text, and the Critic* (Cambridge: Harvard University Press, 1983), 29.

59 Maurie Alieoof and Susan Schouten Levine, "Interview: The Long Walk of Alanis Obomsawin," *Cinema Canada*, June 1987, 10–15.

60 Some of these experiences of racism in the educational system are included in my autobiographical essay, "Tides, Towns and Trains," in *Living the Changes*, ed. Joan Turner (Winnipeg: University of Manitoba Press, 1990), 76–90.

61 Tom Flanagan, *First Nations, Second Thoughts* (Montreal: McGill-Queen's University Press, 2000). Doctrinaire theses such as Flanagan's jolt us to practise anti-racist pedagogy. For an excellent race analysis see Carol Schick, "Keeping the Ivory Tower White: Discourses of racial domination," in *Race, Space, and the Law: Unmapping a White Settler Society*, ed. S. Razack (Toronto: Between the Lines, 2002), 100-119. See also Carol Schick and Verna St. Denis, "Troubling national discourses for anti-racist education," *Journal of Canadian Education* 28, 3 (2005): 296-319.

62 Joyce Green, "Theoretical, Methodological and Empirical Issues in the Study of Indigenous Politics," *Canadian Political Science Association* (2002), 2.

63 Sarain Stump, *There Is My People Sleeping* (Sidney, BC: Grays, 1970).

64 Duchemin, "'Parcel of Whelps'...," 63.

Chapter Two

1 Joyce Green, "Exploring Identity and Citizenship," 25–26.

2 Memmi, *Colonizer and the Colonized*, 52–53.

3 For an insightful psychoanalytical study of the White American habit of addressing Native people as children, see Michael Paul Rogin, *Fathers and Children* (New York: Knopf, 1975). For a Native Canadian perspective, see Harold Cardinal, *The Unjust Society* (Edmonton: Hurtig Publishers, 1969).

4 Duchemin, "Parcel of Whelps," 55.

5 Fanon, *Wretched*, 41.

6 Not insignificantly, Jose de Acosta's work was translated into Italian, French, English, Dutch, and German. See Hugh Honour, *The New Golden Land* (New York: Pantheon Books, 1975).

7 Lewis Henry Morgan, *Ancient Society*, ed. Eleanor Burke Leacock (New York: World, 1963 [1877]).

8 Roy Harvey Pearce, *Savagism and Civilization* (Baltimore: Johns Hopkins University Press, 1965 [1953]), 49.

9 Ibid., 105.

10 Francis Jennings, *Invasion of America: Indians, Colonialism, and the Cant of Conquest* (Chapel Hill: University of North Carolina Press, 1976), 7.

11 Ibid., 8.

12 Ibid.

13 Ibid.

14 For a discussion of scientific racism in relation to the development of Indian imagery, see Robert F. Berkhofer, *The White Man's Indian* (New York: Random House, 1978).

15 Jennings, *Invasion of America*, 9.

16 Ibid.

17 Ibid.

18 Ibid.

19 Ibid., 10.

20 Daniel Francis, *The Imaginary Indian: The Image of the Indian in Canadian Culture* (Vancouver: Arsenal Pulp Press, 1992), 52.

21 Frits Pannekoek, "The Anglican Church and the Disintegration of Red River Society, 1818–1870," In Carl Berger and Ramsay Cook, *The West and the Nation* (Toronto: McClelland and Stewart, 1976), 75.

22 John West, *Substance of a Journal During Residence At The Red River Colony* (London, 1824; rpt. by S.R. Publishers, 1966), 116–117.

23 John McDougall, *Pathfinding on Plain and Prairie* (Toronto, 1898), 80.

24 John McLean, *The Indians of Canada: Their Manners and Customs* (1889, rpt. Coles, 1970), 274.

25 Alexander Ross, *The Red River Settlement: Its Rise, Progress and Present State* (London, 1856; rpt by Ross and Haines, Minneapolis, 1957), 267.

26 Ibid. See pages 205, 206, 79-80, 192, 199, 242, 302, 336, etc.

27 See such descriptions of Native life in George Bryce, *John Black: The Apostle of the Red River* (1898), 46.

28 Alexander Begg, *History of the North-west* (Toronto, 1894), 217.

29 Ibid., 417.

30 Doug Owram, *Promise of Eden: The Canadian Expansionist Movement and the Idea of the West 1856–1900* (Toronto: University of Toronto Press, 1980). Owram begrudgingly allows for this figure: "Man was, in fact, a relatively small presence in this vast area and it is unlikely that there were more than sixty thousand people living between the Rocky Mountains and the head of Lake Superior at

any time in the first half of the nineteenth century. Moreover, the great bulk of this population... was nomadic" (9). However, I do not consider Owram as the most reliable source on Indian populations, as most expansionists underestimate Aboriginal populations to support their civ/sav ideologies, a point Jennings makes convincingly. See Jennings, *Invasion of America*, 146, and chapter 2.

31 Memmi, *Colonizer and the Colonized*.

32 For American historiographic versions, see Henry Nash Smith, *Virgin Land* (Cambridge, MA: Harvard University Press, 1950); Roderick Nash, *Wilderness and the American Mind* (New Haven: Yale University Press, 1967). For a Canadian expansionist view and terminology, see Owram, *Promise of Eden*.

33 Jennings, *Invasion of America*, 15.

34 Quoted in Jennings, *Invasion of America*, 80.

35 Ibid. See Purchas's justification for advancing systematic destruction of Virginia Indians in Pearce, *Savagism*, 6–8.

36 Quoted in Rogin, *Fathers and Children*, 6.

37 Writers often take on the language of the subject they are studying. Owram in *Promise of Eden* often describes the land and Native peoples in such a way as to leave one wondering whether he is simply relaying expansionist attitudes or if he himself is expressing them. The following is a typically unclear comment: "the North West began to be described in terms more... than to a vast *unpeopled* land" (74; emphasis added).

38 For an excellent discussion on this ruling based largely on eighteenth-century bias, see, for example, Frank Cassidy, ed. *Aboriginal Title in British Columbia: Delgamuuko v. The Queen* (Lantzville: Oolichan Books/Montreal: The Institute for Research on Public Policy, 1992).

39 For an early treatment of this, see Pearce, *Savagism and Civilization*, 69–71. Flanagan in *First Nations, Second Thoughts* typically draws on Swiss jurist Emer de Vattel (1758) for his defence of "natural law", that is "civilization" (or re-settler) over hunter (28-47).

40 Ross, *Red River Settlement*, 322.

41 Owram, *Promise of Eden*, 73.

42 Bruce R. Morrison and C. Roderick Wilson, *Native Peoples: The Canadian Experience*, 2nd ed. (Toronto: McClelland and Stewart, 1995), 50.

43 Dickason, *Myth of the Savage*, 273.

44 Nash, *Wilderness*, 24.

45 Ibid., 28.

46 Owram, *Promise of Eden*, 24.

47 Respectively, West, *Substance*, 49; McLean, *Indians of Canada*, 270; Egerton R. Young, *Stories from Indian Wigwams and Northern Campfires* (London, 1893; rpt. Coles, 1974), 12; McDougall, *Pathfinding*, 70.

48 Owram, *Promise of Eden*, 72.

49 Ibid.

50 Begg, *History*, 417.

51 See McLean, *Indians of Canada*, 83, and Wm. Francis Butler, *The Great Lone Land* (1872; Edmonton: Mel Hurtig, 1968).

52 Young, *Stories*, 68–69.

53 James St. G. Walker, "The Indian in Canadian Historical Writing," *Canadian Historical Association Report* 22 (1971): 21–51.

54 See, for example, Lewis O. Saum, *The Fur Trade and the Indian* (Seattle and London: University of Washington Press, 1965).

55 McLean, *Indians of Canada*, 83.

56 Ibid., 61.

57 Ibid., 115.

58 See Roy Harvey Pearce's treatment (*Savagism*, 200–212) of James Fennimore Cooper's *Leatherstocking Tales*, in which the hero is a White frontiersman who must be as cunning a fighter and killer as the imagined savages he must destroy. However, Cooper's White savage Hawkeye is more noble than Richardson's Wacousta.

59 McLean, *Indians of Canada*, 61.

60 See Jennings, *Invasion of America*; Rogin, *Fathers and Children*.

61 Jennings, *Invasion of America*, 146.

62 Even though "squaw" sounds like a mispronounciation of the Algonquian *squoh* (woman), the White male usage of the term, as a rule, has had no resemblance to its origins. See Lutz's conversation with me on this in *Contemporary Challenges: Conversations with Canadian Native Authors* (Saskatoon: Fifth House Publisher, 1991), 181-202.

63 Early colonial writers often referred to Native societies as "nations," though it is not always clear what they meant by that. The *Indian Act*, old anthropology, and Hollywood have been instrumental in demoting Native nations to "tribes" and "bands."

64 Duchemin, "'A Parcel of Whelps.'"

65 Ibid., 54. Compare Brébeuf's "method" of calling the Huron to assembly: "I use the surplice and the square cap, to give more majesty to my appearance." Mealing, ed., *Jesuit Relations*, 46.

66 Duchemin, "'A Parcel of Whelps,'" 51.

67 Ibid., 60.

68 Ibid., 60–61.

69 Ibid., 61.

70 Ibid., 62–63.

71 Ibid., 63.

72 David G. Mandelbaum, *The Plains Cree* (1940; Regina: Canadian Plains Research Centre, 1979).

73 Duchemin, "'A Parcel of Whelps,'" 61.

74 Ibid., 63.

75 Ibid., 68.

76 E.E. Rich, "The Indian Traders," *The Beaver*, Winter 1970, 11, 12, and 17.

77 John C. Ewers, "The Influence of the Fur Trade Upon the Indians of the Northern Plains," *People and Pelts*, ed. Malvina Bolous (Winnipeg: Peguis Publishers, n.d.), 17.

78 Walker, "The Indian in Canadian Historical Writing," 34.

79   West, *Substance*, 68; emphasis added.

80   Ross, *Red River Settlement*, 284–285.

81   Ibid.; emphasis added.

82   Albert Memmi, Edward Said, and Chinua Achebe, among many other analysts, including contemporary sociologists (James Frideres, Rick Ponting) who study the nature of prejudice, have pointed to this easily observable phenomenon in people who oppress or discriminate.

83   Walker, "The Indian in Canadian Historical Writing," 23 and 25–26; emphasis added.

84   Ibid. There have been no new groundbreaking historiographic essays or monographs on Aboriginal peoples since James Walker's (1971). In his follow-up essay (1982) Walker finds that Canadian historians no longer engage in such offensive writing, but, instead, generally avoid treating Aboriginal histories altogether. The more recent approach taken by Robin Jarvis Brownlie in "First Nations Perspectives and Historical Thinking in Canada," in *First Nations, First Thoughts: The Impact of Indigenous Thought in Canada*, ed. Annis May Timpson (2009), is to emphasize a rather electric array of Aboriginal writing and corroborations.

85   Among the seventy-four authors Walker examines are notables such as J.M.S. Careless, D.G. Creighton, W.J. Eccles, F.L. Garneau, L.A. Groulx, A.R.M. Lower, W.S. MacNutt, E.M. McInnis, K.W. McNaught, A.S. Morton, G.F.G. Stanley, and G.M. Wrong.

86   Ibid., 21.

87   Ibid., 22 and 31–37.

88   Carl F. Klinck, "Literary Activity in the Canadas (1812–1841)," *Literary History of Canada: Canadian Literature in English*, Vol. 2, ed. Carl F. Klinck (Toronto: University of Toronto Press, 1965), 195.

89   Compare, for example, Henry the Elder's (1739–1824) gory and graphic description of what White historians call the Michilimackinac massacre of 1763: "from the bodies of some, ripped open, their butchers were drinking the blood... quaffed amid shouts of rage and victory." Quoted in Carl F. Klinck, "Introduction," in John Richardson, *Wacousta* (Philadelphis: Key and Biddle, 1932 rpt. 1967).

90   Margaret E. Turner, *Imagining Culture: New World Narrative and the Writing of Canada* (Montreal and Kingston: McGill-Queen's University Press, 1995), 26.

91   Ibid., 26–27.

92   Ibid., 33.

93   Ibid., 27.

94   Richardson, *Wacousta*, 276–79.

95   Leslie Monkman, *A Native Heritage: Images of the Indian in English Canadian Literature* (Toronto: University of Toronto Press, 1981), 11.

96   Richardson, *Wacousta*, 100.

97   Ralph Connor, *The Foreigner* (1909; rpt. National Library of Canada, 1978), 234.

98   Ibid.

99   Ralph Connor, *The Patrol of the Sun Dance Trail* (Toronto: Westminster Co. Ltd., 1914).

100 Ibid., 191.

Chapter Three

1 Howard Adams, *Prison of Grass* (Toronto: General Publishing, 1975), 11.

2 Walker, "The Indian in Canadian Historical Writing," 99.

3 For similar findings, see Ibid., 21–43.

4 Germaine Warkentin, ed., *Canadian Exploration Literature*: An Anthology (Toronto: Oxford University Press, 1993), x.

5 Ibid. I find the reasoned aloofness with which Warkentin (among others) seeks to balance power politics more trance-forming than transforming; e.g. she writes "Modern Canadians look back…(if they look at all) with mingled feelings; the European discovery…no longer seems a high-minded enterprise…. Like most societies which are the product of European expansionism, we began our social existence by consuming Satan's apple. The knowledge of good—an understandable affection for our own world and the life we have built in history—brought with it the knowledge of evil—the cost of our triumph to the people we attempted to supplant" (ix-x).

6 Emma LaRocque, "On the Ethics of Publishing Historical Records," in Jennifer S.H. Brown and Robert Brightman, eds. *The Orders of the Dreamed* (Winnipeg: University of Manitoba Press, 1988), 199-203.

7 A private letter.

8 James S. Frideres, *Aboriginal Peoples in Canada: Contemporary Conflicts* (Scarborough: Prentice Hall Allyn and Bacon Canada, 1998), 10.

9 Ibid.

10 Ibid., 12.

11 J.M. Blaut, *The Colonizer's Model of the World: Geographical Diffusionism and Eurocentric History* (New York and London: Guilford Press, 1993), 9.

12 For example, *1492: Conquest of Paradise* (1992), *The New World* (2005), *The Last of the Mohicans* (1992), *Dances with Wolves* (1990), *Black Robe* (1991), *Legends of the Fall* (1994), *The Scarlet Letter* (1995), *Squanto: A Warrior's Tale* (1994), *Pocahontas* (1995), *The Indian in the Cupboard* (1995).

13 Michael Hilger, *The American Indian in Film* (Metuchen, NJ and London: Scarecrow Press, 1986), 4.

14 For example, while there were violent confrontations between White and Native peoples, they were neither as violent, as frequent, or Native-originated as they are portrayed in movies. For further comment on this topic, see John E. O'Connor, *The Hollywood Indian* (Trenton: New Jersey State Museum, 1980). For excellent studies of audience inability to distinguish between Hollywood depictions and real Indians, see Berkhofer, *White Man's Indian*; Francis, *Imaginary Indian*; Doxtator, *Fluffs and Feathers*.

15 Blaut, *Colonizer's Model*, 6.

16 Ibid., 7.

17 Ibid., 1.

18 Ibid.

19 See, for example, C. McDiarmid and David Pratt, *Teaching Prejudice* (Toronto: Ontario Institute for Studies in Education, 1971). For a more contemporary assessment of racism in textbooks, see Jon Young, ed., *Breaking The Mosaic: Ethnic Identities in Canadian Schooling* (Toronto: Garamond Press, 1987).

20 Such analysts include Harold Cardinal, Howard Adams, George Manuel, Bruce Sealey and Verna Kirkness, Douglas Cardinal, Jane Willis, and myself, among others.

21 Manitoba Indian Brotherhood, for example, released a report in 1977 on textbook bias entitled *The Shocking Truth About Indians in Textbooks*.

22 Frideres, *Aboriginal Peoples*, 13.

23 For a comparative study of the White image of Aboriginal peoples in Canada, Australia, and New Zealand, see Goldie, *Fear and Temptation*.

24 Margaret Turner does not really pay attention to this rather conspicuous feature of Canadian literature in her treatment of some rather famous Canadian writers (Turner, *Imagining Culture*). There is not much new here from the Native perspective.

25 Monkman, *Native Heritage*, 3.

26 Ibid.

27 Said, *Orientalism*, 3.

28 Ibid., 8–9 and 2.

29 Attempts to exoticize the "Indian" usually take on noble savage, Hollywood, or plastic overtones, depending on the era. See Daniel Francis's discussion of "performing," "celebrity," "plastic," and "childhood" Indians, in which he includes Grey Owl, Pauline Johnson, and E.T. Seton (Francis, *Imaginary Indian*, Chapters 5–7).

30 Gaile McGregor, *The Wacousta Syndrome: Explorations in the Canadian Landscape* (Toronto: University of Toronto Press, 1985). See a similar treatment in Carl F. Klinck, *Literary History of Canada*.

31 Laura Groening, *Listening to Old Woman Speak: Natives and alterNatives in Canadian Literature* (Montreal: McGill-Queen's University Press, 2004), 72.

32 This phrase comes from Fraser J. Pakes, "Seeing With The Stereotypic Eye: The Visual Image of the Plains Indian," *Native Studies Review* 1, 2 (1985): 1–31.

33 Peter Puxley, "The Colonial Experience," in *Dene Nation—The Colony Within*, ed. Mel Watkin (Toronto: University of Toronto Press, 1977), 116.

34 Ibid.

35 Penny Petrone, *Native Literature in Canada*. See especially pp. 112, 117, 118, 120, 134, 135, 158, 162, 178, 182.

36 Ibid., 134, 150, and 162.

37 Ibid., 142 and 130.

38 Ibid., 182.

39 Ibid., 4–7.

40 Ibid., 3.

41 Ibid., 1.

42 See, for example, the review of *Spirit of the White Bison* in the *Winnipeg Free Press*, 10 August 1986.

43 Laura Groening, *Listening to Old Woman Speak* focuses on this debate. For further treatment on this, see also the preface to Lutz, *Contemporary Challenges*; Emma LaRocque, preface to Perreault and Vance, *Writing the Circle*; "Whose Voice Is It,

Anyway? A symposium on who should be speaking for whom," *Books in Canada* 20, 1 (1991): 11–17; Marlene Nourbese Philip, "The Disappearing Debate or How the Discussion of Racism Has Been Taken Over by the Censorship Issue," in *Borrowed Power: Essays on Cultural Appropriation*, ed. Bruce Ziff and Pratima V. Rao (Rutgers University Press, 1997).

44 Bruce Trigger, foreword to George Sioui, *For an American Autohistory* (Montreal and Kingston: McGill-Queen's University Press, 1992).

45 There are timeless observations about this in William Ryan, *Blaming The Victim* (New York: Random House, 1971).

46 Kenneth Coates and Robin Fisher, *Out of the Background: Readings on Canadian Native History*, 2nd ed. (Toronto: Copp Clark, 1996), 3.

47 Blaut, *Colonizer's Model*, 9–10.

48 For a good summary of the constitutional, political, and cultural changes, see Dickason, *Canada's First Nations*, 292–420.

Chapter Four

1 Sherene H. Razack, *Race, Space, and the Law: Unmapping a White Settler Society* (Toronto: Between the Lines: 2002).

2 See especially Chapter 2 in Jennings, *Invasion of America*. Jennings challenges White America's convenient and idelogical view that "savages" are sparsely populated. However, there is no final agreement as to Native populations at various stages of their pre- and post-contact with Europeans. Most historians provide wide-ranging estimates; see, as another example, Gerald Friesen's estimate of 6 to 10 million north of Mexico between 1000 and 1500 CE in *The Canadian Prairies: A History* (Toronto: University of Toronto Press, 1984), 15.

3 Morrison and Wilson, *Native Peoples*, 51.

4 Blaut, *Colonizer's Model*, 184.

5 See Jennings, *Invasion of America*.

6 A.D. Fisher, "A Colonial Education System: Historical Changes and Schooling in Fort Chipewyan," *Canadian Journal of Anthropology* 11, 1 (1981): 37–44.

7 See Waubageshig, ed., *The Only Good Indian* (Don Mills: Mills Press, 1974), 74–102.

8 Frideres, *Aboriginal Peoples*, 7.

9 For an incisive and readable overview of the dispossession, see Geoffrey York, *The Dispossessed: Life and Death in Native Canada* (London: Vintage UK, 1989).

10 Obviously, the Canadian Native experience was/is not like the Jewish experience under Hitler. However, German scholar and critic Hartmut Lutz has observed the White Canadian response (e.g., guilt and denial) to the cultural destruction of Native peoples has been similar to the German response regarding the Holocaust. See Hartmut Lutz's interview with me in *Contemporary Challenges*, 181-202.

11 Governments have imposed modernization schemes on a wide variety of peoples throughout many parts of the world. In this country there has been little understanding about the dramatic effects of forced modernization on Native peoples because of the dearly held notion that "Indians" are inherently anti-development. There is, however, powerful evidence that Native peoples have been battered by industrial assaults. See York, *The Dispossessed*. See also Anastasia M.

Shkilnyk, *A Poison Stronger Than Love: The Destruction of an Ojibwe Community* (New Haven: Yale University Press, 1985). For more personal observations on modernization, see my autobiographical article "Tides, Towns and Trains" In *Living The Changes*, Joan Turner, ed. (Winnipeg: University of Manitoba Press, 1990), 76-90.

12 See Boyce Richardson, *Strangers Devour The Land* (Toronto: Macmillan, 1975); Warner Troyer, *No Safe Place* (Toronto: Clarke, Irwin and Co., 1977); Hugh and Karmel McCallum, *This Land Is Not For Sale* (Toronto: Anglican Book Center, 1975); Boyce Richardson, ed., *Drumbeat: Anger and Renewal in Indian Country* (Toronto: Summerhill Press, Assembly of First Nations, 1989).

13 Kerry Abel and Jean Friesen, eds., *Aboriginal Resource Use in Canada: Historical and Legal Aspects* (Winnipeg: University of Manitoba Press, 1991).

14 *Choosing Life: Special Report on Suicide Among Aboriginal People* (Ottawa: Minister of Supply and Services, 1995), a study released by the Royal Commission on Aboriginal Peoples in 1995, reported that the rate of suicide among Aboriginal people for all age groups is "2 to 3 times higher than the rate among non-Aboriginals," and that it is "5 to 6 times higher among Aboriginal youth than among their non-Aboriginal peers" (1).

15 Peter Puxley, "The Colonial Experience," in *Dene Nation—The Colony Within*, ed. Mel Watkins (Toronto: University of Toronto Press, 1977), 104.

16 Edward Ahenakew, *Voices of the Plains Cree*, ed. R.M. Buck (Toronto: McClelland and Stewart, 1973), 26.

17 Quoted in Moses and Goldie, *Fear and Temptation*, 14.

18 Ibid., 22.

19 Ibid.

20 For a fuller treatment of Shinguaconse, see Janet E. Chute, *The Legacy of Shingwaukonse: A Century of Native Leadership* (Toronto: University of Toronto Press, 1998).

21 Quoted in Petrone, *Native Literature in Canada*, 65.

22 Pauline E. Johnson, *Flint and Feather* (1917; Toronto: Paperjacks, 1987).

23 Ibid., 10–14.

24 Ibid., 15–18.

25 Quoted in Hartwell Bowsfield, ed, *Louis Riel: Rebel of the Western Frontier or Victim of Politics and Prejudice?* (Toronto: Copp Clark, 1969), 35–37.

26 For a good overview of treaties, the *Indian Act*, reserves, residential schools, and Metis loss of lands, see Frideres, *Aboriginal Peoples*; J.R. Miller, *Skyscrapers Hide the Heavens* (Toronto: University of Toronto Press, 1989); Dickason, *Canada's First Nations*, and the Royal Commission on Aboriginal Peoples Report (1996), see especially chapter 4.

27 There are, of course, numerous works and viewpoints on Riel. For an introduction to Riel's thoughts and beliefs, see Thomas Flanagan, ed., *The Diaries of Louis Riel* (Edmonton: Hurtig Publishers, 1976), and Thomas Flanagan, *Louis 'David' Riel: Prophet of the New World* (Toronto: University of Toronto Press, 1979).

28 Petrone, *Native Literature*, 95–111.

29 Edward Ahenakew, *Voices of the Plains Cree*, ed. Ruth M. Buck (Toronto: McClelland and Stewart, 1973).

30 Ibid., 69.

31 Ibid., 13.

32 Harold Cardinal, *The Unjust Society* (Edmonton: Hurtig Publishers, 1969), 1.

33 Ibid., 1–3.

34 Moses and Goldie, *Fear and Temptation*, 14–15.

35 Douglas Cardinal, *Of the spirit*, 44.

36 Much has been learned concerning the real differences between Native and colonizer concepts and treatments of land through the study of legal cases on Aboriginal land rights. Many schools in this field may be consulted: see Bruce A. Cox, ed. *Native People Native Lands* (Ottawa: Carlton University Press, 1987); Frank Cassidy, ed. *Aboriginal Title in British Columbia* (1992); Keith Thor Carlson, *You Are Asked to Witness: The Stó:lô in Canada's Pacific Coast History* (Chilliwack: Stó:lô Heritage Trust, 1997).

37 Quoted in Petrone, *Native Literature*, 37.

38 Negotiated agreements were certainly not alien to Aboriginal politics or cultures. Historians (e.g., Abraham Rotstein, Jean Friesen, Olive Dickason, Arthur J. Ray) have noted the Aboriginal tradition of gift exchange and ceremony, which often attended the conclusion of trade or verbal agreements. These rituals signified the central importance of keeping one's word.

39 Beatrice Culleton Mosionier, *In Search of April Raintree* (Winnipeg: Pemmican Publications, 1983).

40 Maria Campbell, *Halfbreed* (Toronto: McClelland and Stewart, 1973), 11.

41 Duncan Mercredi, *Dreams of the Wolf in the City* (Winnipeg: Pemmican Publications, 1992), 1 and 3.

42 Ibid., 3-4.

43 Ibid., 50-51.

44 Duncan Mercredi, *Wolf and Shadows* (Winnipeg: Pemmican, 1995), 50.

45 George Kenny, *Indians Don't Cry* (Toronto: Chimo Publishing, 1977), 6.

46 Ibid.

47 Jeannette Armstrong, "Death Mummer," in Connie Fife, ed. *The Colour of Resistance* (Toronto: Sister Vision Press, 1993), 10.

48 Ibid., 10–11.

49 Sarain Stump, *There Is My People Sleeping* (Sidney, B.C.: Grays, 1970).

Chapter Five

1 In "The Gift," Dumont writes of watching her father revisit and linger over a beloved spot of land he had long ago lost. See Perreault and Vance, eds., *Writing The Circle*, 44–46.

2 Emma LaRocque, "Long Way From Home," *Ariel* 25.1 (January 1994), 122-126.

3 Quoted in Marty Dunn, *Red on White: The Biography of Duke Redbird* (Toronto: New Press, 1971), 84–86.

4 Quoted in Petrone, *Native Literature in Canada*, 93. See also Moses and Goldie *An Anthology of Canadian Native Literature in English* (Toronto: Oxford University Press, 1990).

5   Petrone provides examples of such.

6   Quoted in Catherine Soneegoh Sutton, "Letter," in *An Anthology of Canadian Native Literature*, ed. Daniel David Moses and Terry Goldie (Don Mills: Oxford University Press, 1992), 26.

7   Ibid, 26–27.

8   Constance Stevenson, "Prejudice (Or, In-Laws)" in Perreault and Vance, eds., *Writing the Circle*, 265.

9   Jennings, *Invasion*, 12.

10 Walker, "Indians in Canadian Historical Writing," 33.

11 Berkhofer, *The White Man's Indian*, 13.

12 Ibid.

13 Dickason, *Myth of the Savage*, 59.

14 Ibid.

15 Ibid., 63–64.

16 Cardinal, *Unjust Society*, 53.

17 Cardinal, *Of the Spirit*, 43.

18 Green, "Exploring Identity and Citizenship," 26.

19 Jane Willis, *Geneish: An Indian Girlhood* (Toronto: New Press, 1973), 67–68.

20 Howard Adams, *Prison of Grass* (Toronto: General Publishing, 1975), 16.

21 Campbell, *Halfbreed*, 50.

22 Ibid., 103.

23 Ibid., 117.

24 Ibid., 133.

25 Ibid., 134–135.

26 Adams, *Prison*, 142–143.

27 Ibid., 144. For the most part, I find Adams's treatment of the "White Ideal" compelling; however, he does generalize a lot, especially in Chapter 13. Much of the data or sociological commentary upon which he based his argument in 1975 is, of course, no longer applicable in whole.

28 Campbell, *Halfbreed*, 9.

29 Ernie Louttit, "Disadvantage to Advantage," in *Voices: Being Native in Canada*, ed. Linda Jaine and Drew Hayden Taylor (Saskatoon: University of Saskatchewan, 1992), 100–105.

30 Ibid., 100.

31 Ibid., 103.

32 Jeannette Armstrong, *Slash* (Penticton: Theytus Books, 1985), 35.

33 Deborah Doxtator, *Fluffs and Feathers: An Exhibit on the Symbols of Indianness* (Brantford: Woodland Cultural Centre, 1992).

34 From a speech broadcast on radio in 1925 by Six Nations Native activist Levi General (1873–1925). Quoted in Petrone, *Native Literature in Canada*, 103.

35 Quoted in Moses and Goldie, *Native Literature in English*, 110.

36 Chief Dan George, *My Heart Soars* (Saanichton, BC: Hancock House, 1974), 24.

37 Ibid., 42.

38 Ibid., 72.

39 George Kenny, *Indians Don't Cry*, 35.

40 Shilling, perhaps because he was passionate about painting and colour, emphasized "the beauty of my people" in *The Ojibway Dream* (Montreal: Tundra Books, 1986). Kenny, while highlighting the humanity of Native peoples, tends to dwell on the no-so-beautiful effects of colonization on "his people."

41 Kenny, *Indians Don't Cry*, 7.

42 Ibid., 7–10.

43 Ibid., 71.

44 See especially poems "Legacy" and "Death Bird" in *Indians Don't Cry*.

45 Ibid., 5.

46 Ibid., 78.

47 Loretta Todd, "What More Do They Want?" in *Indigena: Contemporary Native Perspectives*, ed. Gerald McMaster and Lee-Ann Martin (Vancouver: Douglas and McIntyre, 1992), 71.

48 Rita Joe, *Poems of Rita Joe* (Halifax: Abenaki Press, 1978), 2.

49 Quoted in Dickason, *Myth of the Savage*, 30.

50 Alexander Begg, *History of the North West, Vol. I* (Toronto, 1894), 217.

51 LaRocque, "Preface," xxii.

52 See Petrone, *Native Literature*.

53 D. Bruce Sealey and Verna J. Kirkness, *Indians Without Tipis*, ed. D. Bruce Sealey and Verna J. Kirkness (Agincourt: 1973), 55.

54 Joe, *Poems*, 3.

55 Ibid., 21.

56 Gloria Cranmer Webster, "From Colonization to Repatriation," in *Indigena*, ed. McMaster and Martin, 25.

57 Ibid., 25.

58 Louise Bernice Halfe, *Bear Bones and Feathers* (Regina: Coteau Books, 1994), 98.

59 Joane Cardinal-Shubert, speech quoted in Ormond McKague, ed. *Racism in Canada* (Saskatoon: Fifth House Publishers, 1991), 7.

60 Quoted in Moses and Goldie, *Native Literature in English*, 17–24.

61 Ibid.; emphasis in original.

62 Johnson, *Flint and Feather*, 10-14.

63 Alfred Groulx, in Joel T. Maki, ed. *Steal My Rage* (Vancouver: Douglas and McIntyre, 1995), 18.

64 Duke Redbird, in Marty Dunn, *Red on White: The Biography of Duke Redbird* (Toronto: New Press, 1971), 86.

65 Adams, *Prison of Grass*, 18.

66 Ibid., 19.

67 Daniel N. Paul, *We Were Not the Savages* (Halifax: Nimbus Publishing, 1993), 64.

68 Ibid., 108.

69 Ibid.

70 Ibid., 340; emphasis in original.

71 Jeannette Armstrong, in Moses and Goldie, *Native Literature in English,* 203–204.

72 Jeannette Armstrong, "This Is My Story" in *All My Relations,* ed. T. King (Toronto: McClelland and Stewart, 1990), 129.

73 Ibid., 133.

74 George Melnyk, introduction to Cardinal, *Of the Spirit,* 10–22.

75 Cardinal, *Of the Spirit,* 64.

76 Memmi, *Colonizer and the Colonized,* 86.

Chapter Six

1 George Copway, *Recollections of a Forest Life,* or *Life and Travels of KAH-GE-GA-GAH-BOWH* (London: C. Gilpin, 5, Bishopsgate Street Without, 1851, 2nd Edition), 10-12.

2 Puxley, "The Colonial Experience," 116.

3 In addition to Fanon's and Memmi's expositions on internalization, my study of the Afro-American experience, especially as articulated by Malcolm X, Eldridge Cleaver, Toni Morrison, Alice Walker, and Maya Angelou, has contributed to my understanding of the internalization problem. And, of course, the more recent postcolonial studies have enriched our treatment of the "subaltern." But most of all, I owe my understanding to my Native colleagues, who, by their honesty, confirmed my own experiences and research.

4 Quoted in Petrone, *Native Literature in Canada,* 49.

5 Ibid.

6 Dee Horne, *Contemporary American Indian Writing: Unsettling Literature* (New York: Peter Lang Pub., 1999), 13.

7 Helen Hoy cautions against "assimilating Nature narratives into the mainstream" in *How Should I Read These* (Toronto: University of Toronto Press, 2001), 9.

8 Johnson, *Flint and Feather,* 1–3.

9 Ibid.

10 Ibid., 4–6.

11 Ibid.

12 Doxtator, *Fluffs and Feathers,* 24. See also Daniel Francis, *The Imaginary Indian,* 111-123.

13 See Ojibway poet Armand Garnet Ruffo's *Grey Owl: The Mystery of Archie Belaney* (Regina: Coteau, 1997).

14 Quoted in Waubageshig, 184–188.

15 George Ryga, *The Ecstasy of Rita Joe and other plays* (Don Mills: General Publishing, 1971), 85.

16 Francis, *Imaginary Indian,* 53.

17 Berkhofer, *White Man's Indian,* 90.

18 Francis, *Imaginary Indian,* 53.

19 Ibid. Also see Edward S. Curtis, *Visions of a Vanishing.* Text by Florence Curtis Graybill and Victor Boesen (Boston: Houghton Mifflin Company, 1976).

20 Berkhofer, *White Man's Indian*, 90.

21 Francis, *Imaginary Indian*, 39.

22 Berkhofer, *White Man's Indian*, 77.

23 Ibid., 91.

24 See Seton's *Two Little Savages, Being the Adventures of Two Boys Who Lived as Indians and What They Learned* (New York: Grosset and Dunlap, 1903) and *The Gospel of the Redman* (London: Psychic Press, 1937). See also Francis, *Imaginary Indian*, 144–168.

25 Kateri Damm, "Says Who: Colonialism, Identity and Defining Indigenous Literature," in *Looking at the Words of our People: First Nations Analysis of Literature*, ed. Jeannette Armstrong (Penticton: Theytus Books, 1993), 14.

26 Francis, *Imaginary Indian*, 4.

27 Quoted in Ibid., 2.

28 Redbird, in Dunn, *Red on White: Biography of Duke Redbird*, 53.

29 Ibid., Preface.

30 George, *My Heart Soars*, 63.

31 Ibid., 30.

32 Rita Joe, *Poems of Rita Joe* (Halifax: Abenaki Press, 1978), Poem # 10.

33 Ibid.

34 Copway, *Recollections*, 12.

35 Halfe, *Blue Marrow* (Regina: Coteau Books, 2004).

36 Doxtator, in *Fluffs and Feathers*, 13.

37 George Sioui, *For an American Indian Autohistory* (Montreal: McGill-Queen's University Press, 1992), 61 and 8.

38 Ibid., 31 and 38.

39 Ibid., 37.

40 Ibid., 36.

41 Ibid., 37.

42 Ibid., 38.

43 This is a long-standing problem for Native peoples—whether it is us struggling to fit or whether others are posing as "Indian." See Doxtator, *Fluffs and Feathers* and Daniel Francis, *The Imaginary Indian*.

44 Marilyn Dumont, "Popular Images Of Nativeness" in *Looking at the Words of Our People*, ed. J. Armstrong, 49.

45 Jeannette Armstrong, "Land Speaking," in *Speaking for the Generations: Native Writers on Writing*, ed. Simon J. Ortiz (Tucson: University of Arizona Press, 1998), 175–76.

46 See Joyce Green, "Cultural and Ethnic Fundamentalism: The Mixed Potential for Identity, Liberation, and Oppression" in *Right Thinking: Fundamentalism Across Themes*, ed. Carol Schick, JoAnn Jaffe, Ailsa Watkinson (Halifax: Fernwood Publishing, 2004), 19-34.

47 Howard Adams, *A Tortured People: The Politics of Colonization* (Penticton: Theytus Books, 1995), 34.

48 That the Cree of James Bay used snowmobiles (instead of dogsleds) to travel to their camps was used against them by lawyers defending the James Bay Hydro in Quebec.

See Boyce Richardson, *Strangers Devour the Land* (Toronto: MacMillan of Canada, 1975). Notions of difference and tradition have been used spuriously in other areas too; see Emma LaRocque, "Re-examining Culturally Appropriate Models in Criminal Justice Applications," in *Aboriginal and Treaty Rights in Canada*, ed. Michael Asch (Vancouver: University of British Columbia Press, 1997), 75–96.

49 Memmi, *Colonizer and the Colonized*, 71.

50 Ashcroft, Griffiths, and Tiffin, *The Empire Writes Back*, 11.

51 Arguments for "cultural differences" (as a basis for culturally appropriate programs) are also popular in proposals for self-government; see the Royal Commission on Aboriginal Peoples (Canada, 1995), see Frideres, *Aboriginal Peoples in Canada*, 245–246.

52 Kimberly M. Blaeser, "Native Literature: Seeking A Critical Center" in *Looking at the Words of Our People*, ed. J. Armstrong, 51-61.

53 Ashcroft, Griffiths, and Tiffin, *Key Concepts*, 60–61.

54 Doxtator, *Fluffs and Feathers*, 12.

55 Ibid.

56 Victor J. Ramraj, "Preface," in *Concert of Voices: An Anthology of World Writing in English*, ed. Victor J. Ramraj (Peterborough: Broadview Press, 1995), xxix.

57 Puxley, "The Colonial Experience," 111.

58 Quoted in Perreault and Vance, xxii.

59 Gloria Cranmer Webster, "From Colonization to Repatriation," in *Indigena: Contemporary Native Perspectives*, ed. Gerald McMaster and Lee-Ann Martin (Vancouver: Douglas and McIntyre, 1992), 36–37.

Chapter Seven

1 Jeannette Armstrong, *Whispering in Shadows*, (Penticton: Theytus Books, 2001), 19.

2 For example, see the critical works by Renate Eigenbrod, Julia Emberly, Margery Fee, Laura Groening, Barbara Godard, Dee Horne, Helen Hoy, Lynette Hunter, Hartmut Lutz.

3 In the early 1990s, several critics focussed repeatedly and almost exclusively on Armstrong, Campbell, Culleton, and Maracle. See, for example, essays by Margery Fee, Barbara Godard, Agnes Grant, and Noel Elizabeth Currie in W.H. New, *Native Writers and Canadian Literature*. Such a focus led to further studies focussing again on these writers. What this meant at that time was many other Native writers, including Slipperjack, did not receive the critical attention they deserved. Much has changed in criticism since the 1990s, as Note 2 indicates.

4 Armstrong, *Slash*, 24.

5 Ibid., 58–121.

6 Ibid., 179–218.

7 Ruby Slipperjack, *Honour the Sun* (Winnpeg: Pemmican Publications, 1987), 1–169.

8 Ibid., 35–37, 87–94, and 105–113.

9 Ibid., 35–37.

10 Ibid., 181–210.

11 Ibid., 223–224.

12 Ibid., 181.

13 Ibid., 159-160.

14 Lutz, *Contemporary Challenges*, 208.

15 Ibid., 208–209.

16 Ibid., 14.

17 Ibid., 16.

18 Ibid.

19 Ibid.

20 Thomas King, "Introduction," *All My Relations*, ed. Thomas King (Toronto: McClelland and Stewart, 1990).

21 See, for example, Basil Johnston, Thomson Highway, Lenore Keeshig-Tobias, Louis Owens, Gerald Vizenor.

22 Dickason, *Canada's First Nations*, 419.

23 It is actually notoriously difficult to get exact statistics on Aboriginal urbanization. Frideres, for example, cites 1991 studies that show that 38.2 percent of Status Indians are off-reserve. This, though, does not take into account other Aboriginal peoples (Status and non-Status Indians, Inuitl and Metis). Such stats are further complicated by failure to specify terms. Frideres often uses the normally inclusive term "Aboriginal" when he is reffering to "on- or off-reserve Indians." Other times he uses "Aboriginal" to include the Metis but not the Inuit. Generally, Aboriginal urbanization varies considerably from region to region.

24 Blaut, *The Colonizer's Model of the World*, 1–3.

25 Paul Levine, "Frantz Fanon: The Politics of Skin," in *Divisions* (Toronto: The Hunter Rose Company for CBC Publications), 37.

26 Among the scholars who have advanced this historically grounded thesis are Francis Jennings, James Axtell, Cornelius Jaenen, Jack Weatherford, Robin Ridington, and James M. Blaut.

27 See Toni Morrison, *Playing in the Dark: Whiteness and the Literary Imagination* (Cambridge: Harvard University Press, 1992). See also Henry Louis Gates Jr., ed., *Black Literature and Literary Theory* (New York: Methuen, 1984).

28 Harlow, *Resistance Literature*, 30.

29 Jeannette Armstrong, "The Disempowerment of First North American Native Peoples and Empowerment Through Their Writing," in Moses and Goldie, eds., *Native Literature in English*, 211.

30 As he put it in a film with the same title. Shilling died in 1986 from heart failure at the age of forty-five but not before he could produce *The Ojibway Dream*, a book mixing poetry and art.

31 Arthur Shilling, *The Ojibway Dream* (Montreal: Tundra Books, 1986), 20.

32 Richard Wagamese, *Quality of Light* (Toronto: Doubleday Canada, 1997), 3.

33 Armstrong, "Disempowerment," 208.

34 In *Native Literature in Canada* Penny Petrone produced an extensive library of Aboriginal authors and works covering the period from the 1820s to 1990. Since 1990 hundreds of Native authored writings, fiction and non-fiction, have appeared, such that we need an updated critical survey of Canadian Aboriginal Literatures. What's

more, a growing number of these writers are publishing multiple works or genres; they include Richard Wagamese, Ruby Slipperjack, Lee Maracle, Louise Halfe, Thomas King, Jeannette Armstrong, Richard Van Camp, Drew Hayden Taylor, Gregory Scofield, Duncan Mercredi, Annaharte Marie Baker, Marilyn Dumont, Eden Robinson, Warren Cariou, Neal McLeod, Joseph Boyden, Beatrice Culleton Mosionier, among others.

Postscript

1   Maria Campbell, *Stories of the Road Allowance People* (Penticton: Theytus Books, 1995), 143.

2   Green, "Exploring Identity and Citizenship," 26.

3   Ashcroft, Griffiths, and Tiffin, *The Empire Writes Back*.

4   *Mooneow* in my community refers to White people, but not in terms of colour. Rather, it connotes commodity or money.

5   Jeanne Perreault, "Notes from the Co-editors," *Ariel: A Review of International English Literature* 25, 1 (1994): 10.

6   Lynette Hunter, *Outsider Notes: Feminist Approaches to Nation State Ideology, Writers/Readers and Publishing* (Vancouver: Talonbooks, 1996), 159.

7   W.H. New, editorial, *Native Writers and Canadian Writing: Canadian Literature Special Issue*, ed. W.H. New (Vancouver: University of British Columbia Press, 1990), 4.

8   Ibid., 8.

9   Blaut affirms Wolf for providing a "useful and important survey," showing how "unconvincing is the theory that non-European civilizations, historically, were stagnant and unprogressive." But Blaut criticizes Wolf for stopping short of "questioning the truly crucial Eurocentric belief that Europeans were *more* progressive than non-Europeans." Blaut, *Colonizer's Model*, 137n15.

10   In this context, voice and victim have been used interchangeably in reference to Native peoples.

11   I mean this in the profoundest sense of the word "knowledge," knowledge that is uniquely indigenous but not caricatured, confined, nor congealed. See my article "From the Land to the Classroom: Broadening Aboriginal Epistemology" in eds., Jill Oakes, Rick Riewe, Marlyn Bennet and Brenda Chisholm, *Pushing the Margins* (Winnipeg: Native Studies Press, 2001). See also Linda Tuhiwai Smith, *Decolonizing Methodologies: Research and Indigenous Peoples* (London: ZED Books, 1999).

12   Harlow, *Resistance Literature*, 7.

13   The following is a tiny sampling of Aboriginal histories that are simply outstanding in their respect for Aboriginal peoples and knowledge, research, and meticulous detail. They include: Kerry M. Abel, *Changing Places: History, Community, and Identity in Northeastern Ontario* (2006); Kerry Abel, *Drum Songs: Glimpses of Dene History* (2005); Keith Thor Carlson, ed., *You Are Asked To Witness: The Stó:lō in Canada's Pacific Coast History* (1997).

14   Peter Kulchyski, professor in the Department of Native Studies, University of Manitoba, a political science specialist, has long put into practice his engaged research with Native northerners. His extraordinary appreciation of Native-land-knowledge is evident in his works. See especially *Like the Sound of a Drum*, 2005.

15 Ashcroft, Griffiths, and Tiffin, "Introduction," *Empire*, 32.

16 Greg Young-Ing, "Aboriginal People's Estrangement: Marginalization in the Publishing Industry" in J. Armstrong, ed., *Looking at the Words*, 182.

17 Hunter, *Outsider Notes*, 145.

18 See Brydon's and Hutcheon's articles in Ashcroft, Griffiths, and Tiffin, eds., *Post-Colonial Studies Reader*.

19 See, for example, Ashcroft et al., Gaile McGregor, Leslie Monkman, and Margaret Turner.

20 Francis, *Imaginary Indian*, 224.

21 Renate Eigenbrod, *Travelling Knowledges* (Winnipeg: University of Manitoba Press, 2005), 206.

22 Laura Groening in *Listening to Old Woman Speak* devotes a chapter on "The Healing Aesthetic of Basil Johnston." She does not define what she means by the phrase "healing aesthetic." See also Lewis Mehl-Madrona, PhD, *Narrative Medicine: The Use of History and Story in the Healing Process* (Rochester: Bear and Company, 2007); Jo-Ann Episkenew, *Taking Back Our Spirits: Indigenous Literature, Public Policy and Healing* (Winnipeg: University of Manitoba Press, 2009).

23 Native writers have tended to use caricature, often humorous, in their characterization of the colonizer. Margo Kane "makes faces" at the colonizer through her scathingly humorous treatment of stereotypes in *Moonlodge*. There are sprinkles of colonialist (usually White) characters in other Native works; the most extensive is Armand Garnet Ruffo's playful study of Grey Owl. Basil Johnston also pokes fun at the colonizer in *Moose Meat and Wild Rice*. Richard Wagamese deals with the White psyche to some degree, but the issue remains ripe for treatment.

24 Blaeser, "Native Literature: Seeking a Critical Center," 51–62.

25 Gaile McGregor, *The Wacousta Syndrome: Explorations in the Canadian Landscape* (Toronto: University of Toronto Press, 1985), 200–201.

26 Emma LaRocque, "Long Way from Home," *Ariel: A Review of International English Literature* 25, 1 (1994): 122–126.

Bibliography

Abel, Kerry. *Changing Places: History, Community, and Identity in Northeastern Ontario.* Montreal: McGill-Queen's University Press, 2006.

_____. *Drum Songs: Glimpses of Dene History.* 2nd ed. Montreal: McGill-Queen's University Press, 2005.

Abel, Kerry, and Jean Friesen, eds. *Aboriginal Resource Use in Canada: Historical and Legal Aspects.* Winnipeg: University of Manitoba Press, 1991.

Abelove, Henry, et al., eds. *Visions of History.* Manchester: Manchester University Press, 1983.

Achebe, Chinua. "Colonialist Criticism." In *The Post-Colonial Studies Reader,* ed. Bill Ashcroft, Gareth Griffiths, and Helen Tiffin. London and New York: Routledge, 1995.

Achimoona. Introduced by Maria Campbell. Saskatoon: Fifth House, 1985.

Acoose, Janice. *Iskwewak: Kah' Ki Yaw Ni Wahkomakanak.* Toronto: Women's Press, 1995.

_____. "Post Halfbreed: Indigenous Writers as Authors of Their Own Realities." In *Looking at the Words of our People: First Nations Analysis of Literature,* ed. Jeannette Armstrong. Penticton: Theytus Books, 1993.

Adams, Howard. *A Tortured People: The Politics of Colonization.* Penticton: Theytus Books, 1995.

_____. *Prison of Grass.* Toronto: General Publishing, 1975.

Ahenakew, Edward. *Voices of the Plains Cree.* Edited by Ruth M. Buck. Toronto: McClelland and Stewart, 1973.

Alfred, Gerald R. *Heeding the Voices of Our Ancestors.* Toronto: Oxford University Press, 1995.

Alfred, Taiaiake (Gerald). "Redressing Racist Academics, Or, Put Your Clothes Back on, Please!" (review of *Disrobing the Aboriginal Industry* by Frances Widdowson and Albert Howard). http://www.taiaiake.com/42 (accessed 11 June 2009).

Alieoof, Maurie, and Susan Schouten Levine. "Interview: The Long Walk of Alanis Obomsawin." *Cinema Canada*, June 1987, 10–15.

Allan, Luke. *Blue Pete: Rebel.* London: Herbert Jenkins, 1940.

Allen, Paula Gunn. *The Sacred Hoop: Recovering the Feminine in American Indian Traditions.* Boston: Beacon Press, 1986.

Angelou, Maya. *The Complete Collected Poems of Maya Angelou.* New York: Random House, 1994.

_____. *I Know Why The Caged Bird Sings.* New York: Bantam Books, 1970.

Armstrong, Jeannette. *Whispering in Shadows.* Penticton: Theytus Books, 2001.

_____. "Land Speaking." In *Speaking for the Generations: Native Writers on Writing,* ed. Simon J. Ortiz. Tucson: University of Arizona Press, 1998.

_____. *Breath Tracks.* Toronto: Williams-Wallace Publishers, 1991.

_____. "This Is A Story." In *All My Relations: An Anthology of Canadian Native Fiction,* ed. Thomas King. Toronto: McClelland and Stewart, 1991.

_____. *Slash.* Penticton: Theytus Books, 1985.

_____. "The Disempowerment of First North American Native Peoples and Empowerment Through Their Writing." In *An Anthology of Canadian Native Literature in English,* ed. Daniel David Moses and Terry Goldie. Toronto: Oxford University Press, 1992.

Armstrong, Jeannette, ed. *Looking at the Words of our People: First Nations Analysis of Literature.* Penticton: Theytus Books, 1993.

Armstrong, Jeannette C., and Lally Grauer, eds. *Native Poetry in Canada: A Contemporary Anthology.* Peterborough: Broadview Press, 2001.

Asch, Michael. *Aboriginal and Treaty Rights in Canada: Essys on Law, Equity, and Respect for Difference.* Vancouver: University of British Columbia Press, 1997.

_____. *Home and Native Land: Aboriginal Rights and the Canadian Constitution.* Toronto: Methuen, 1984.

Ashcroft, Bill, and Gareth Griffiths, Helen Tiffin. *Key Concepts in Post-Colonial Studies.* London and New York: Routledge, 1998.

_____. *The Empire Writes Back: Theory and Practice in Post-Colonial Literature.* New York: Routledge, 1989.

Bill Ashcroft, Gareth Griffiths, and Helen Tiffin, eds. *The Post-Colonial Studies Reader.* London and New York: Routledge, 1995.

Atwood, Margaret and Robert Weaver. *The New Oxford Book of Canadian Short Stories in English.* Toronto: Oxford University Press, 1997.

Axtell, James. *Natives and Newcomers: The Cultural Origins of North America.* New York: Oxford University Press, 2001.

_____. *The Invasion Within: The Contest of Cultures in Colonial North America.* New York: Oxford University Press, 1985.

Bailey, A.G. *The Conflict of European and Eastern Algonkian Cultures 1504–1700.* Toronto: University of Toronto Press, 1969.

Baker, Marie Annaharte. *Being On The Moon.* Winlaw, BC: Polestar Press, 1990.

Baldwin, James. *Notes of a Native Son.* Boston: Beacon Press, 1949.

Bannerji, Himani. *Returning the Gaze: Essays on Racism, Feminism and Politics.* Toronto: Sister Vision Press, 1993.

Battiste, Marie, ed. *Reclaiming Indigenous Voice and Vision.* Vancouver: University of British Columbia Press, 2000.

Begg, Alexander. *History of the North-west.* 3 vols. Toronto: Hunter and Rose, 1894.

_____. *Alexander Begg's Red River Journal and Other Papers Relative to the Red River Resistance of 1869–70.* Edited by W.L. Morton. Toronto: Champlain Society, 1956.

Berger, Carl, and Ramsay Cook, eds. *The West and the Nation.* Toronto: McClelland and Stewart, 1976.

Berger, Thomas. *Northern Frontier, Northern Homeland: The Report of the Mackenzie Valley Pipeline Inquiry: Volume One.* Ottawa: Minister of Supply and Services, 1977.

Berkes, Fikret. "Traditional Ecological Knowledge in Perspective." In *Traditional Ecological Knowledge: Concepts and Cases,* ed. Julian T. Inglis. Ottawa: International Program on Traditional Ecological Knowledge and International Development Research Centre, 1993.

Berkhofer, Robert F. *The White Man's Indian.* New York: Random House, 1978.

Berton, Pierre. *Hollywood's Canada.* Toronto: McClelland and Stewart, 1975.

Bhabba, Homi K. "Cultural Diversity and Cultural Differences." In *The Post-Colonial Studies Reader,* ed. Bill Ashcroft, Gareth Griffiths, and Helen Tiffin. London and New York: Routledge, 1995.

Blaeser, Kimberly M. "Native Literature: Seeking a Critical Center." In *Looking at the Words of our People: First Nations Analysis of Literature,* ed. Jeannette Armstrong. Penticton: Theytus Books, 1993.

Blaut, J.M. *The Colonizer's Model of the World: Geographical Diffusionism and Eurocentric History.* New York and London: Guilford Press, 1993.

Bolt, Christine. *Victorian Attitudes To Race.* Toronto: University of Toronto Press, 1971.

Boon, T.C. *The Anglican Church From the Bay to the Rockies.* Toronto: Ryerson Press, 1962.

Bowsfield, Hartwell, ed. *Louis Riel: Rebel of the Western Frontier or Victim of Politics and Prejudice?* Toronto: Copp Clark, 1969.

Brant, Beth, ed. *A Gathering of Spirit: Writing and Art of North American Indian Women.* Toronto: Women's Press, 1988.

Brant, Beth. "A Long Story." In *An Anthology of Canadian Native Literature in English*, ed. Daniel David Moses and Terry Goldie. Toronto: Oxford University Press, 1992.

_____. *Mohawk Trail*. Ithaca, NY: Firebrand Books, 1985.

Brant Castellano, Marlene. "Vocation or Identity: The Dilemma of Indian Youth." In *The Only Good Indian*, ed. Waubageshig. Revised ed. Don Mills, ON: New Press, 1974.

Brodribb, Somer. "The Traditional Roles of Native Women in Canada and the Impact of Colonization." *Canadian Journal of Native Studies* 4, 1 (1984): 85–103.

Brown, Dee. *Bury My Heart at Wounded Knee*. New York: Holt, Rinehart and Winston, 1970.

Brown, Leslie, and Susan Strega, eds. *Research as Resistance: Critical, Indigenous, and Anti-Oppressive Approaches*. Toronto: Canadian Scholars' Press, 2005.

Brown, Jennifer S.H., and Elizabeth Vibert. *Reading Beyond Words: Contexts for Native History*. Peterborough: Broadview Press, 1998.

Brown, Jennifer S.H., and Robert Brightman. *"The Orders of the Dreamed": George Nelson on Cree and Northern Ojibwa Religion and Myth, 1823*. Winnipeg: University of Manitoba Press, 1988.

Brownlie, Robin Jarvis. "First Nations Perspectives and Historical Thinking in Canada." In *First Nations, First Thoughts—New Challenges*, ed. Annis May Timpson. Vancouver: University of British Columbia Press, 2009. 21-50

Bryce, George. *John Black: The Apostle of the Red River*. 1898.

Butler, Wm. Francis. *The Great Lone Land*. 1872. Edmonton: Hurtig Publishers, 1968.

Cameron, Ann (Cam Hubert). *Dreamspeaker and Tem Eyos Ki and the Land Claims Question*. Toronto: Clarke, Irwin, 1978.

Campbell, Maria. *Stories of the Road Allowance People*. Penticton: Theytus Books, 1995.

_____. *Halfbreed*. Toronto: McClelland and Stewart, 1973.

Cardinal, Douglas. *Of the Spirit*. Edited by George Melnyk. Edmonton: NeWest Press, 1977.

Cardinal, Harold. *The Rebirth of Canada's Indians*. Edmonton: Hurtig Publishers, 1976.

_____. *The Unjust Society*. Edmonton: Hurtig Publishers, 1969.

Cardinal-Schubert, Joane. "Surviving As a Native Woman Artist." In *Racism in Canada*, ed. Ormond McKague, Saskatoon: Fifth House Publishers, 1991.

Cariou, Warren. "Haunted Prairie: Aboriginal 'Ghosts' and the Spectres of Settlement." *University of Toronto Quarterly* 75, 2 (2006): 727–734.

_____. *Lake of the Prairies: Stories of Belonging*. Scarborough, ON: Doubleday Canada, 2002.

_____. *The Exalted Company of Roadside Martyrs: Two Novellas*. Regina: Coteau Books, 1999.

Carlson, Keith Thor. *You Are Asked to Witness: The Stó:lô in Canada's Pacific Coast History*. Chilliwack, BC: Stó:lô Heritage Trust, 1997.

Carter, Sarah. *Lost Harvests: Prairie Indian Reserve Farmers and Government Policy.* Montreal: McGill-Queen's University Press, 1990.

_____. "The Missionaries' Indian: The Publications of John McDougall, John Maclean and Egerton Ryerson Young." *Prairie Forum* 9, 1 (1984): 27–44.

Cassidy, Frank, ed. *Aboriginal Title in British Columbia: Delgamuukw v. The Queen.* Lantzville, BC: Oolichan Books, 1992.

Christian, Barbara. "The Race for Theory." In *The Post-Colonial Studies Reader*, ed. Bill Ashcroft, Gareth Griffiths, and Helen Tiffin. London and New York: Routledge, 1995.

Chute, Janet E. *The Legacy of Shingwaukonse: A Century of Native Leadership.* Toronto: University of Toronto Press, 1998.

Clark, Kenneth. *Civilisation.* New York: Harper and Row, 1969.

Cleaver, Eldridge. *Soul on Ice.* New York: Dell, 1968.

Clutesi, George. *Potlatch.* Sidney, BC: Grays, 1969.

Colorado, Pam. "Bridging Native and Western Science." *Convergence* 21, 2–3 (1988): 49–67.

Connor, Ralph. *The Foreigner.* 1909. Ottawa: National Library of Canada, 1978.

_____. *The Patrol of the Sun Dance Trail.* Toronto: Westminster Co. Ltd., 1914.

Cook, Ramsay, Craig Brown, and Carl Berger, eds. *Approaches to Canadian History.* Toronto: University of Toronto Press, 1967.

Cooper, James Fennimore. *The Last of the Mohicans.* 1826. London: Pan Books, 1977.

Copway, George. *The Traditional History and Characteristic Sketches of the Ojibway Nation.* New York: AMS Press, 1972.

_____. *Recollections of a Forest Life: or, The life and travels of Kah-ge-ga-gah-bowh, or, George Copway, Chief of the Ojibway Nation.* 2nd ed. London: C. Gilpin, 1851.

_____. *The life, history and travels of Kah-ge-ga-bowh (George Copway): a young Indian chief of the Ojebwa nation, a convert to the Christian faith and a missionary to his people for twelve years; with a sketch of the present state of the Ojebwa nation in regard to Christianity and their future prospects: also, an appeal with all the names of the chiefs now living, who have been christianized, and the missionaries now laboring among them.* 6th ed. Philadelphia: J. Harmstead, 1847.

Craven, Margaret. *I Heard the Owl Call My Name.* Toronto: Clarke, Irwin, 1967.

Culhane-Speck, Dara. *An Error in Judgement.* Vancouver: Talonbooks, 1987.

Culleton Mosionier, Beatrice. *Spirit of the White Bison.* Winnipeg: Pemmican Publications, 1985.

_____. *In Search of April Raintree.* Winnipeg: Pemmican Publications, 1983.

Cumming, Peter A., and Neil H. Mickenberg. *Native Rights in Canada.* Toronto: General Publishing, 1970.

Currie, Elizabeth Noel. "Jeannette Armstrong and the Colonial Legacy." In *Native Writers and Canadian Writing: Canadian Literature Special Issue*, ed. W.H. New. Vancouver: University of British Columbia Press, 1990.

Cuthand, Beth. *Voices in the Waterfall.* Penticton: Theytus Books, 1989.

Damm, Kateri. "Says Who: Colonialism, Identity and Defining Indigenous Literature." In *Looking at the Words of our People: First Nations Analysis of Literature*, ed. Jeannette Armstrong. Penticton: Theytus Books, 1993.

_____. "Dispelling and Telling: Speaking Native Realities in Maria Campbell's Halfbreed and Beatrice Culleton's In Search of April Raintree." In *Looking at the Words of our People: First Nations Analysis of Literature*, ed. Jeannette Armstrong. Penticton: Theytus Books, 1993.

Day, David, and Marilyn Bowering, eds. *Many Voices: An Anthology of Contemporary Canadian Indian Poetry*. Vancouver: J.J. Douglas, 1977.

Deloria, Philip J. *Playing Indian*. New Haven and London: Yale University Press, 1998.

Dene Nation. *Denendeh: A Dene Celebration*. Yellowknife: Dene Nation, 1984.

Dickason, Olive Patricia. *The Native Imprint: The Contribution of First Peoples to Canada's Character*. 2 vols. Athabasca, AB: Athabasca University, 1995.

_____. *Canada's First Nations: A History of Founding Peoples from Earliest Times*. Toronto: McClelland and Stewart, 1992.

_____. *The Myth of the Savage and the Beginnings of French Colonialism in the Americas*. Edmonton: University of Alberta Press, 1984.

Donovan, Kathleen M. *Feminist Readings of Native North American Literature: Coming to Voice*. Tucson: University of Arizona Press, 1998.

Doxtator, Deborah. *Fluffs and Feathers: An Exhibit on the Symbols of Indianness*. Brantford, ON: Woodland Cultural Centre, 1992.

Duchemin, Parker. "'A Parcel of Whelps': Alexander Mackenzie among the Indians." In *Native Writers and Canadian Writing: Canadian Literature Special Issue*, ed. W.H. New. Vancouver: University of British Columbia Press, 1990.

_____. "Stealing History." *Briarpatch*, October 1988, 17–23.

Dumont, Marilyn. *A Really Good Brown Girl*. London, ON: Brick Books, 1996.

_____. "Popular Images of Nativeness." In *Looking at the Words of our People: First Nations Analysis of Literature*, ed. Jeannette Armstrong. Penticton: Theytus Books, 1993.

_____. "The Gift." In *Writing The Circle: Native Women of Western Canada*, ed. Jeanne Perreault and Sylvia Vance. Edmonton: NeWest Publishers, 1990.

Dunn, Marty. *Red on White: The Biography of Duke Redbird*. Toronto: New Press, 1971.

Eagleton, Terry. *Ideology: An Introduction*. London: Verso, 1991.

Easingwood, Peter, Konrad Gross, and Hartmut Lutz, eds. *Informal Empire? Cultural Relations between Canada, the United States and Europe*. Kiel, Germany: I and F Verlag, 1998.

Eigenbrod, Renate. *Travelling Knowledges: Positioning the Im/migrant Reader of Aboriginal Literatures in Canada*. Winnipeg: University of Manitoba Press, 2005.

_____. "Can 'The Subaltern' Be Read? The Role of the Critic in Postcolonial Studies." *Acolit*, 2 (1996): 97–102.

_____. "The Oral in the Written: A Literature Between Two Cultures." *Canadian Journal of Native Studies* 15, 1 (1995): 89–102.

Eigenbrod, Renate, and Jo-Ann Episkenew, eds. *Creating Community: A Roundtable on Canadian Aboriginal Literature*. Penticton and Brandon: Theytus and Bearpaw, 2002.

Emberly, Julia V. *Thresholds of Difference: Feminist Critique, Native Women's Writings, Postcolonial Theory*. Toronto: University of Toronto Press, 1993.

Episkenew, Jo-Ann. *Taking Back Our Spirits: Indigenous Literature, Public Policy, and Healing*. Winnipeg: University of Manitoba Press, 2009.

Ewers, John C. "The Influence of the Fur Trade Upon the Indians of the Northern Plains." In *People and Pelts*, ed. Malvina Bolous. Winnipeg: Peguis Publishers, 1972.

Fanon, Frantz. *Black Skin, White Masks*. 1952. New York: Grove Press, 1967.

_____. *The Wretched of the Earth*. New York: Grove Press, 1963.

Fee, Margery. "Who Can Write as Other?" In *The Post-Colonial Studies Reader*, ed. Bill Ashcroft, Gareth Griffiths, and Helen Tiffin. London and New York: Routledge, 1995.

_____. "Upsetting Fake Ideas: Jeannette Armstrong's 'Slash' and Beatrice Culleton's 'April Raintree.'" In *Native Writers and Canadian Writing: Canadian Literature Special Issue*, ed. W.H. New. Vancouver: University of British Columbia Press, 1990.

Ferguson, Russell. "Introduction: Invisible Center." In *Out There: Marginalisation and Contemporary Cultures*, ed. Russell Ferguson et al. New York: New Museum of Contemporary Art, 1990.

Fiddler, Don, and Linda Jaine, eds. *Gatherings*. 6 vols. Penticton: Theytus Publishers, 1995

Fife, Connie. *The Colour of Resistance: A Contemporary Collection of Writing by Aboriginal Women*. Toronto: Sister Vision Press, 1993.

Fisher, A.D. "A Colonial Education System: Historical Changes and Schooling in Fort Chipewyan." *Canadian Journal of Anthropology* 11, 1 (1981): 37–44.

Fisher, Robin, and Kenneth Coates, eds. *Out of the Background: Readings on Canadian Native History*. Toronto: Copp Clark Pitman, 1996 [1988].

Flanagan, Thomas. *First Nations? Second Thoughts*. Montreal: McGill-Queen's University Press, 2000.

_____. *Louis 'David' Riel: Prophet of the New World*. Toronto: University of Toronto Press, 1979.

Flanagan, Thomas, ed. *The Diaries of Louis Riel*. Edmonton: Hurtig Publishers, 1976.

Forer, Mort. *The Humpback*. Toronto: McClelland and Stewart, 1969.

Francis, Daniel. *The Imaginary Indian: The Image of the Indian in Canadian Culture*. Vancouver: Arsenal Pulp Press, 1992.

Friar, Ralph, and Natasha Friar. *The Only Good Indian: The Hollywood Gospel*. New York: Drama Book Publishers, 1972.

Frideres, James S. *Aboriginal Peoples in Canada: Contemporary Conflicts.* Scarborough, ON: Prentice Hall Allyn and Bacon Canada, 1998.

Friesen, Gerald. *The Canadian Prairies: A History.* Toronto: University of Toronto Press, 1984.

Friesen, Jean. "Magnificient Gifts: The Treaties of Canada with the Indians of the Northwest 1869–70." *Transactions of the Royal Society of Canada* 5, 1 (1986): 41–51.

Gagné, Marie-Anik. *A Nation Within A Nation: Dependency and the Cree.* Montreal: Black Rose Books, 1994.

Gates, Henry Louis, Jr. *Black Literature and Literary Theory.* New York: Methuen, 1984.

George, Chief Dan. *My Heart Soars.* Saanichton, BC: Hancock House, 1974.

———. "My Very Good Dear Friends..." In *The Only Good Indian,* ed. Waubageshig. Revised ed. Don Mills, ON: New Press, 1974.

Gillmor, Don, and Pierre Turgeon. *Canada: A People's History, Volume One.* Toronto: McClelland and Stewart, 2001.

Give Back: First Nations Perspectives on Cultural Practice. Vancouver: Gallerie Publications, 1992.

Godard, Barbara. "The Politics of Representation: Some Native Canadian Women Writers." In *Native Writers and Canadian Writing: Canadian Literature Special Issue,* ed. W.H. New. Vancouver: University of British Columbia Press, 1990.

———. *Talking About Ourselves: The Literary Productions of the Native Women of Canada.* Ottawa: Canadian Research Institute For the Advancement of Women, 1985.

Goddard, John. *Last Stand of the Lubicon Cree.* Vancouver: Douglas and McIntyre, 1991.

Goldie, Terry. *Fear and Temptation: The Image of the Indigene in Canadian, Australian, and New Zealand Literatures.* Montreal: McGill-Queen's University Press, 1989.

Gooderham, Kent, ed. *I Am An Indian.* Toronto: J.M. Dent and Sons, 1969.

Granatstein, J.L. *Who Killed Canadian History?* Toronto: Harper Collins Publishers Ltd., 1998.

Grant, Agnes. "Contemporary Native Women's Voices." In *Native Writers and Canadian Writing: Canadian Literature Special Issue,* ed. W.H. New. Vancouver: University of British Columbia Press, 1990.

Grant, Agnes, ed. *Our Bit of Truth: An Anthology of Canadian Native Literature.* Winnipeg: Pemmican Publications, 1990.

Green, Joyce A. "Cultural and Ethnic Fundamentalism: The Mixed Potential for Identity, Liberation and Oppression." In *Right Thinking: Fundamentalism Across Themes.* Ed. Carol Schick, JoAnn Jaffe, and Ailsa Watkinson. Halifax: Fernwood Press, 2004.

———. "Transforming at the Margins of the Academy." In *Women in the Canadian Academic Tundra,* ed. Elena Hannah, Linda Joan Paul, and Swani Vethamany-Globus. Montreal: McGill-Queen's University Press, 2002.

_____."Theoretical, Methodological and Empirical Issues in the Study of Indigenous Politics." *Canadian Political Science Association*, 2002.

_____. "Exploring Identity and Citizenship: Aboriginal Women, Bill C-31 and the Sawridge Case." PhD diss., University of Alberta, 1997.

_____. "Towards A Detente With History: Confronting Canada's Colonial Legacy." *International Journal of Canadian Studies* 12 (Fall 1995): 85-105.

Groening, Laura. *Listening to Old Woman Speak: Natives and alterNatives in Canadian Literature*. Montreal: McGill-Queen's University Press, 2004.

Haley, Alex. *Roots*. New York: Bantam Books, 1977.

Halfe, Louise. *Blue Marrow*. Toronto: McClelland and Stewart, 1998.

_____. *Bear Bones and Feathers*. Regina: Coteau Books, 1994.

Harjo, Joy, and Gloria Bird. *Reinventing the Enemy's Language: Contemporary Native Women's Writings of North America*. New York: W.W. Norton, 1997.

Harlow, Barbara. *Resistance Literature*. New York: Methuen, 1987.

Harrison, Julia D. *Metis: People Between Two Worlds*. Vancouver: Douglas and McIntyre, 1985.

Highway, Tomson. *Kiss of the Fur Queen*. Toronto: Doubleday Canada, 1998.

_____. *Dry Lips Oughta Move to Kapuskasing*. Saskatoon: Fifth House, 1989.

_____. *The Rez Sisters*. Saskatoon: Fifth House, 1988.

Hilger, Michael. *The American Indian in Film*. Metuchen, NJ: The Scarecrow Press, 1986.

Hitchcock, Peter. *Dialogics of the Oppressed*. Minneapolis: University of Minnesota Press, 1993.

Hodgson, Heather. *Seventh Generation*. Penticton: Theytus Books, 1989.

Honour, Hugh. *The New Golden Land*. New York: Pantheon Books, 1975.

hooks, bell. *Feminist Theory: From Margin to Center*. Boston: South End Press, 1984.

Horne, Dee. *Contemporary American Indian Writing: Unsettling Literature*. New York: Peter Lang Publishing, 1999.

Hoy, Helen. "'Nothing But the Truth': Discursive Transparency in Beatrice Culleton." *Ariel* 25, 1 (1994): 155–184.

Hulan, Renee, ed. *Native North America: Critical and Cultural Perspectives*. Toronto: ECW Press, 1999.

Hulan, Renee, and Renate Eigenbrod, eds. *Aboriginal Oral Traditions: Theory, Practice, Ethics*. Black Point, NS: Fernwood Publishing, 2008.

Hunter, Lynette. *Literary value/cultural power: verbal arts in the twenty-first century*. Manchester and New York: Manchester University Press, 2001.

_____. *Outsider Notes: Feminist Approaches to Nation State Ideology, Writers/Readers and Publishing*. Vancouver: Talonbooks, 1996.

Hutcheon, Linda. "Circling the Downspout of Empire." In *The Post-Colonial Studies Reader*, ed. Bill Ashcroft, Gareth Griffiths, and Helen Tiffin. London and New York: Routledge, 1995.

Jaenen, Cornelius J. "Amerindindian Views of French Culture in the Seventeenth Century." *Canadian Historical Review* 55, 3 (1974): 261–291.

Jaine, Linda, and Drew Hayden Taylor, eds. *Voices: Being Native in Canada.* Saskatoon: University of Saskatchewan, Extension Divsion, 1992.

Jannetta, Armando E. "'Travels through forbidden geography': Metis Trappers and Traders Louis Goulet and Ted Trindell." *Ariel* 25, 2 (1994): 60–74.

Jennings, Francis. *Invasion of America: Indians, Colonialism, and the Cant of Conquest.* Chapel Hill: University of North Carolina Press, 1976.

Joe, Rita. *Song of Rita Joe: Autobiography of a Mi'kmaq Poet.* Charlottetown: Ragweed Press, 1996.

_____. *The Song of Eskasoni: More Poems of Rita Joe.* Charlottetown: Ragweed Press, 1988.

_____. *Poems of Rita Joe.* Halifax: Abenaki Press, 1978.

Johnson, Pauline E. *Flint and Feather.* 1917. Toronto: Paperjacks, 1987.

Johnston, Basil. "One Generation From Extinction." In *Native Writers and Canadian Writing: Canadian Literature Special Issue*, ed. W.H. New. Vancouver: University of British Columbia Press, 1990.

_____. *Moose Meat and Wild Rice.* Toronto: McClelland and Stewart, 1978.

Kane, Margo. "Moonlodge." In An Anthology of Canadian Native Literature in English, ed. Daniel David Moses and Terry Goldie. Toronto: Oxford University Press, 1992.

Karrer, Wolfgang, and Hartmut Lutz, eds. *Minority Literatures in North America: Contemporary Perspectives.* New York: P. Lang, 1990.

Keeshig-Tobias, Lenore. "Trickster Beyond 1992: Our Relationship." In *Indigena: Contemporary Native Perspectives*, ed. Gerald McMaster and Lee-Ann Martin. Vancouver: Douglas and McIntyre, 1992.

_____. "Stop Stealing Native Stories." *Globe and Mail*, 26 January 1990, A7.

Keller, Betty. *Pauline: A Biography of Pauline Johnson.* Halifax: Goodread Biographies, 1981.

Kenny, George. *Indians Don't Cry.* Toronto: Chimo Publishing, 1977.

Keon, Orville, Wayne Keon, and Ronald Keon. *Sweetgrass: A Modern Anthology of Indian Poetry.* Elliot Lake, ON: Algoma Printing Service, 1971.

King, Thomas. "Godzilla vs Post-Colonial." In *New Contexts of Canadian Criticism.* Ed. Ajay Heble, Donna Palmateer Pennee and J.R. Struthers. Peterborough: Broadview Press, 1997.

_____. *Green Grass, Running Water.* Toronto: Harper Collins Publishers, 1993.

_____. *One Good Story That One.* Toronto: Harper Collins Publishers, 1993.

_____. *All My Relations.* Toronto: McClelland and Stewart, 1990.

_____. *Medicine River.* Toronto: Penguin Books, 1989.

Kinsella, W.P. *Dance Me Outside.* Ottawa: Oberon Press, 1977.

Kirkness, Verna J. *Education of Indians in Federal and Provincial Schools.* Ottawa: Canada, Department of Indian Affairs and Northern Development, 1978.

Klinck, Carl F. "Literary Activity in the Canadas (1812–1841)." In *Literary History of Canada: Canadian Literature in English*, ed. Carl F. Klinck. Vol. 1. Toronto: University of Toronto Press, 1965.

Kroetsch, Robert. "Unhiding the Hidden." In *The Post-Colonial Studies Reader*, ed. Bill Ashcroft, Gareth Griffiths, and Helen Tiffin. London and New York: Routledge, 1995.

Krupat, Arnold. *Ethnocriticism: Ethnography History Literature*. Berkeley: University of California Press, 1992.

_____. *For Those Who Come After: A Study of Native American Autobiography*. Berkeley: University of California Press, 1985.

Kulchyski, Peter. "The Emperor's Old Clothes" (review of *Disrobing the Aboriginal Industry* by Frances Widdowson and Albert Howard). *Canadian Dimension* 43, 2 (2009): 46–48.

_____. *Like The Sound of a Drum: Aboriginal Cultural Politics in Denendeh and Nunavut*. Winnipeg: University of Manitoba Press, 2005.

LaRocque, Emma. "When the 'Wild West' is Me: Re-Viewing Cowboys and Indians." In *Challenging Frontiers: The Canadian West*. Ed. Lorry Felske and Beverly Rasporich. Calgary: University of Calgary Press, 2004.

_____. "Teaching Aboriginal Literature: The Discourse of Margins and Mainstreams." In *Creating Community: A Roundtable on Canadian Aboriginal Literature*. Ed. R. Eigenbrod and J. Episkenew. Penticton, BC and Brandon, Mb: Theytus and Bearpaw, 2002.

_____. "From the Land to the Classroom: Broadening Epistemology." In *Pushing the Margins: Native and Northern Studies*, ed. Jill Oakes et al. Winnipeg: University of Manitoba, Native Studies Press, 2001.

_____. "Native Identity and the Metis: Otehpayimsuak Peoples." In *A Passion for Identity: Canadian Studies for the 21st Century*. Ed. David Taras and Beverly Rasporich. Scarborough: Nelson, Thomson Learning, 2001.

_____. "Re-examining Culturally Appropriate Models in Criminal Justice Applications." In *Aboriginal and Treaty Rights in Canada: Essays on Law, Equality and Respect for Difference*. Ed. Michael Asch. Vancouver: University of British Columbia Press, 1997.

_____. "When the Other Is Me: Native Writers Confronting Canadian Literature." In *Issues in the North*, ed. Jill Oakes and Rick Riewe. Occasional Publication Number 40. Canadian Circumpolar Institute, 1996.

_____. "Long Way From Home." *Ariel: A Review of International English Literature* 25, 1 (1994): 122–126.

_____. "Preface—or—Here Are Our Voices Who Will Hear?" In *Writing The Circle: Native Women of Western Canada*, ed. Jeanne Perreault and Sylvia Vance. Edmonton: NeWest Publishers, 1990.

_____. "Tides, Towns and Trains." In *Living the Changes*, ed. Joan Turner. Winnipeg: University of Manitoba Press, 1990.

_____. "On The Ethics of Publishing Historical Records." In *"The Orders of the Dreamed": George Nelson on Cree and Northern Ojibwa Religion and Myth, 1823*, ed. Jennifer S.H. Brown and Robert Brightman. Winnipeg: University of Manitoba Press, 1988.

_____. "The Metis in English Canadian Literature." *Canadian Journal of Native Studies* 3.1 (1983): 85-94.

_____. *Defeathering the Indian*. Agincourt, ON: Book Society of Canada, 1975.

Laurence, Margaret. *The Diviners*. Toronto: McClelland and Stewart, 1974.

Lee, Bobbi. *Bobbi Lee: Indian Rebel*. Richmond: LSM Information Center, 1975. Rpt under Lee Maracle by Toronto: Women's Press, 1980.

Levine, Paul. "Frantz Fanon: The Politics of Skin." In *Divisions*. Toronto: Canadian Broadcasting Corp., 1975.

Louttit, Ernie. "Disadvantage to Advantage." In *Voices: Being Native in Canada*, ed. Linda Jaine and Drew Hayden Taylor. Saskatoon: University of Saskatchewan, Extension Divsion, 1992.

Lutz, Hartmut. *Approaches, Approaches, Approaches: Essays in Native North American Studies and Literatures*. Augsburg: Wibner-Verlag, 2002.

_____. "Confronting Cultural Imperialism: First Nations People Are Combatting Continued Cultural Theft." *Multiculturalism in North America and Europe: Social Practices-Literary Visions*, ed. Hans Braun and Wolfgang Klooss. Tries, Germany: Wissenschafthicher Verlag Tries, 1995.

_____. "Contemporary Native Literature in Canada and 'The Voice of the Mother.'" In *O Canada: Essays on Canadian Native Literature and Culture*, ed. Jorn Carlsen. Aarhus, Denmark: Aarhus University Press, 1995.

_____. *Contemporary Challenges: Conversations with Canadian Native Authors*. Saskatoon: Fifth House Publishers, 1991.

Lutz, Hartmut, ed. *Four Feathers: Poems And Stories By Canadian Native Authors*. O.B.E.M.A. No. 7 Bilingual edition. Osnabruck: Druck-& Verlagscooperative 85 GmbH, 1993.

MacEwan, Grant. *Metis Makers of History*. Saskatoon: Western Producer Prairie Books, 1981.

Maki, Joel T., ed. *Steal My Rage*. Vancouver: Douglas and McIntyre, 1995.

Malcolm X. *Malcolm X Speaks: Selected Speeches and Statements*. Edited by George Breitman. New York: Grove Press, 1965.

Mandelbaum, David G. *The Plains Cree*. 1940. Regina: Canadian Plains Research Centre, 1979.

Manitoba. *The Report of Aboriginal Justice Inquiry of Manitoba*. Winnipeg: Government of Manitoba, 1991.

Manitoba Indian Brotherhood. *The Shocking Truth About Textbooks in Manitoba*. Winnipeg: Manitoba Indian Cultural Centre, 1977.

Mannoni, O. *Prospero and Caliban*. New York: Frederick A. Praeger, 1964.

Manuel, George, and Michael Posluns. *The Fourth World*. Toronto: Collier, 1974.

Maracle, Lee. *Ravensong.* Vancouver: Press Gang Publishers, 1993.

_____. "Oratory: Coming to Theory." In *Give Back: First Nations Perspectives on Cultural Practice.* Vancouver: Gallerie Publications, 1992.

_____. *Sundogs.* Penticton: Theytus Books, 1992.

_____. *Sojourner's Truth and Other Stories.* Vancouver: Press Gang Publishers, 1990.

_____. *I Am Woman.* Vancouver: Write-On Press, 1988.

Martin, Calvin, ed. *The American Indian and the Problem of History.* New York: Oxford University Press, 1987.

Mason, Peter. *Deconstructing America: Representation of the Other.* New York: Routledge, 1990.

McCallum, Hugh, and Karmel McCallum. *This Land Is Not For Sale.* Toronto: Anglican Book Center, 1975.

McCallum, Hugh, Karmel McCallum, and John Olthius. *Moratorium: Justice, Energy, The North and Native People.* Toronto: Anglican Book Center, 1977.

McDiarmid, C., and David Pratt. *Teaching Prejudice.* Toronto: Ontario Institute for Studies in Education, 1971.

McDougall, John. *Pathfinding on Plain and Prairie.* Toronto: W. Briggs, 1898.

McGregor, Gaile. *The Wacousta Syndrome: Explorations in the Canadian Landscape.* Toronto: University of Toronto Press, 1985.

McKague, Ormond, ed. *Racism in Canada.* Saskatoon: Fifth House Publishers, 1991.

McLean, John. *The Indians of Canada: Their Manners and Customs.* 1889. Rpt. Coles, 1970.

McLeod, John. *Beginning Postcolonialism.* Manchester and New York: Manchester University Press, 2000.

McLeod, Neal. *Cree Narrative Memory: From Treaties to Contemporary Times.* Saskatoon: Purich Publishing, 2007.

McMaster, Gerald, and Lee-Ann Martin, eds. *Indigena: Contemporary Native Perspectives.* Vancouver: Douglas and McIntyre, 1992.

Mealing, S.R., ed. *The Jesuit Relations and Allied Documents: A Selection, 1632–73.* Toronto: McClelland and Stewart, 1965.

Mehl-Madrona, Lewis. *Narrative Medicine: The Use of History and Story in the Healing Process.* Rochester, VT: Bear and Company, 2007.

Memmi, Albert. *The Colonizer and the Colonized.* Boston: Beacon Press, 1957.

Mercredi, Duncan. *Wolf and Shadows.* Winnipeg: Pemmican, 1995.

_____. *Dreams of the Wolf in the City.* Winnipeg: Pemmican, 1992.

_____. *Spirit of the Wolf.* Winnipeg: Pemmican, 1991.

Michelet, Jules. *History of the French Revolution.* Edited by Gordon Wright. Chicago: University of Chicago Press, 1967.

Miller, Christine, and Patricia Chuchryk, eds. *Women of the First Nations: Power, Wisdom and Strength.* Winnipeg: University of Manitoba Press, 1997.

Miller, J.R. *Skyscrapers Hide the Heavens*. Toronto: University of Toronto Press, 1989.

Monkman, Leslie. *A Native Heritage: Images of the Indian in English Canadian Literature*. Toronto: University of Toronto Press, 1981.

Monture-Angus, Patricia. *Thunder in My Soul: A Mohawk Woman Speaks*. Halifax: Fernwood, 1995.

Morgan, Lewis Henry. *Ancient Society*. 1877. Edited by Eleanor Burke Leacock. New York: World, 1963.

Morrison, Bruce R., and C. Roderick Wilson. *Native Peoples: The Canadian Experience*. 2nd ed. Toronto: McClelland and Stewart, 1995.

Morrison, Toni. *Playing in the Dark: Whiteness and the Literary Imagination*. Cambridge: Harvard University Press, 1992.

Morton, W.L. "The Canadian Metis." *Beaver*, September 1950, 3–7.

Moses, Daniel David, and Terry Goldie. *An Anthology of Canadian Native Literature in English*. Toronto: Oxford University Press, 1992.

Mowat, William, and Christine, eds. *Native Peoples in Canadian Literature*. Toronto: Macmillan of Canada, 1975.

Mukherjee, Arun. *Oppositional Aesthetics: Readings from a Hyphenated Space*. Toronto: TSAR, 1994.

Murray, David. *Forked Tongues: Speech, Writing and Representation in North American Indian Texts*. Bloomington: Indiana University Press, 1991.

Murray, Laura J., and Keren Rice, eds. *Talking on the Page: Editing Aboriginal Oral Texts*. Toronto: University of Toronto Press, 1999.

Nash, Roderick. *Wilderness and the American Mind*. New Haven: Yale University Press, 1967.

National Indian Brotherhood. *Indian Control of Indian Education*. Ottawa: National Indian Brotherhood, 1972.

New, W.H. *A History of Canadian Literature*. London: Macmillan, 1989.

New, W.H., ed. *Native Writers and Canadian Writing: Canadian Literature Special Issue*. Vancouver: University of British Columbia Press, 1990.

Ngugi wa Thiong'o. *Decolonising The Mind*. London: James Curray, 1986.

O'Connor, John E. *The Hollywood Indian*. Trenton: New Jersey State Museum, 1980.

Overall, Christine. *A Feminist I: Reflections from Academia*. Peterborough: Broadview Press, 1998.

Owens, Louis. *Other Destinies: Understanding the American Indian Novel*. Norman: University of Oklahoma Press, 1992.

Owram, Doug. *Promise of Eden: The Canadian Expansionist Movement and the Idea of the West 1856–1900*. Toronto: University of Toronto Press, 1980.

Pakes, Fraser J. "Seeing With The Stereotypic Eye: The Visual Image of the Plains Indian." *Native Studies Review* 1, 2 (1985): 1–31.

Pannekoek, Frits. *A Snug Little Flock: The Social Origins of the Riel Resistance 1869–70*. Winnipeg: Watson and Dwyer Publishing, 1991.

Patterson, Palmer E. *The Canadian Indian: A History Since 1500.* Toronto: Collier-Macmillan Canada, 1972.

Paul, Daniel N. *We Were Not The Savages.* Halifax: Nimbus Publishing, 1993.

Pearce, Roy Harvey. *Savagism and Civilization.* 1953. Baltimore: Johns Hopkins University Press, 1965.

Pelletier, Wilfred, and Ted Poole. *No Foreign Land.* New York: Pantheon, 1973.

Perreault, Jeanne. "Notes from the Co-editors." *Ariel: A Review of International English Literature* 25, 1 (1994): 9–11.

_____. *Writing Selves: Contemporary Feminist Autography.* Minneapolis: University of Minnesota Press, 1995.

Perreault, Jeanne, and Sylvia Vance, eds. *Writing The Circle: Native Women of Western Canada.* Edmonton: NeWest Publishers, 1990.

Peters, Jacob. *Journal of the Reverend Peter Jacobs, Indian Wesleyan missionary, from Rice Lake to the Hudson's Bay territory, and returning: commencing May, 1852. with a brief account of his life, and a short history of the Wesleyan mission in that country.* New York: Carlton and Phillips, 1855.

Peterson, Jacqueline. "Many Roads to Red River: Metis Genesis in the Great Lakes Region, 1680-1815." In *The New Peoples: Being and Becoming Metis in North America,* ed. Jacqueline Peterson and Jennifer S.H. Brown. Winnipeg: University of Manitoba Press, 1985.

Peterson, Jacqueline, and Jennifer S.H. Brown, eds. *The New Peoples: Being and Becoming Metis in North America.* Winnipeg: University of Manitoba Press, 1985.

Petrone, Penny. "Aboriginal Literature, Native and Metis Literature." In *Oxford Companion To Canadian Literature,* ed. E. Benson and William Toye. Toronto: Oxford University Press, 1997.

_____. *Native Literature in Canada.* Toronto: Oxford University Press, 1990.

_____. "Indian Literature." In *Oxford Companion to Canadian Literature,* ed. William Toye. Toronto: Oxford University Press, 1983.

Philip, M. Nourbese. *Frontiers: Essays and Writings on Racism and Culture.* Stratford, ON: Mercury Press, 1992.

Ponting, J. Rick, ed. *Arduous Journey: Canadian Indians and Decolonization.* Toronto: McClelland and Stewart, 1986.

_____. *First Nations in Canada: Perspectives on Opportunity, Empowerment, and Self-Determination.* Toronto: McGraw-Hill Ryerson, 1997.

Prucha, Francis Paul. *The American Indian Policy in the Formative Years.* Cambridge, MA: Harvard University Press, 1962.

Puxley, Peter. "The Colonial Experience." *Dene Nation—The Colony Within,* ed. Mel Watkins. Toronto: University of Toronto Press, 1977.

Ramraj, Victor J. *Concert of Voices: An Anthology of World Writing in English.* Peterborough, ON: Broadview Press, 1995.

Rasporich, Beverly. "Native Women Writing: Tracing the Patterns." *Canadian Ethnic Studies* 28, 1 (1996): 37–51.

Ray, Arthur J. *Indians in the Fur Trade: Their Role as Trappers, Hunters, and Middlemen in the Lands Southwest of Hudson Bay 1660–1870.* Toronto: University of Toronto Press, 1974.

Ray, Arthur J., and Donald Freeman. *"Give Us Good Measure": An Economic Analysis of Relations Between the Indians and the Hudson's Bay Company before 1763.* Toronto: University of Toronto Press, 1978.

Razack, Sherene H. *Race, Space, and the Law: Unmapping a White Settler Society.* Toronto: Between the Lines, 2002.

Redbird, Duke. *Loveshine and Red Wine.* Cutler, Ont.: Woodland Studios Publishing, 1981.

Rich, E.E. "The Indian Traders." *Beaver*, Winter 1970, 4–20.

Richardson, Boyce. *Strangers Devour The Land.* Toronto: Macmillan, 1975.

Richardson, Boyce, ed. *Drumbeat: Anger and Renewal in Indian Country.* Toronto: Summerhill Press, Assembly of First Nations, 1989.

Richardson, John. *Wacousta or, The Prophecy: A Tale of the Canadas.* London: T. Cadell, 1832.

_____. *Wau-Nan-Gee, or The Massacre of Chicago.* New York: H. Long, 1852.

Ridington, Robin. "Cultures in Conflict: Problems in Discourse." In *Native Writers and Canadian Writing: Canadian Literature Special Issue*, ed. W.H. New. Vancouver: University of British Columbia Press, 1990.

_____."Technology, World View, and Adaptive Strategy in a Northern Hunting Society." In *The Native Imprint: The Contribution of First Peoples to Canada's Character*, ed. Olive P. Dickason. Athabasca, AB: Athabasca University, 1995.

Robinson, Eden. *Monkey Beach.* Toronto: Alfred A. Knopf Canada, 2000.

Rockhill, Kathleen. "The Chaos of Subjectivity in the Ordered Halls of Academe." *Canadian Woman Studies* 8, 4 (1987): 12–17.

Rogin, Michael Paul. *Fathers and Children.* New York: Knopf, 1975.

Ross, Alexander. *The Red River Settlement: Its Rise, Progress and Present State.* London, 1856. Rpt. Ross and Haines, Minneapolis, 1957.

Rotstein, A. "Trade and Politics: An Institutional Approach." *Western Canadian Journal of Anthropology* 3, 1 (1972): 1–28.

Royal Commission on Aboriginal Peoples. *Report of the Royal Commission on Aboriginal Peoples.* Ottawa. Supply and Services Canada, 1996.

_____. *Choosing Life: Special Report on Suicide Among Aboriginal People.* Ottawa: Minister of Supply and Services, 1995.

Ruffo, Armand Garnet, ed. *(Ad)dressing our Words: Aboriginal Perspectives on Aboriginal Literatures.* Penticton: Theytus Books, 2001.

_____. *Grey Owl: The Mystery of Archie Belaney.* Regina: Coteau, 1997.

Ryan, William. *Blaming The Victim.* New York: Random House, 1971.

Ryga, George. *The Ecstasy of Rita Joe and other plays.* Don Mills, ON: General Publishing, 1971.

Said, Edward W. *Representations of the Intellectual.* New York: Vintage Books, 1996.

_____. *Culture and Imperialism.* New York: First Vintage Books, 1994.

_____. *The World, The Text, and the Critic.* Cambridge: Harvard University Press, 1983.

_____. *Orientalism.* London: Routledge and Kegan Paul, 1978.

Sanders, D. "The Rights of the Aboriginal Peoples of Canada." *Canadian Bar Review* 6.1 (1983): 314-338.

Satz, Ronald N. *American Indian Policy in the Jacksonian Era.* Lincoln: University of Nebraska Press, 1975.

Saul, John Ralston. *A Fair Country.* Toronto: Viking Canada, 2008.

Saum, Lewis O. *The Fur Trade and the Indian.* Seattle: University of Washington Press, 1965.

Sawchuk, Joe, Patricia Sawchuk, Terry Ferguson, and the Metis Association of Alberta. *Metis Land Rights in Alberta: A Political History.* Edmonton: Metis Association of Alberta, 1981.

Schick, Carol. "Keeping the Ivory Tower White: Discourses of racial domination." In *Race, Space, and the Law: Unmapping a White Settler Society*, ed. S. Razack. Toronto: Between the Lines, 2002.

Schick, Carol, and Verna St. Denis. "Troubling national discourses for anti-racist education." *Journal of Canadian Education* 28, 3 (2005): 296-319.

Scofield, Gregory. *Singing Home the Bones.* Vancouver: Raincoast Books, 2005.

_____. *Thunder Through My Veins: Memories of a Métis Childhood.* Toronto: Perennial, 1999.

_____. *The Gathering: Stones for the Medicine Wheel.* Vancouver: Polestar Press, 1993.

Sealey, D. Bruce, and Antoine S. Lussier. *The Metis: Canada's Forgotten People.* Winnipeg: Manitoba Metis Federation, 1975.

Sealey, D. Bruce, and Verna J. Kirkness, eds. *Indians Without Tipis.* Agincourt, ON: 1973. Book Society of Canada, 1974.

Seton, E.T. *The Gospel of the Redman: An Indian Bible.* London: Psychic Press, 1937.

_____. *Two Little Savages, Being the Adventures of Two Boys Who Lived as Indians and What They Learned.* New York: Grosset and Dunlap, 1903.

Sheehan, Bernard W. *Seeds of Extinction.* Chapel Hill: University of North Carolina Press, 1973.

Shilling, Arthur. *The Ojibway Dream.* Montreal: Tundra Books, 1986.

Shkilnyk, Anastasia M. *A Poison Stronger Than Love: The Destruction of an Ojibwe Community.* New Haven: Yale University Press, 1985.

Siggins, Maggie. *Riel: A Life of Revolution.* Toronto: Harper Collins, 1994.

Sioui, George. *For an American Autohistory.* Montreal: McGill-Queen's University Press, 1992.

Slattery, Brian. "Understanding Aboriginal Rights." *Canadian Bar Review* 66 (1987): 727–83.

Slipperjack, Ruby. *Dog Tracks.* Saskatoon: Fifth House, 2008.

_____. *Weesquachak and the lost ones.* Penticton: Theytus Books, 2000.

_____. *Silent Words.* Saskatoon: Fifth House Publishers, 1992.

_____. *Honour The Sun.* Winnpeg: Pemmican Publications, 1987.

Smith, Allen. "Seeing Things: Race, Image and National Identity in Canadian and American Movies and Television." *American Review of Canadian Studies* 26, 3 (1996): 376–390.

Smith, Donald B. *Le Sauvage. The Native People in Quebec: Historical Writings on the Heroic Period (1534–1663) of New France.* Ottawa: National Museums of Canada, 1974.

Smith, Henry Nash. *Virgin Land.* Cambridge, MA: Harvard University Press, 1950.

Stalker, Jacqueline, and Susan Prentice. *The Illusion of Inclusion: Women in Post-Secondary Education.* Halifax: Fernwood Publishing, 1998.

Stanley, George F. *The Birth of Western Canada: A History of the Riel Rebellion.* Toronto: University of Toronto Press, 1960.

Stedman, Raymond William. *Shadows of the Indian: Stereotypes in American Culture.* Norman: University of Oklahoma Press, 1982.

Stevenson, Michael. "Columbus and the War on Indigenous People." *Race and Class* 32.3 (1992): 27-45.

Stump, Sarain. *There Is My People Sleeping.* Sidney, BC: Grays, 1970.

Taylor, Drew H. *Me Funny.* Vancouver: Douglas and McIntyre, 2005.

_____. *Funny, You Don't Look Like One.* Penticton: Theytus Books, 1996.

_____. "Pretty Like A White Boy: The Adventures of a Blue-Eyed Ojibway." In *An Anthology of Canadian Native Literature in English,* ed. Daniel David Moses and Terry Goldie. Toronto: Oxford University Press, 1992.

Thistle, Paul C. *Indian-European Trade Relations in the Lower Saskatchewan River Region to 1840.* Winnipeg: University of Manitoba Press, 1986.

Tiffin, Chris, and Alan Lawson, eds. *De-scribing Empire: Post-colonialism and Textuality.* London: Routledge, 1994.

Tobias, John L. "Protection, Civilization, Assimilation: An Outline History of Canada's Indian Policy." *Western Canadian Journal of Anthropology* 6, 2 (1976): 13–30.

_____. "The Subjugation of the Plains Cree, 1879–1885." *Canadian Historical Review* 64, 4 (1983): 519–48.

Todd, Loretta. "What More Do They Want?" In *Indigena: Contemporary Native Perspectives,* ed. Gerald McMaster and Lee-Ann Martin. Vancouver: Douglas and McIntyre, 1992.

Trigger, Bruce G. "Champlain Judged by His Indian Policy: A Different View of Early Canadian History." In *The Native Imprint: The Contribution of First Peoples to Canada's Character,* ed. Olive P. Dickason. Athabasca, AB: Athabasca University, 1995.

_____. "The Historians' Indian: Native Americans in Canadian Historical Writing from Charlevoix to the Present." In *The Native Imprint: The Contribution of First Peoples to Canada's Character,* ed. Olive P. Dickason. Athabasca, AB: Athabasca University, 1995.

_____. *Native and Newcomers: Canada's "Heroic Age" Reconsidered*. Montreal and Kingston: McGill-Queen's University Press, 1985.

Trott, Christopher G. "The Dialectic of 'Us' and 'Other': Anglican Missionary Photographs of the Inuit." *American Review of Canadian Studies* 31 (2001): 171–190.

Troyer, Warner. *No Safe Place*. Toronto: Clarke, Irwin, 1977.

Turner, Dale. *This Is Not a Peace Pipe: Towards a Critical Indigenous Philosophy*. Toronto: University of Toronto Press, 2006.

Turner, Frederick Jackson. *The Significance of the Frontier in American History* [1893]. Edited by Harold P. Simonson. New York: Frederick Ungar, 1963.

Turner, Margaret E. *Imagining Culture: New World Narrative and the Writing of Canada*. Montreal: McGill-Queen's University Press, 1995.

Twigg, Alan. *Aboriginality: The Literary Origins of British Columbia, Vol 2*. Vancouver: Ronsdale Press, 2005.

Valaskakis, Gail Guthrie. *Indian Country: Essays on Contemporary Native Culture*. Waterloo: Wilfrid Laurier University Press, 2005.

Van Camp, Richard. *The Moon of Letting Go and Other Stories*. Winnipeg: Enfield and Wizenty, 2009.

_____. *The Lesser Blessed*. Vancouver: Douglas and McIntyre, 1996.

Van Kirk, Sylvia. *"Many Tender Ties": Women in Fur-Trade Society 1670–1870*. Norman: University of Oklahoma Press, 1980.

Vizenor, Gerald. "Crows Written on the Poplars: Autocritical Autobiographies." In *I Tell You Now: Autobiographical Essays by Native American Writers*, ed. Brian Swann and Arnold Krupat. Lincoln: University of Nebraska Press, 1987.

Wagamese, Richard. *One Native Life*. Vancouver/Toronto/Berkeley: Douglas and McIntyre, 2008.

_____. *Dream Wheels*. Toronto: Doubleday Canada, 2006.

_____. *For Joshua*. Toronto: Doubleday Canada, 2002.

_____. *Quality of Light*. Toronto: Doubleday Canada, 1997.

_____. *Keeper 'n Me*. Toronto: Doubleday Canada, 1994.

Waldram, James, B. *As Long As The Rivers Run: Hydroelectric Development and Native Communities in Western Canada*. Winnipeg: University of Manitoba Press, 1988.

Walker, Alice. *The Color Purple*. New York: Pocket Books, 1982.

Walker, James St. G. "The Indian in Canadian Historical Writing." *Canadian Historical Association Report* 22 (1971): 21–51.

Warkentin, Germaine, ed., *Canadian Exploration Literature: An Anthology*. Toronto: Oxford University Press, 1993.

Warrior, Emma Lee. "Compatriots." In *An Anthology of Canadian Native Literature in English*, ed. Daniel David Moses and Terry Goldie. Toronto: Oxford University Press, 1992.

Watkins, Mel, ed. *Dene Nation—The Colony Within*. Toronto: University of Toronto Press, 1977.

Waubageshig. "The Comfortable Crisis." In *The Only Good Indian*, ed. Waubageshig. Revised ed. Don Mills, ON: New Press, 1974.

Waubageshig, ed. *The Only Good Indian*. Revised ed. Don Mills, ON: New Press, 1974.

Weatherford, Jack. *Indian Givers: How the Indians of the Americas Transformed the World*. New York: Ballantine Books, 1989.

Webster, Gloria Cranmer. "From Colonization to Repatriation." In *Indigena: Contemporary Native Perspectives*, ed. Gerald McMaster and Lee-Ann Martin. Vancouver: Douglas and McIntyre, 1992.

Welsh, Christine. "Women in the Shadows: Reclaiming a Metis Heritage." *Descant* 24, 3 (1993): 89–104.

West, John. *Substance of a Journal During Residence At The Red River Colony*. London, 1824. Rpt. S.R. Publishers, 1966.

Wheeler, Jordan. *Brothers in Arms*. Winnipeg: Pemmican Publications, 1989.

"Whose Voice Is It, Anyway? A symposium on who should be speaking for whom." *Books in Canada* 20, 1 (1991): 11–17.

Widdowson, Frances, and Albert Howard. *Disrobing the Aboriginal Industry: The Deception Behind Indigenous Cultural Preservation*. Montreal: McGill-Queen's University Press, 2008.

Wiebe, Rudy. *The Scorched Wood People*. Toronto: McClelland and Stewart, 1977.

Williams, David. *The Burning Wood*. Toronto: Anansi, 1975.

Williamson, Janice. *Sounding Differences: Conversations with Seventeen Canadian Women Writers*. Toronto: University of Toronto Press, 1993.

Williamson, Norman J. "The Indian in the Canadian Novel in English in the Period 1860–1918." MA thesis, University of Manitoba, 1976.

Willis, Jane. *Geneish: An Indian Girlhood*. Toronto: New Press, 1973.

Wilson, Betty. *Andre Tom McGregor*. Toronto: Macmillan, 1976.

Woodcock, George. "Prairie Writers and the Metis: Rudy Wiebe and Margaret Laurence." *Canadian Ethnic Studies* 14, 1 (1982): 9–22.

Wolfe, Eric R. *Europe and the People Without History*. Berkeley: University of California Press, 1982.

York, Geoffrey. *The Dispossessed: Life and Death in Native Canada*. Toronto: Lester and Orpen Dennys, 1989.

Young, Egerton R. *Stories from Indian Wigwams and Northern Campfires*. London, 1893. Rpt. Coles, 1974.

Young, Jon, ed. *Breaking The Mosaic: Ethnic Identities in Canadian Schooling*. Toronto: Garamond Press, 1987.

Young, Robert J.C. *Postcolonialism: A Very Short Introduction*. Oxford: Oxford University Press, 2003.

Young Man, Alfred. "The Metaphysics of North American Indian Art." In *Indigena: Contemporary Native Perspectives*, ed. Gerald McMaster and Lee-Ann Martin. Vancouver: Douglas and McIntyre, 1992.

Index